PATHFINDER
AN AMERICAN SAGA

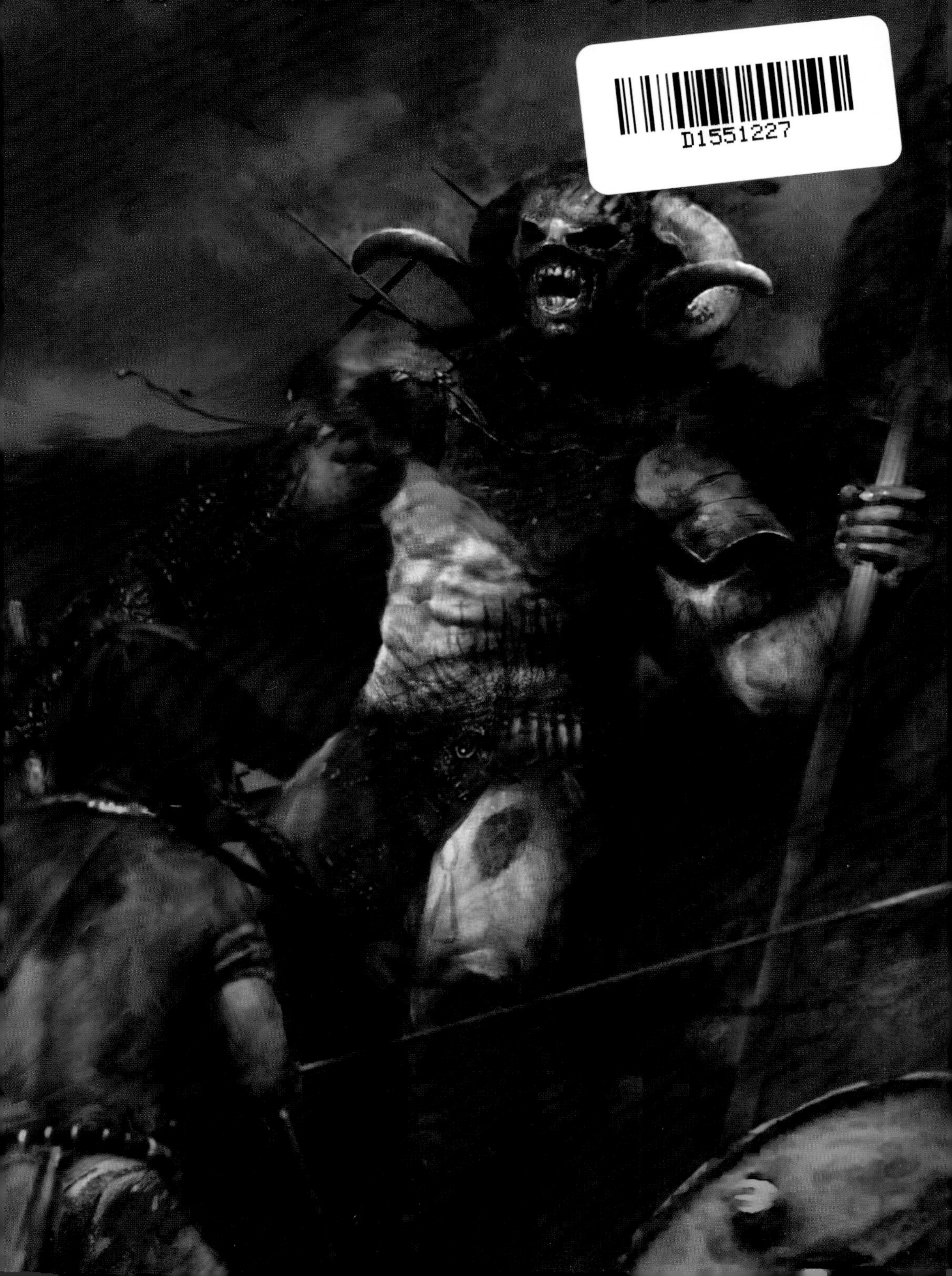

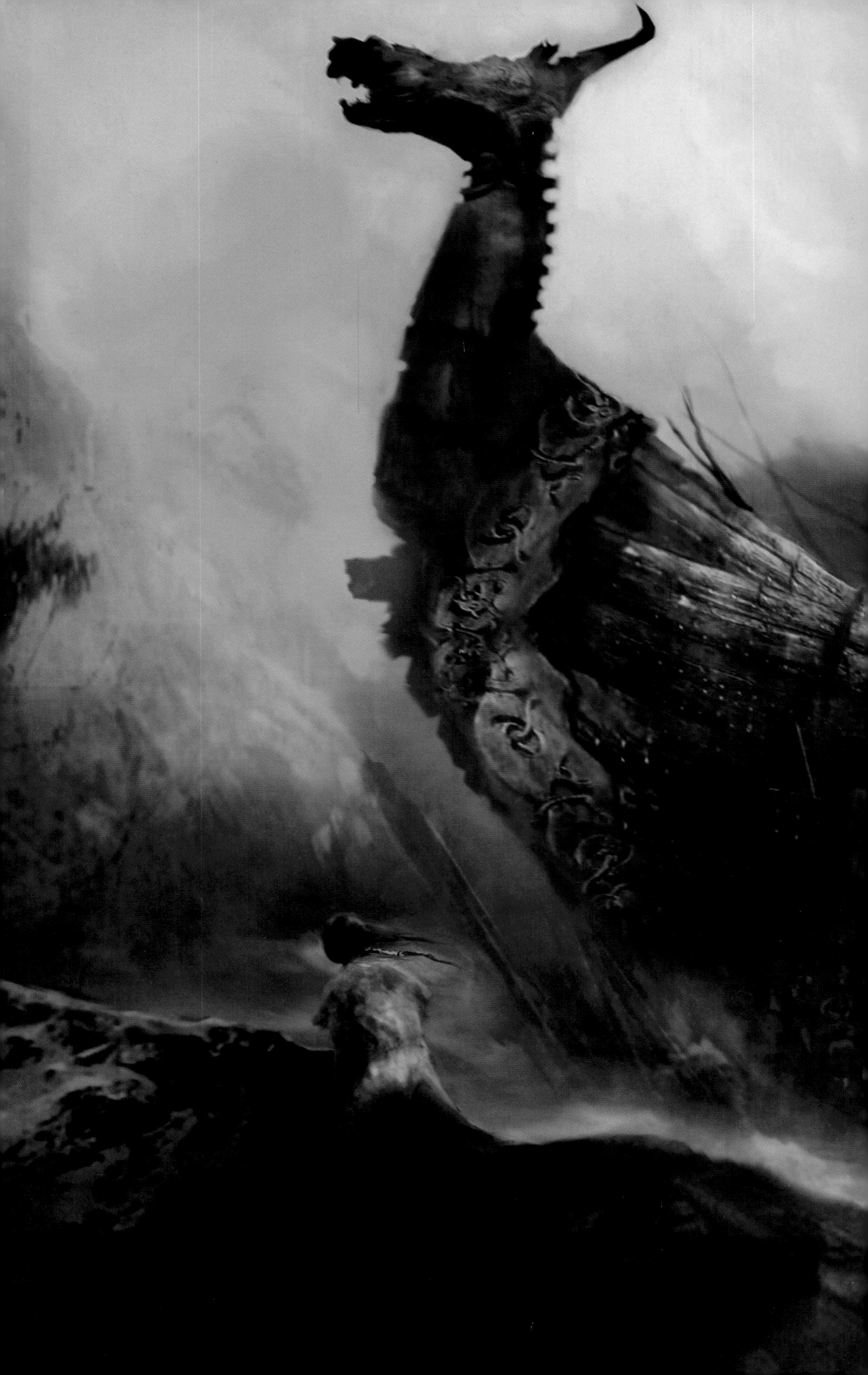

PATHFINDER
AN AMERICAN SAGA

directed by
MARCUS NISPEL

adapted from the screenplay by
LAETA KALOGRIDIS

art by
CHRISTOPHER SHY

final edit by
JASON PARK

graphic novel produced by
JERRY DIGBY

story edited by
VICTORIA FOSTER

production consultation by
MATT REILLY and MAX RIEDL

Dark Horse Books™

FOREWORD

When I was growing up in the suburbs of Frankfurt in the '70s, it still took a year for a movie to make it from America to Germany.

In the meantime, we played with *Star Wars* action figures in the dirt, pored over *Star Wars* comic books, and listened to the disco version of John Williams' score for many months—rabid fans even before seeing the movie. This process of imagining a movie before seeing it was my film school.

A few years later I came to America to illustrate comics. My first job interview was with *Mad* magazine on Madison Avenue. Let's just say that I failed miserably. When I started to direct, I was always drawn to graphic novel material. Most of what I found was too over the top, but what about a real-life superhero stuck in a real-life predicament that is stranger than fiction in a war between Vikings and Indians?! Nobody from N. C. Wyeth to Frank Frazetta had ever painted this picture. American history books didn't even depict the possibility. Yet two weeks after the completion of the script, proof was found that Vikings made it to American shores, as far down the coast as Boston and New York City. Whether reality or myth, it was American lore from a time before the Western—or even Christopher Columbus for that matter. I was fascinated with an American saga older than King Arthur or the *Nibelungenlied*—an imagined, untold history.

I met Christopher Shy when I was thinking about translating his latest graphic novel *Ascend* for the big screen. I asked him to do the same for me—to create images about a clash of two ancient cultures, which had never before been depicted.

The images poured in.

Ten pages . . . twenty . . . forty . . . sixty . . . characters, costumes, and set pieces were defined. We quickly agreed on a realistic portrayal of Indians, but wanted to take some artistic license with the Vikings. There would be contrivances, but they would be our contrivances—nothing we or anybody else would ever have seen before. More *Predator* than *Hägar*. Horns? Yes! But our way—more feral, primitive— not like something out of a Richard Wagner opera. As his conceptualizations trickled in, we went into production on the film, and not only the studio, but also the various departments caught his fire—art, costumes, makeup, hair, props, and construction. My production designer, Greg Blair, and art director Geoff Wallace were in daily communication with Chris about every possible detail. How would our dragon ship look as a wreck? How would the Indian dwellings have been constructed hundreds of years before the John Ford-Western "wigwams"?

As his artwork stacked up, it was clear what had to happen—we needed to fill in the blanks and I needed to fulfill my lifelong dream of putting together a graphic novel. This is Christopher's interpretation of our movie, and the movie is our interpretation of his artwork. At some point we were so in synch that pages would come in looking exactly like a scene as we were shooting it. Sometimes we would surprise ourselves with how differently we each envisioned the same page. It was an extraordinarily inspirational situation—telling a story on paper and celluloid at the same time.

I don't care about the Oscars. I dream of plastic action figures with extendable lightsabers, model kits, and comic books, and maybe one day a spoof in *Mad* magazine. I don't want my work to hang in a museum, but rather turn into a real experience in other people's hands—Christopher's, or anyone else's who feels like playing.

Marcus Nispel
Director, *Pathfinder*

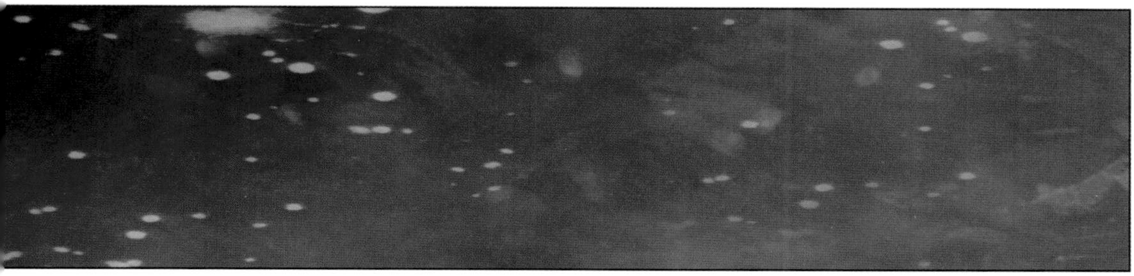

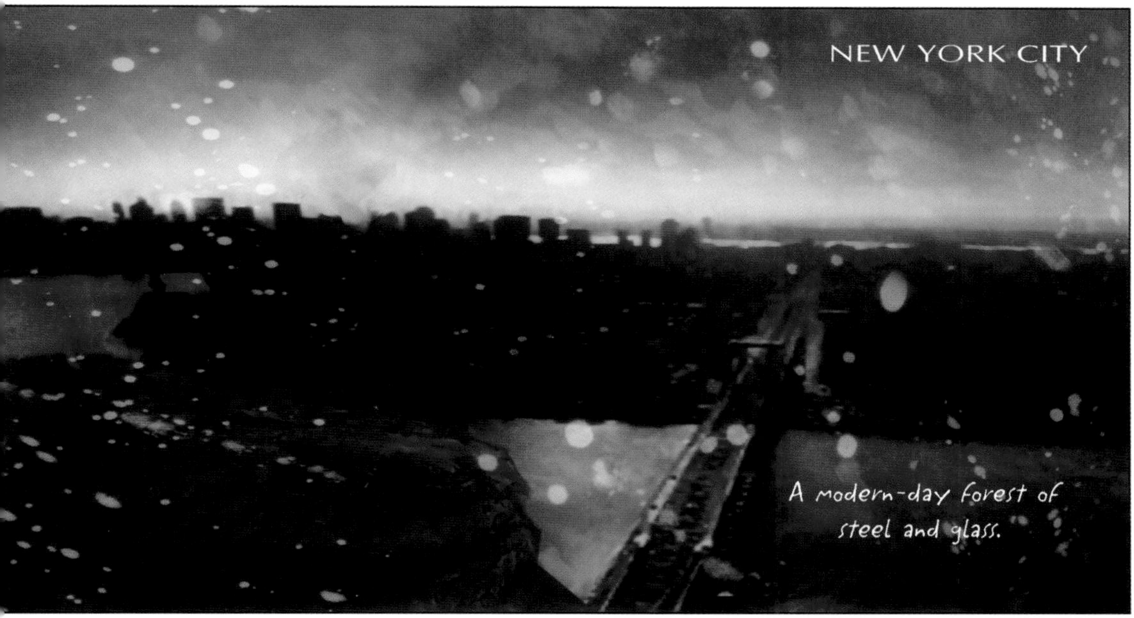
NEW YORK CITY
A modern-day forest of steel and glass.

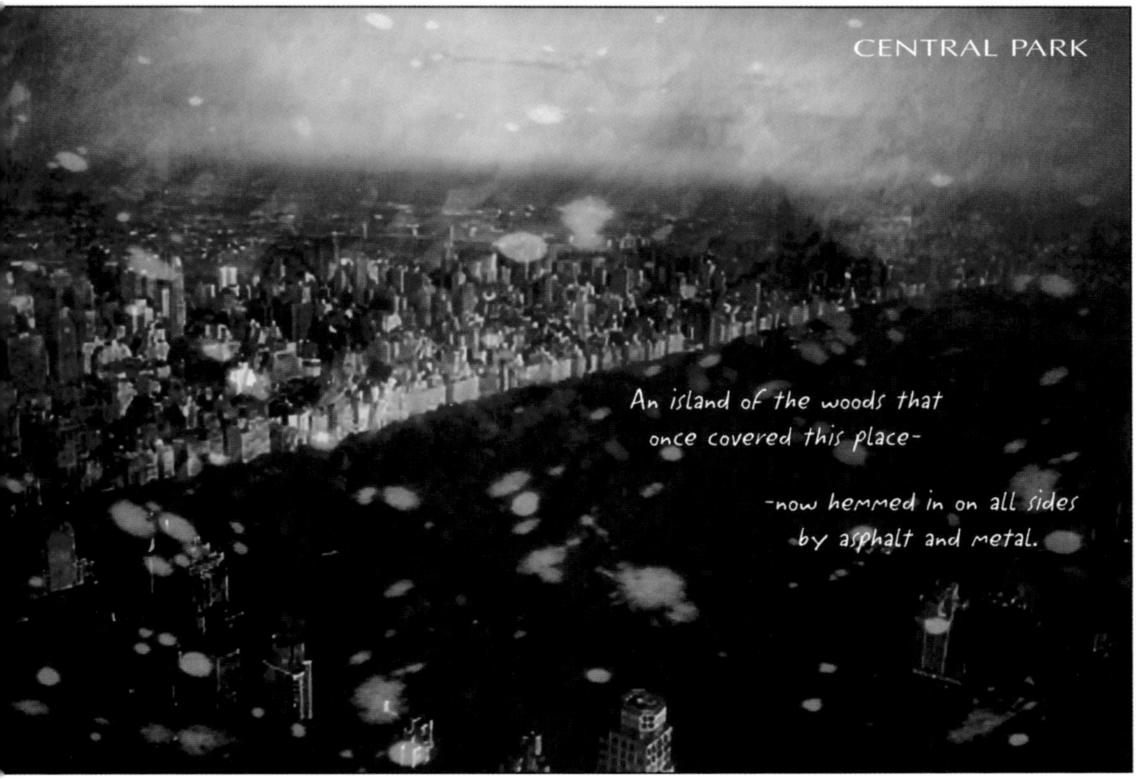
CENTRAL PARK
An island of the woods that once covered this place-
-now hemmed in on all sides by asphalt and metal.

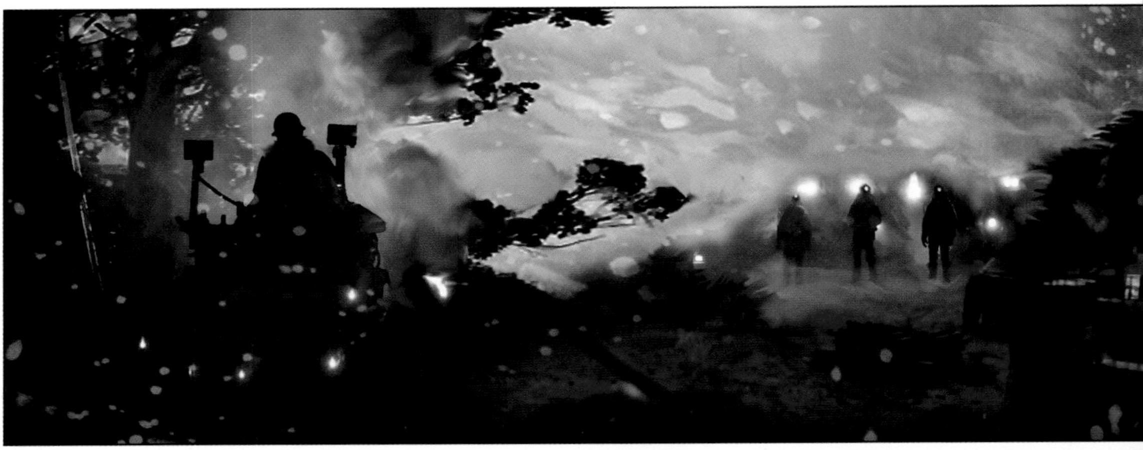

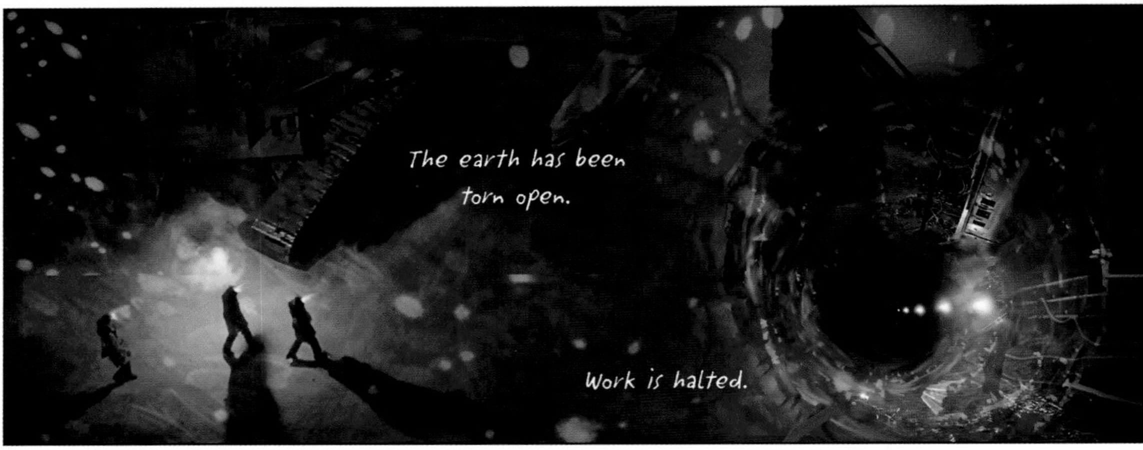
The earth has been torn open.
Work is halted.

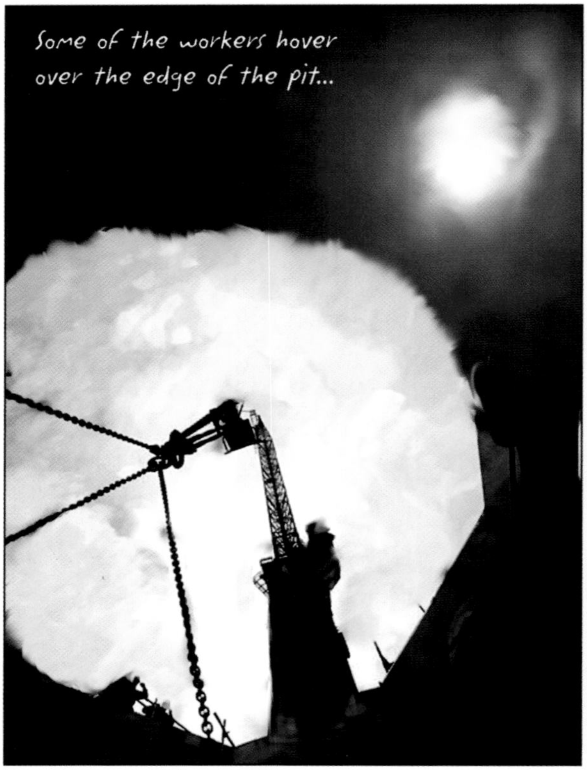
Some of the workers hover over the edge of the pit...

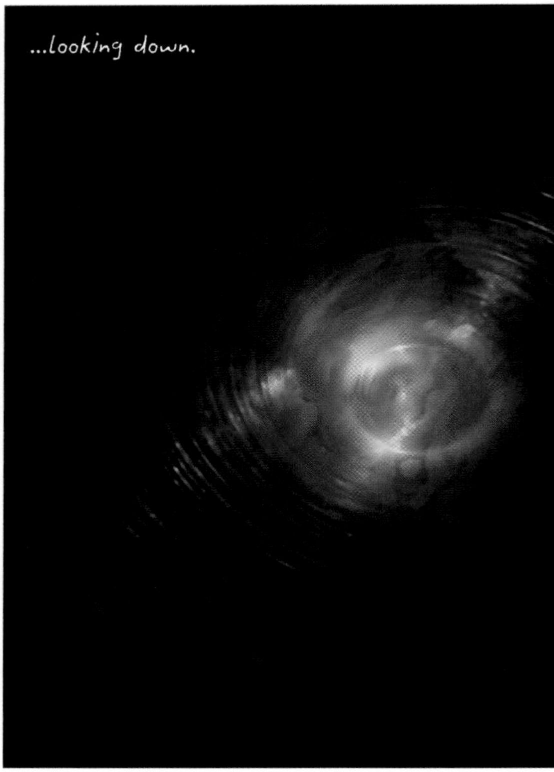
...looking down.

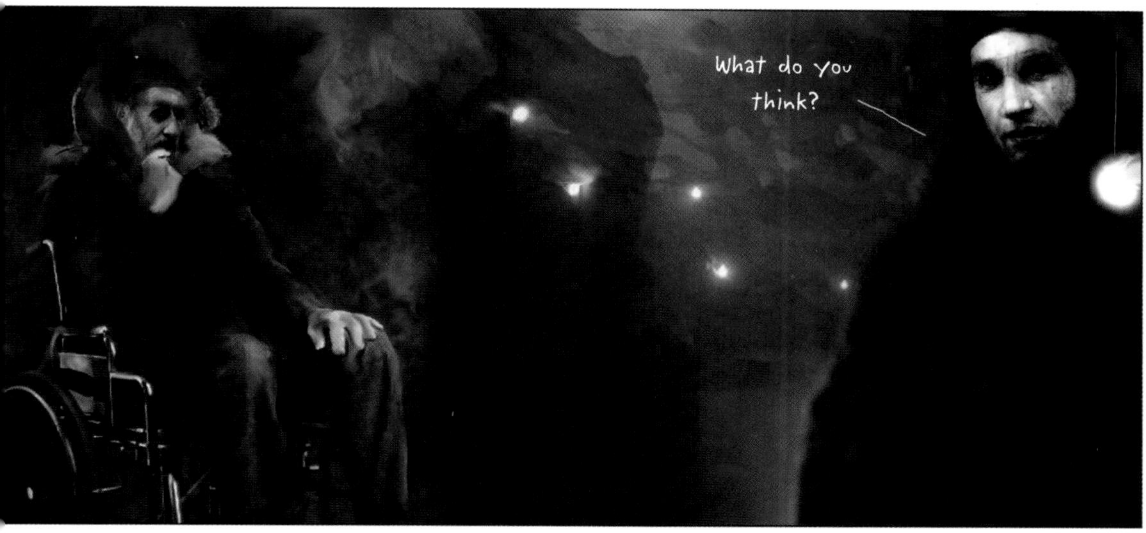
What do you think?

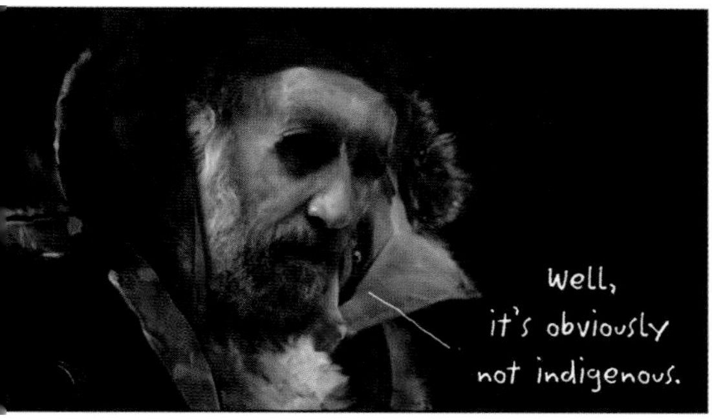
Well, it's obviously not indigenous.

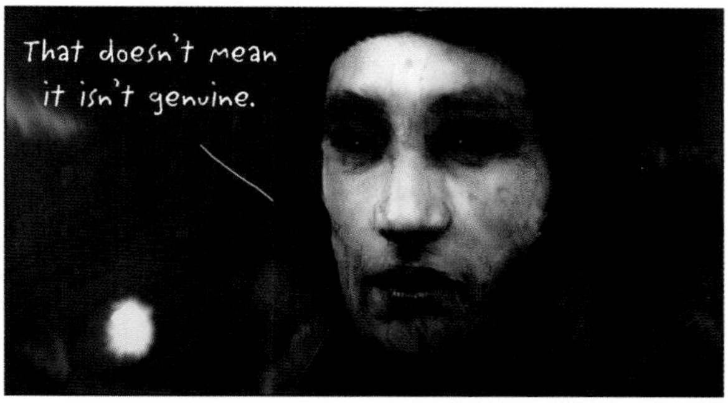
That doesn't mean it isn't genuine.

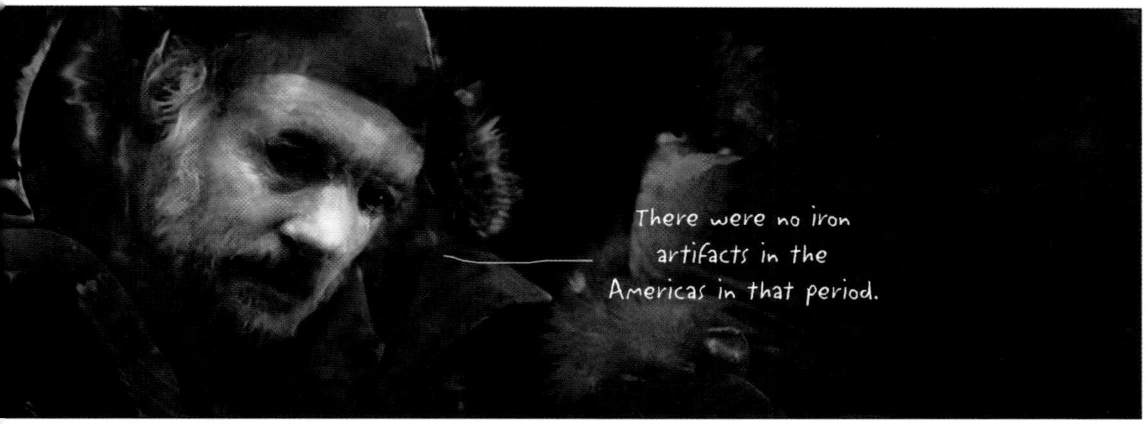
There were no iron artifacts in the Americas in that period.

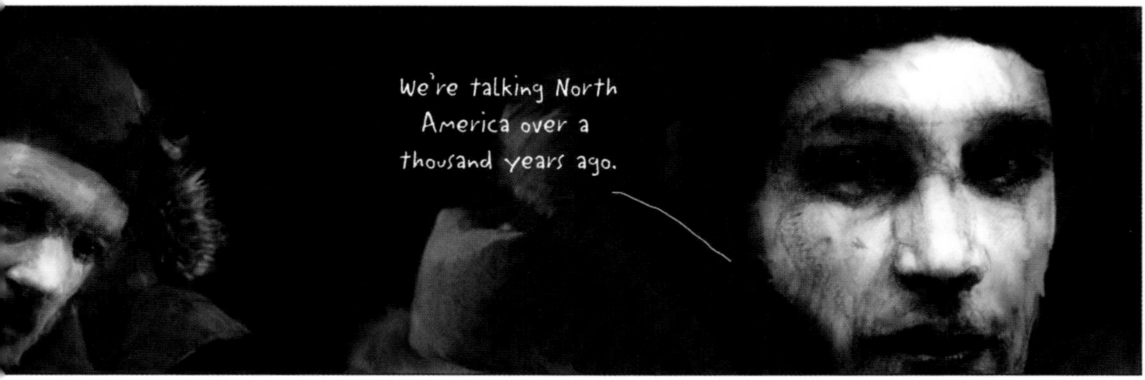
We're talking North America over a thousand years ago.

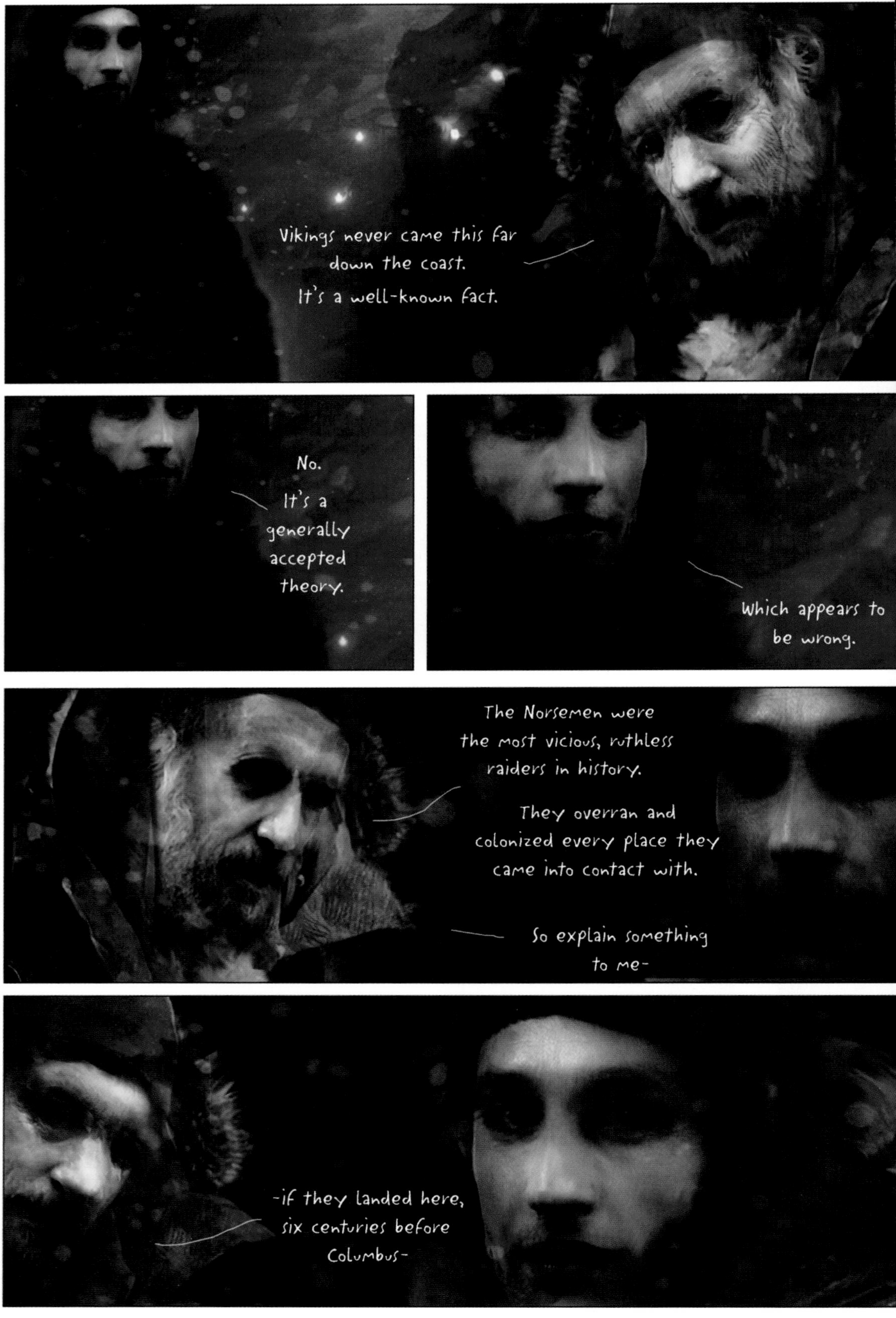
Vikings never came this far down the coast.
It's a well-known fact.
No.
It's a generally accepted theory.
Which appears to be wrong.
The Norsemen were the most vicious, ruthless raiders in history.
They overran and colonized every place they came into contact with.
So explain something to me-
-if they landed here, six centuries before Columbus-

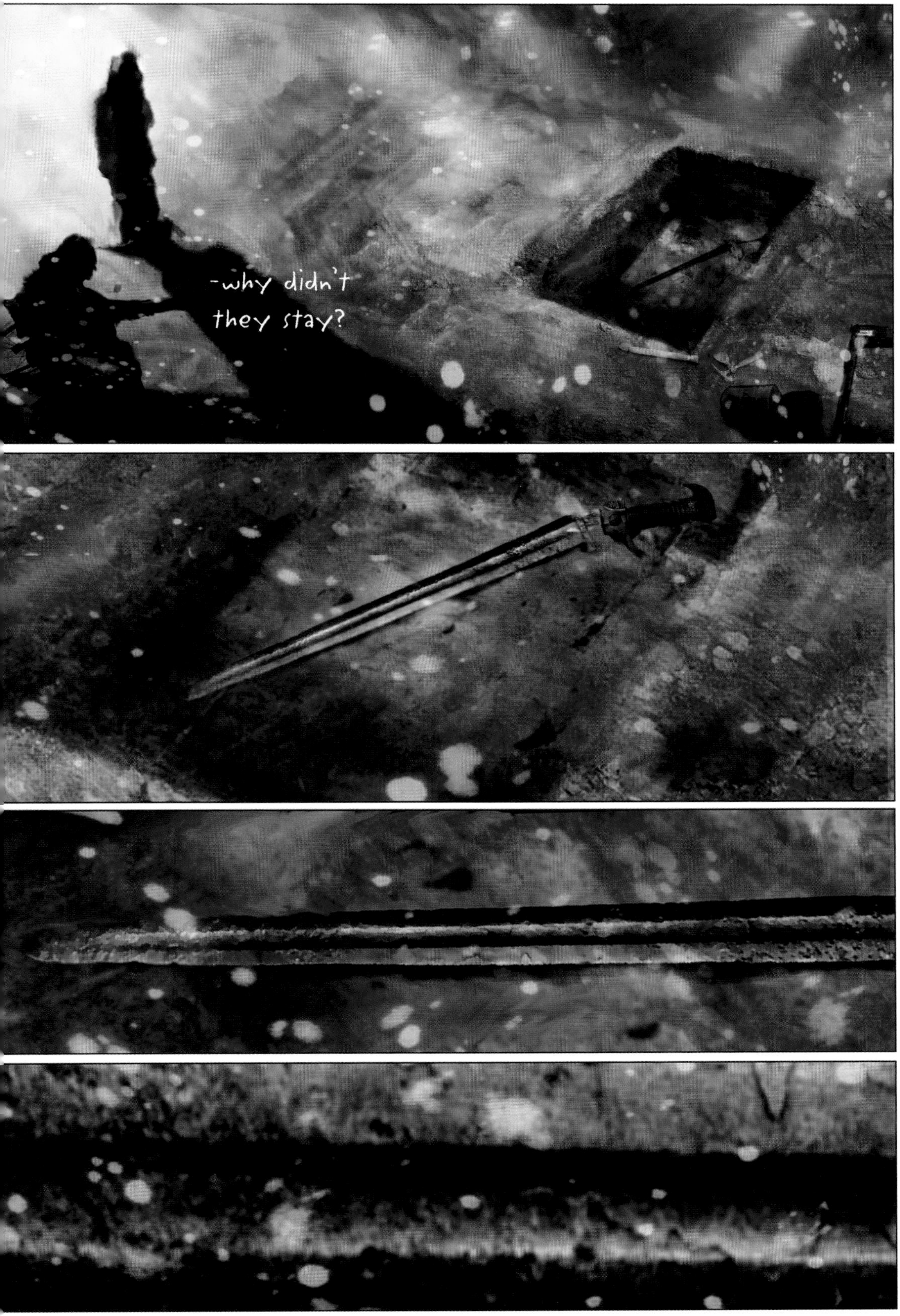
-why didn't
they stay?

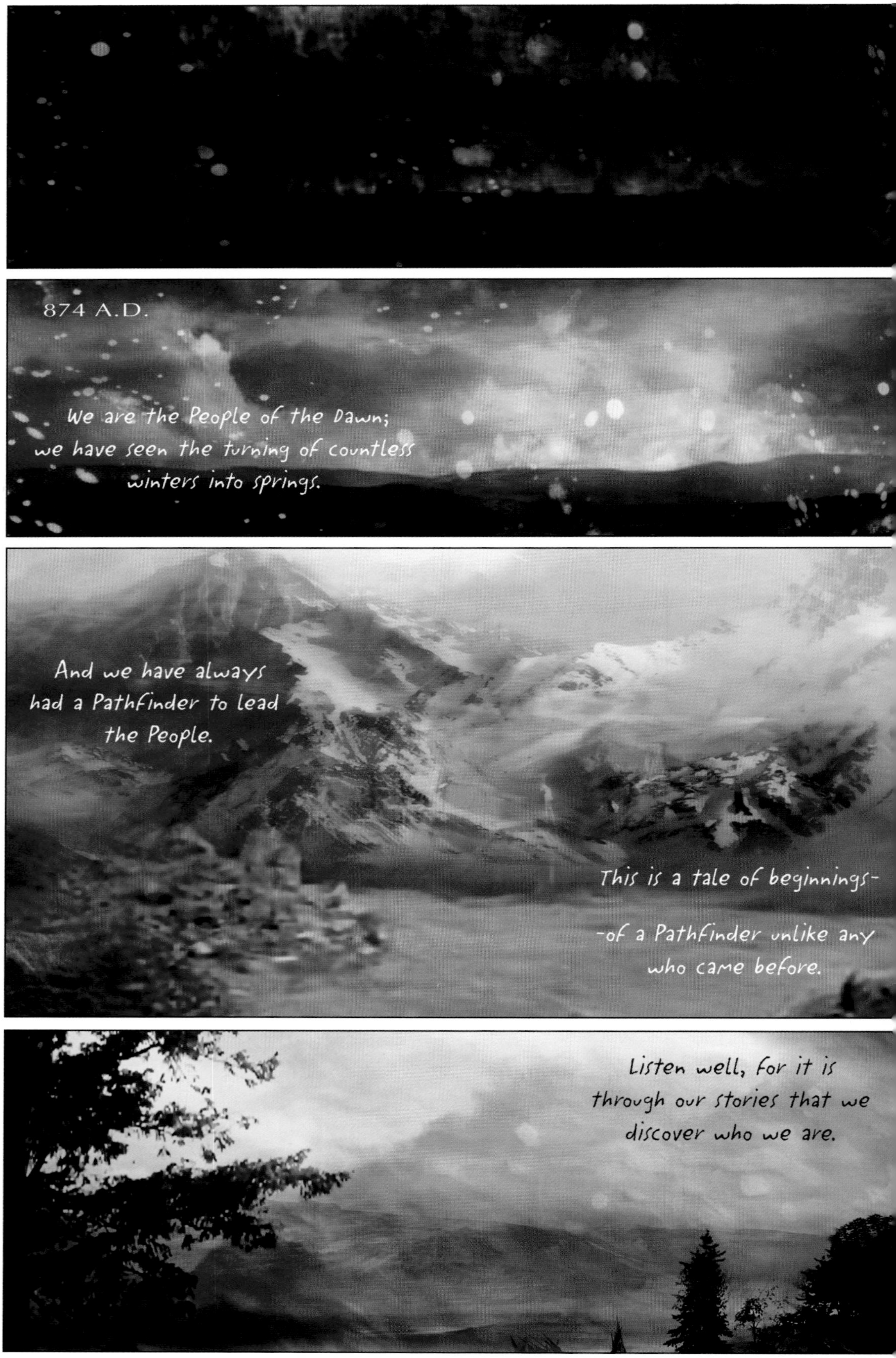
874 A.D.
We are the People of the Dawn; we have seen the turning of countless winters into springs.
And we have always had a Pathfinder to lead the People.
This is a tale of beginnings-
-of a Pathfinder unlike any who came before.
Listen well, for it is through our stories that we discover who we are.

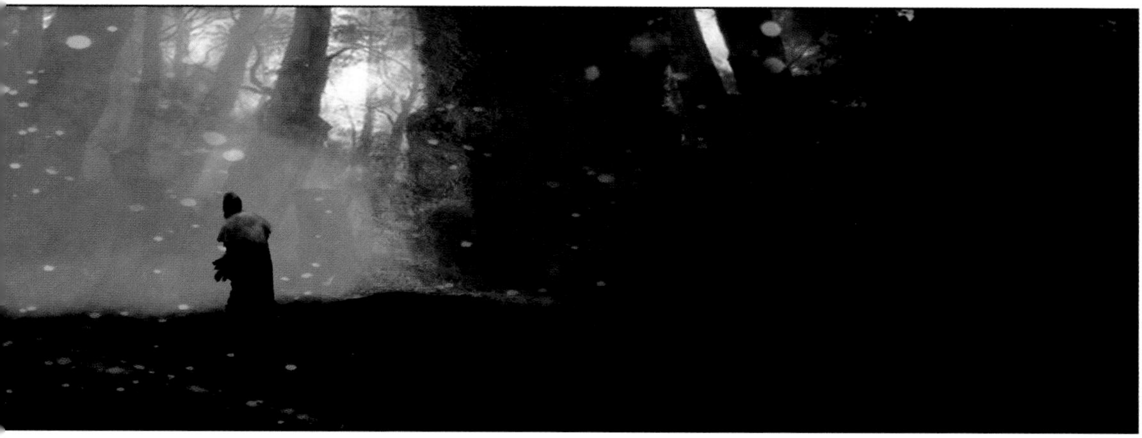

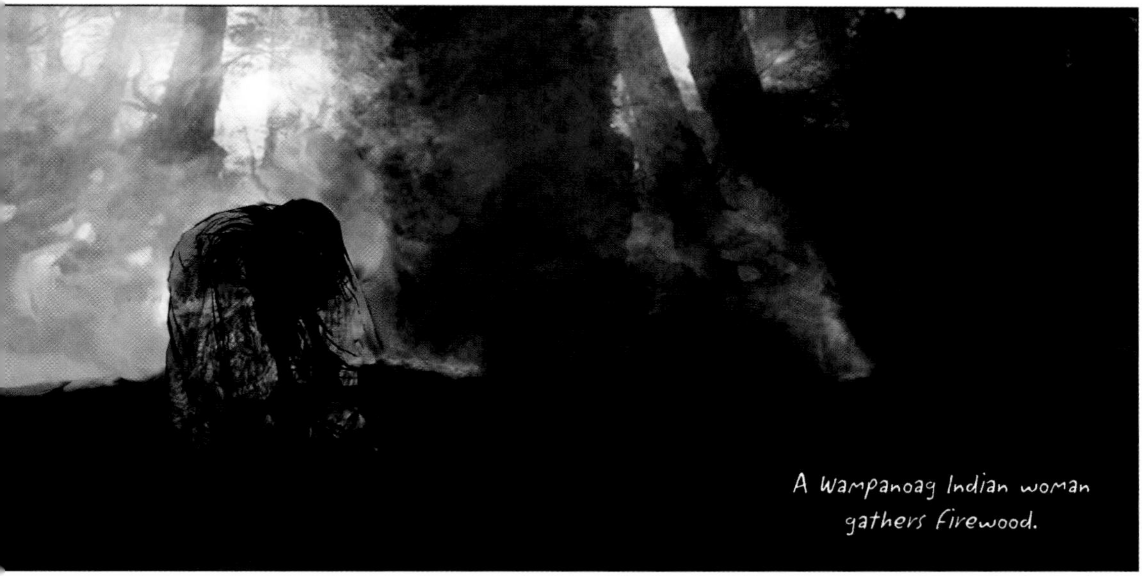
A Wampanoag Indian woman gathers firewood.

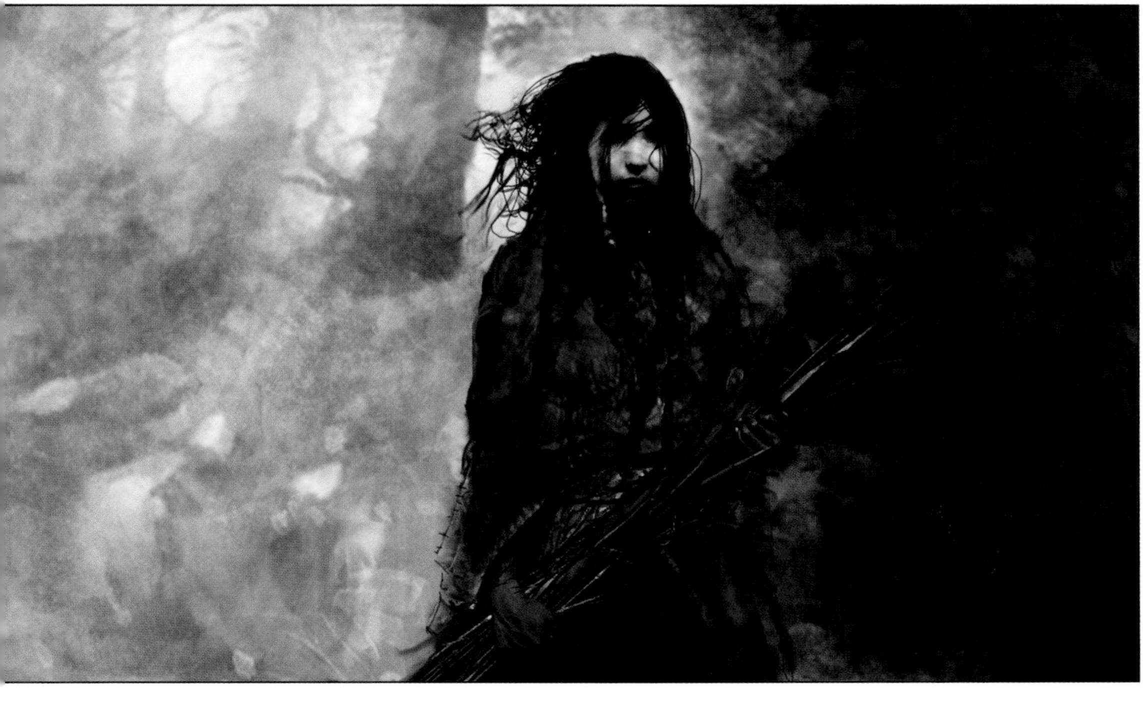

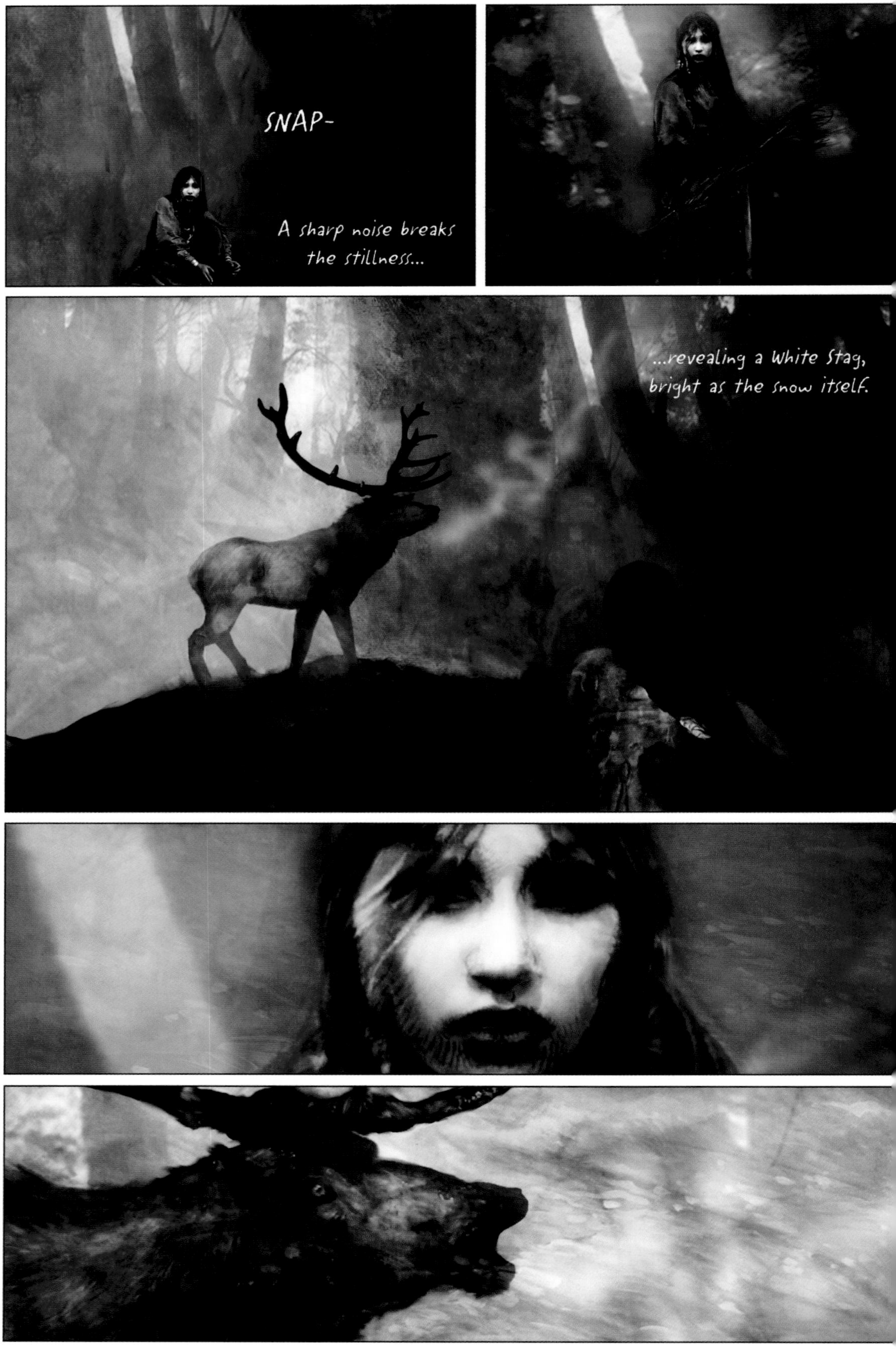
SNAP-
A sharp noise breaks the stillness...
...revealing a White Stag, bright as the snow itself.

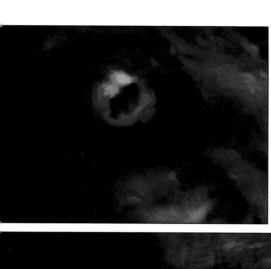
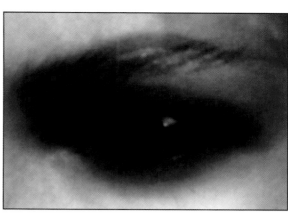

Suddenly—

13

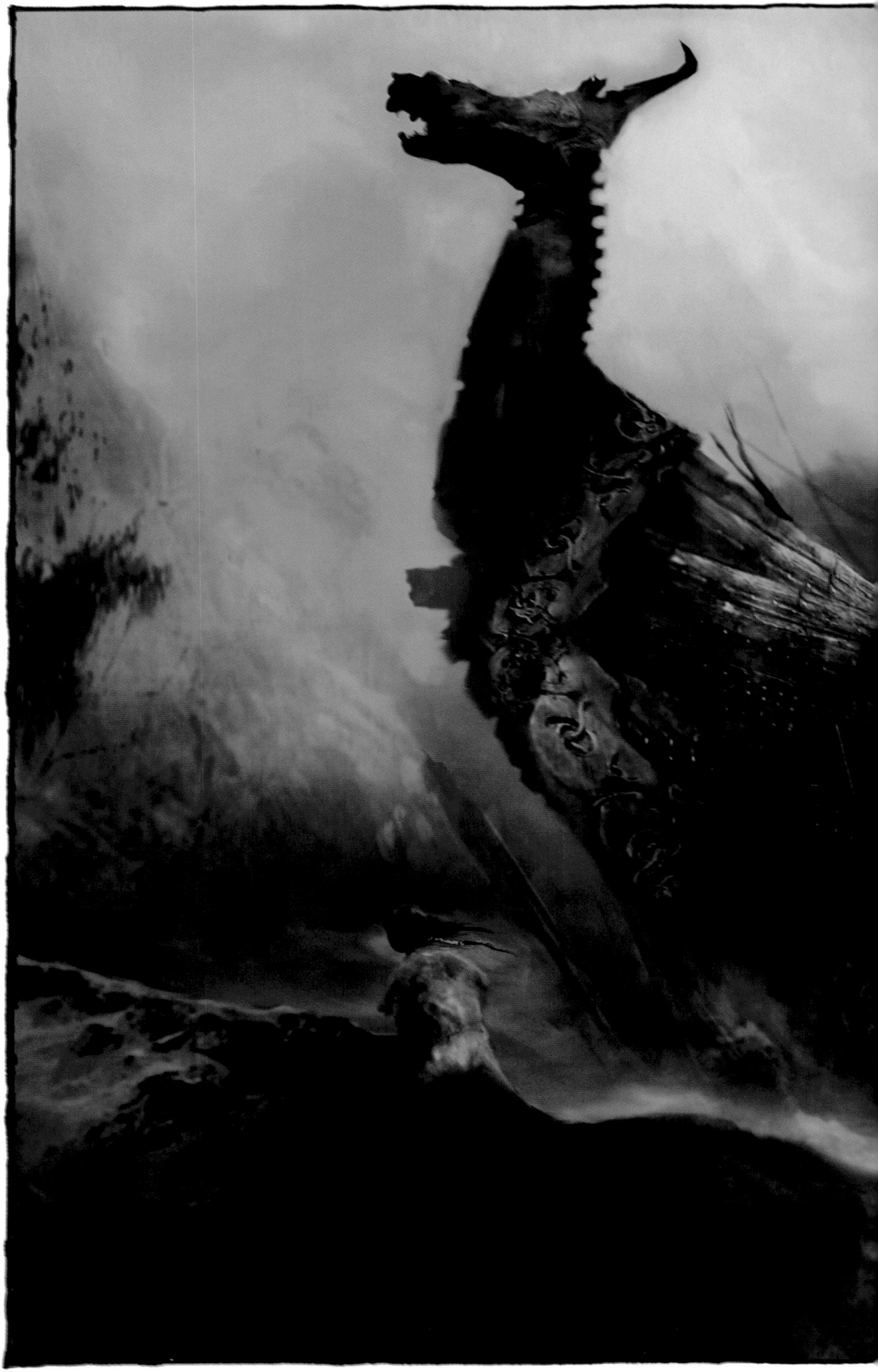

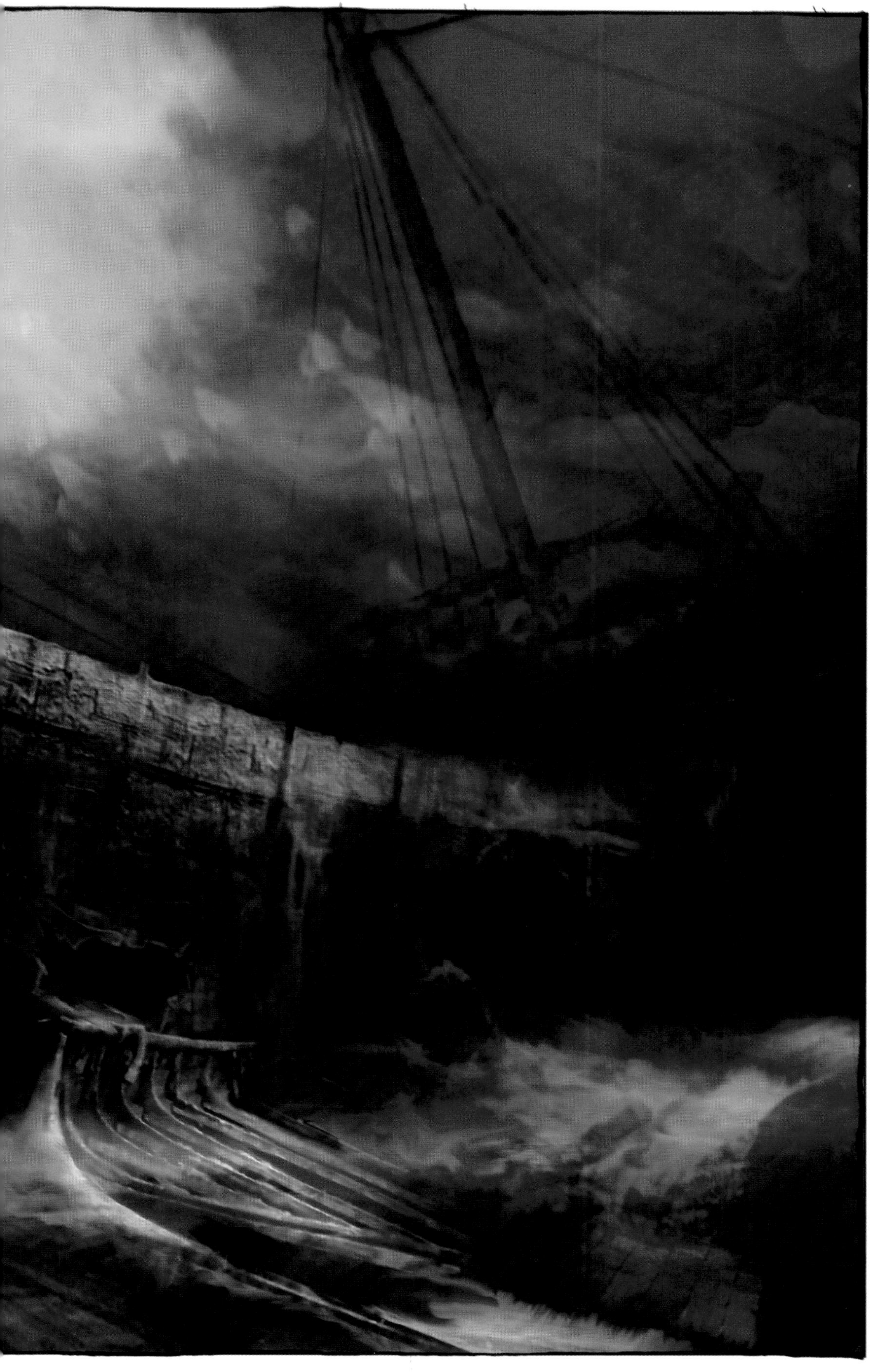

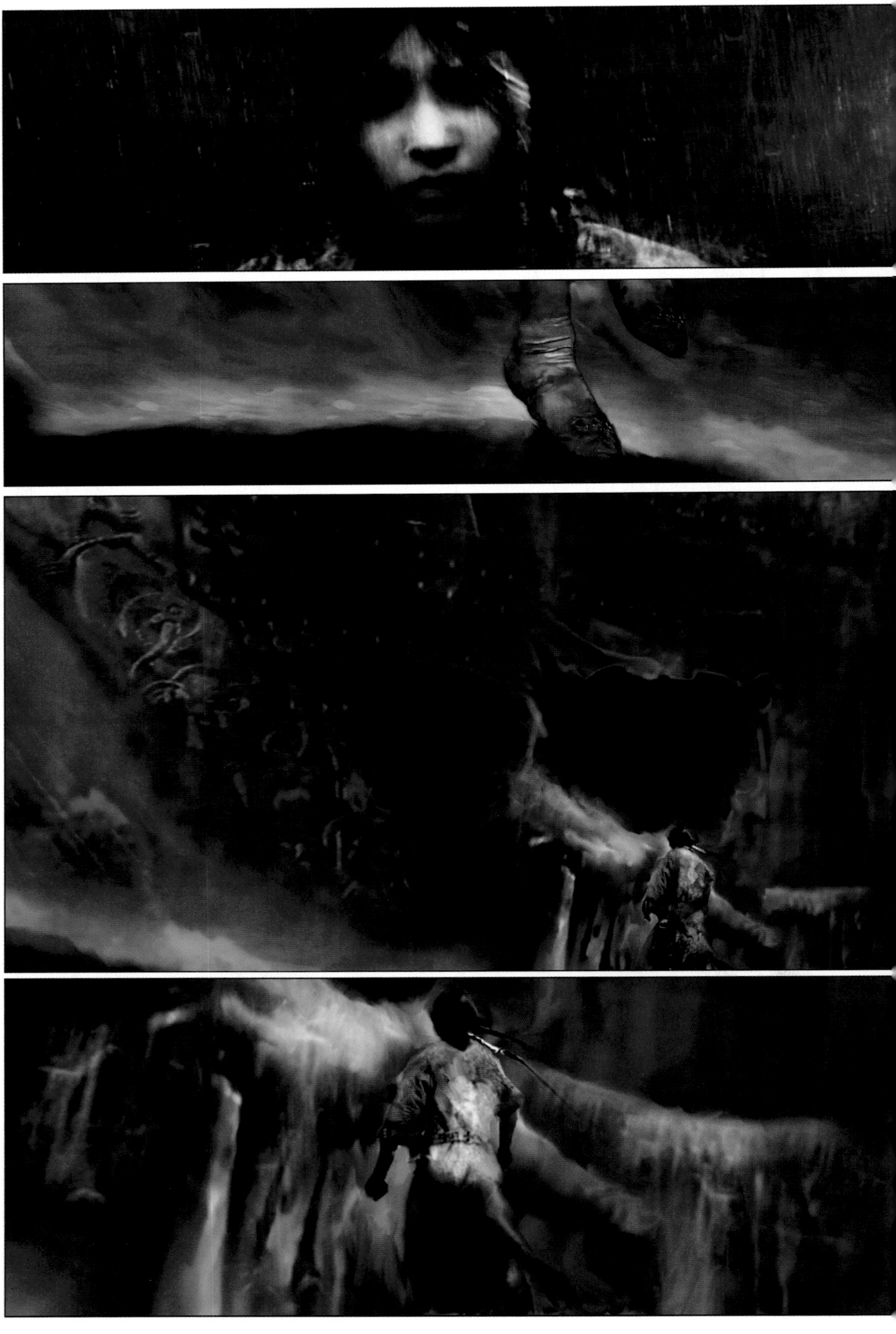

The ship's hold...

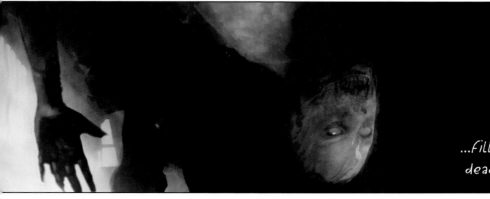

...filled with
dead bodies.

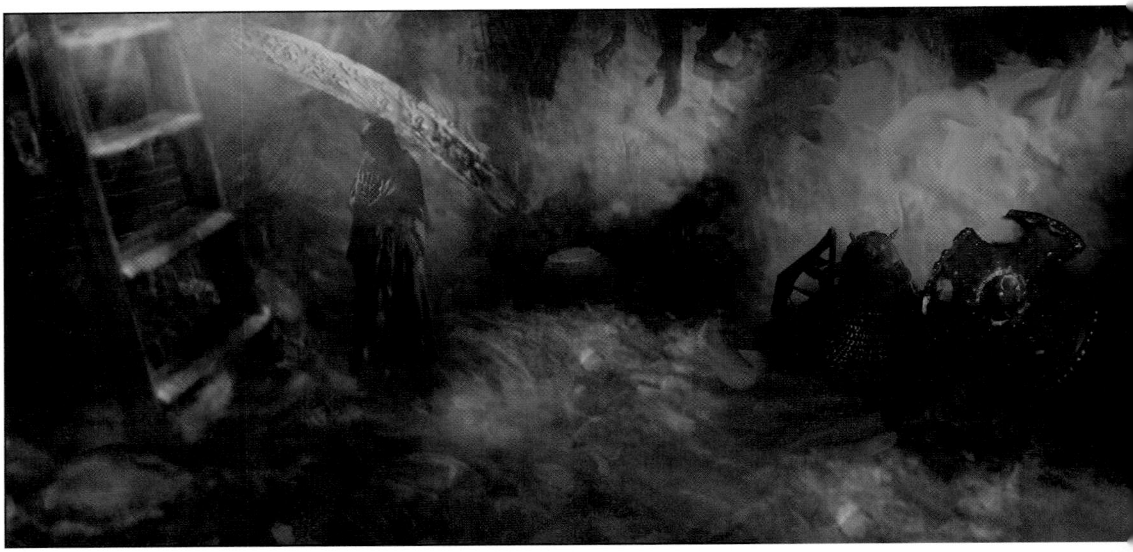

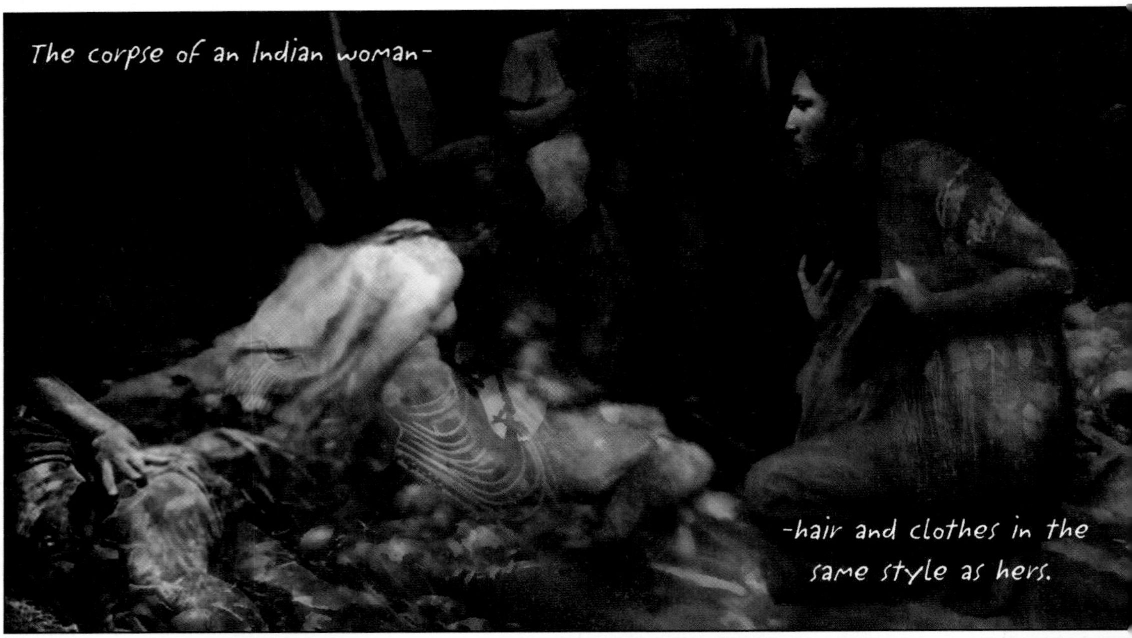
The corpse of an Indian woman-
-hair and clothes in the same style as hers.

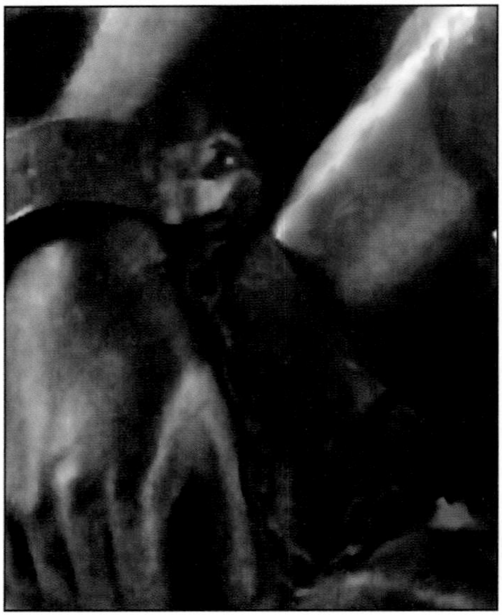

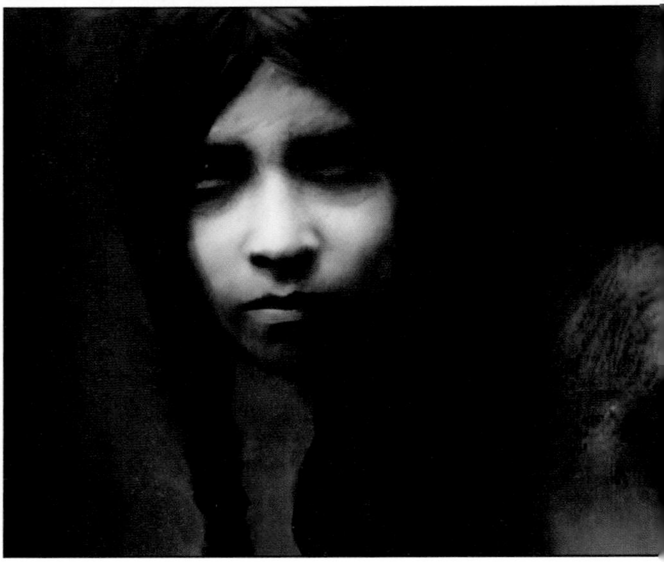

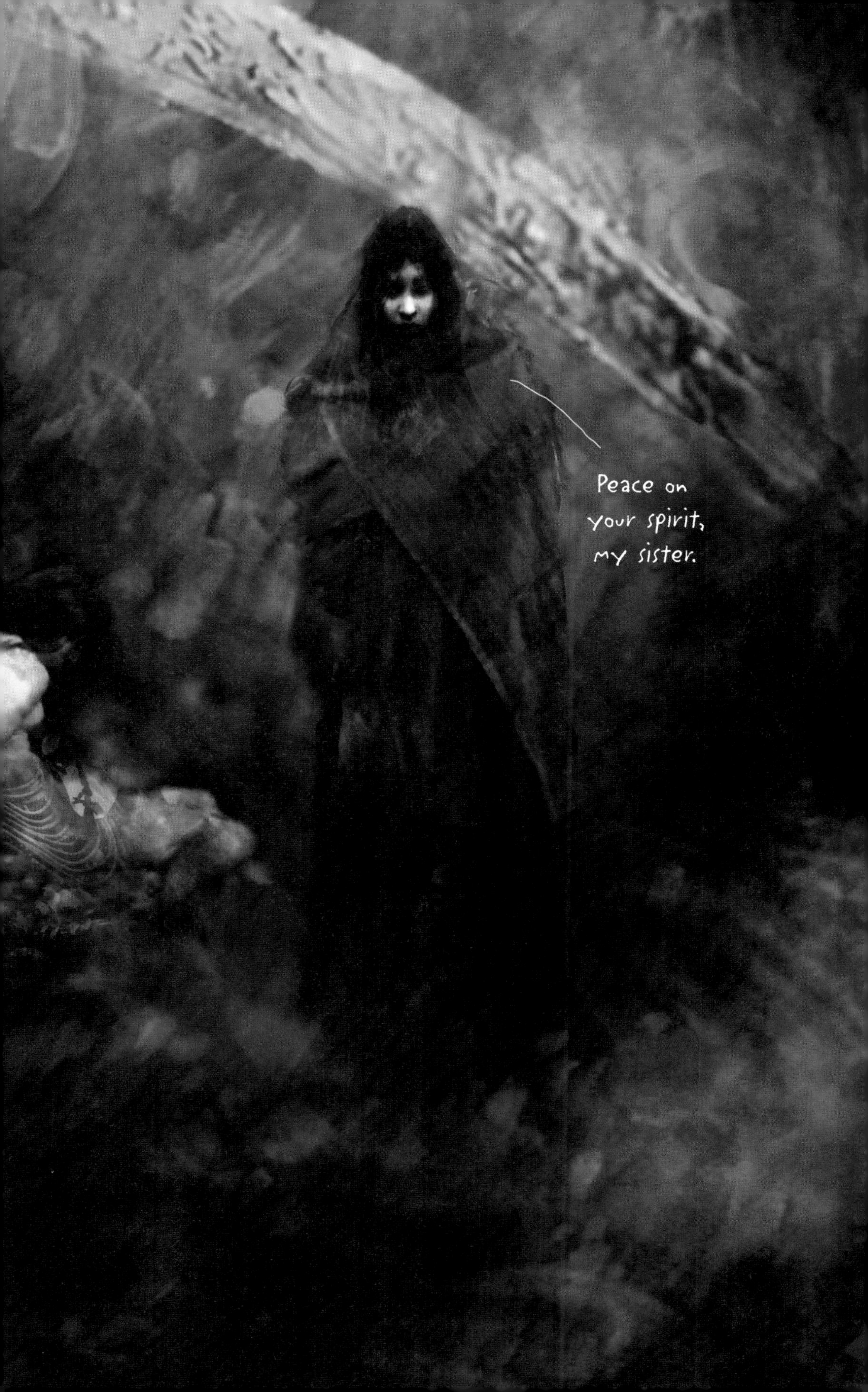
Peace on your spirit, my sister.

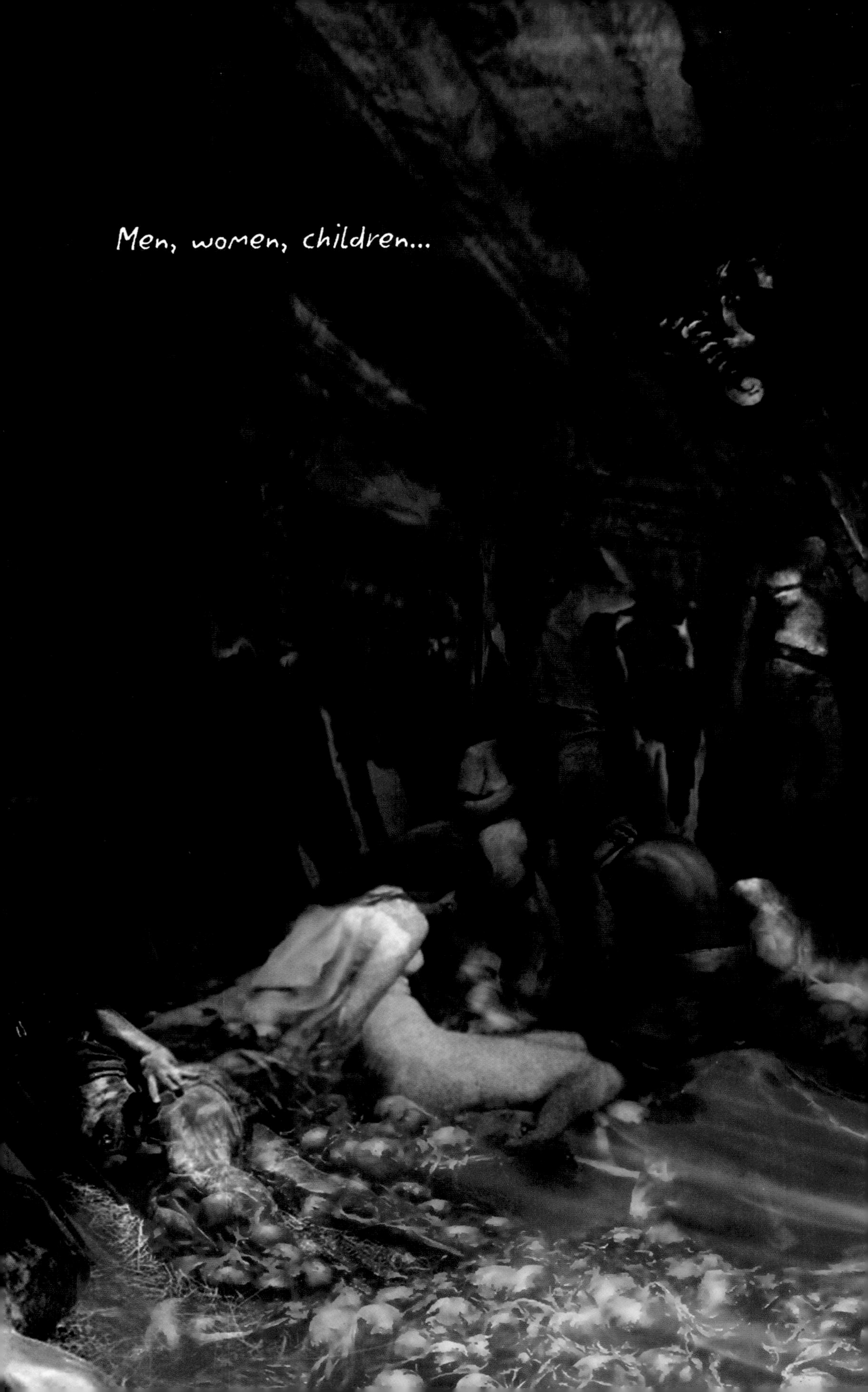
Men, women, children...

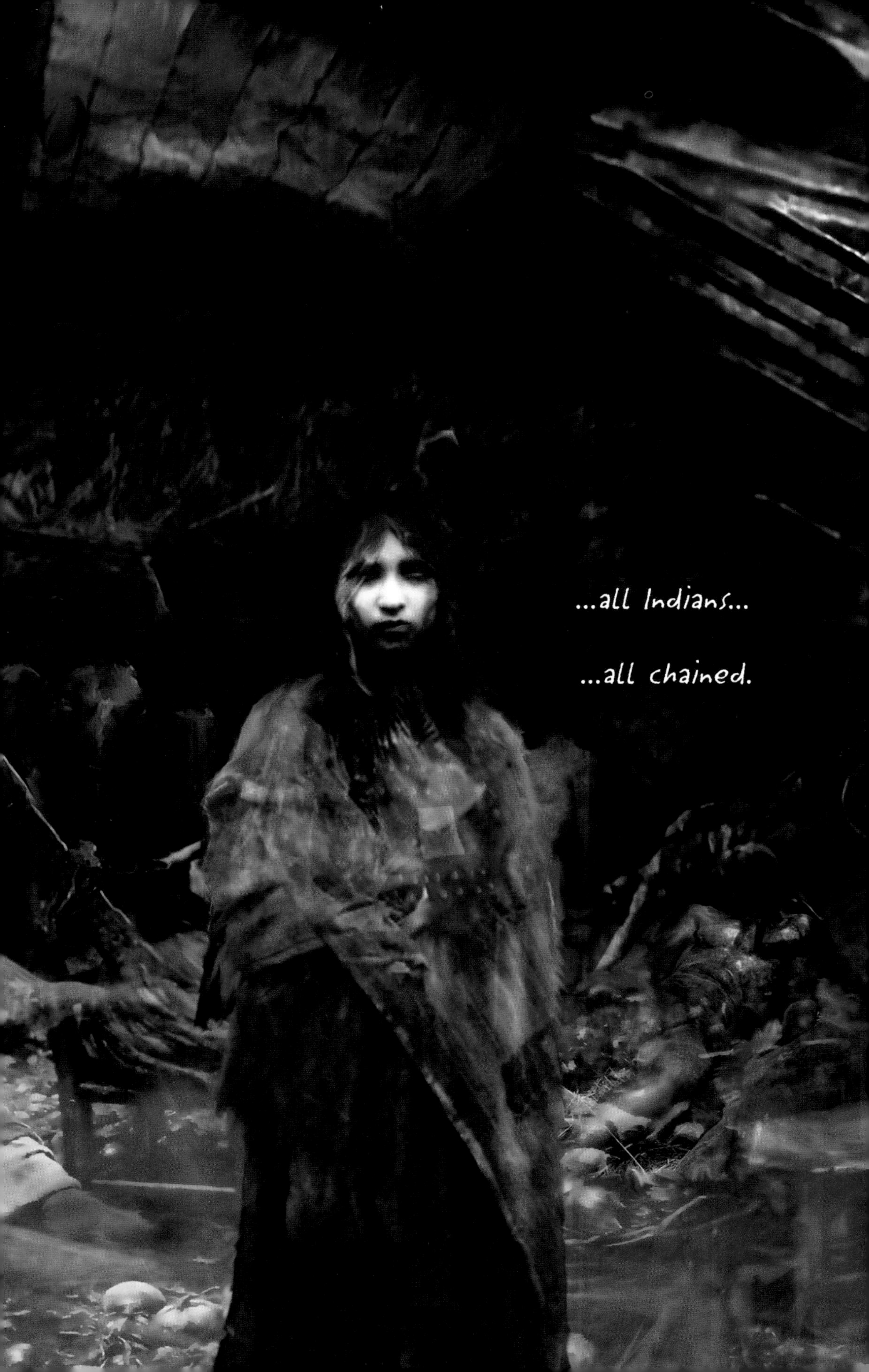
...all Indians...
...all chained.

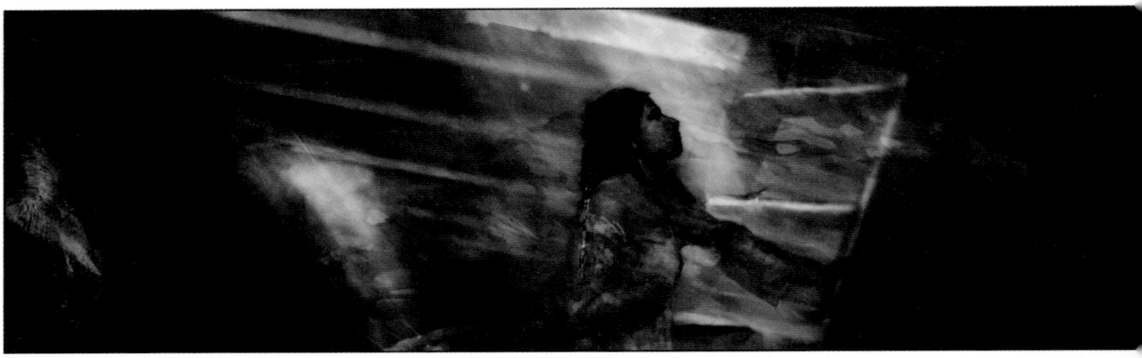

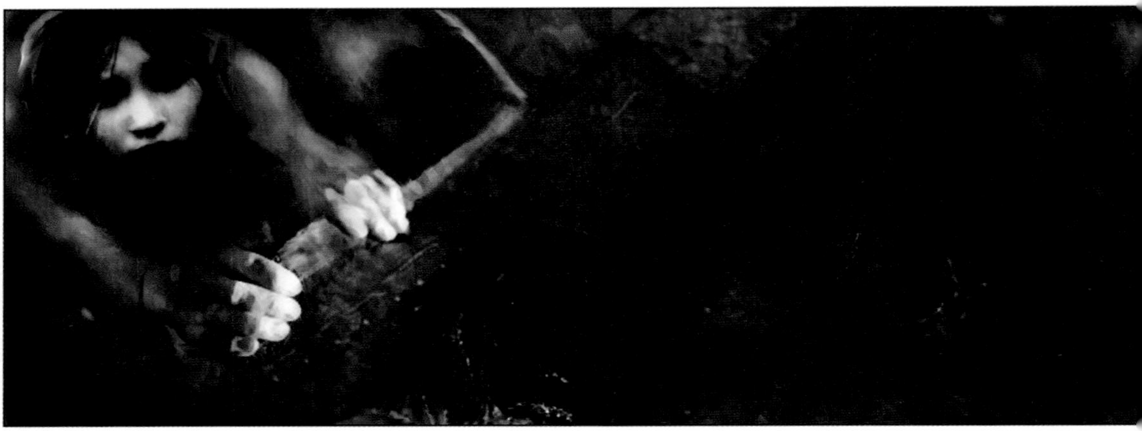

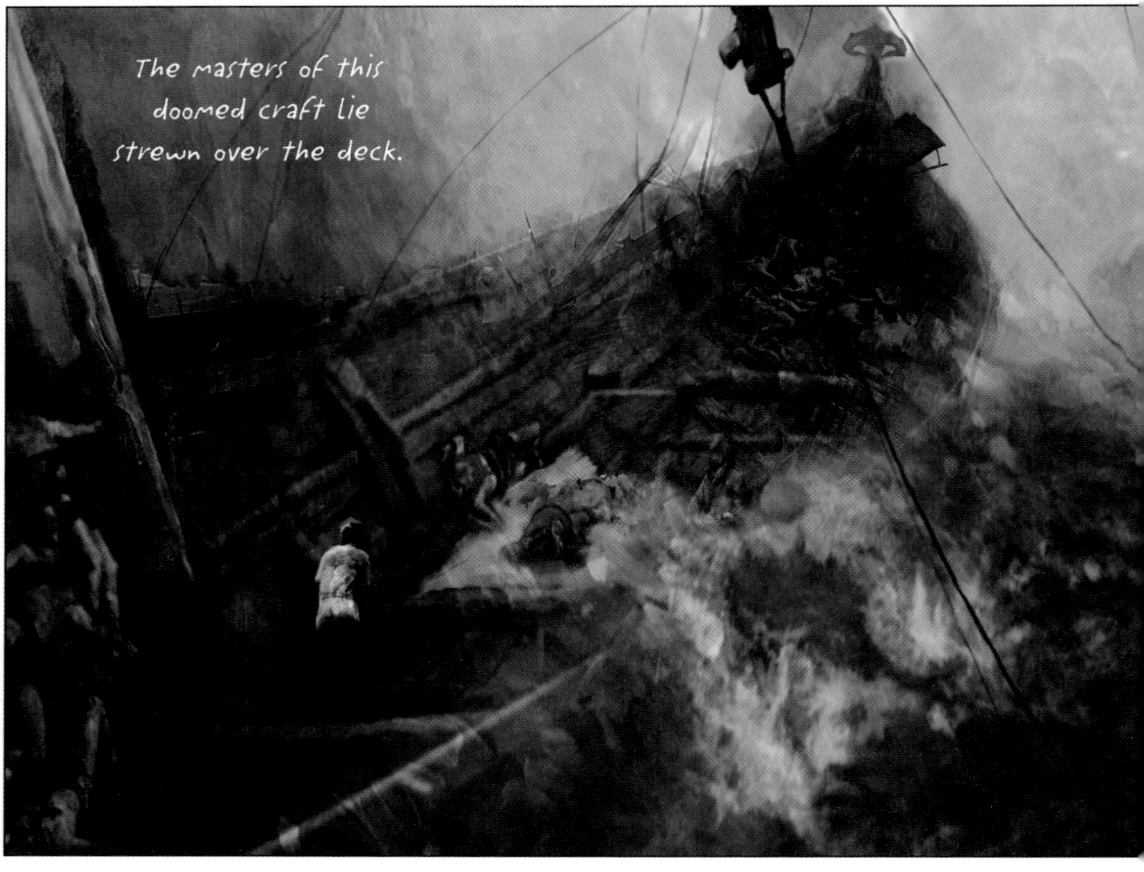
The masters of this doomed craft lie strewn over the deck.

Their swords, their shields...

...she's never seen
anything like this before.

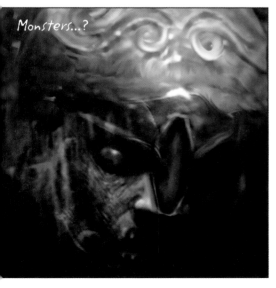

Monsters...?

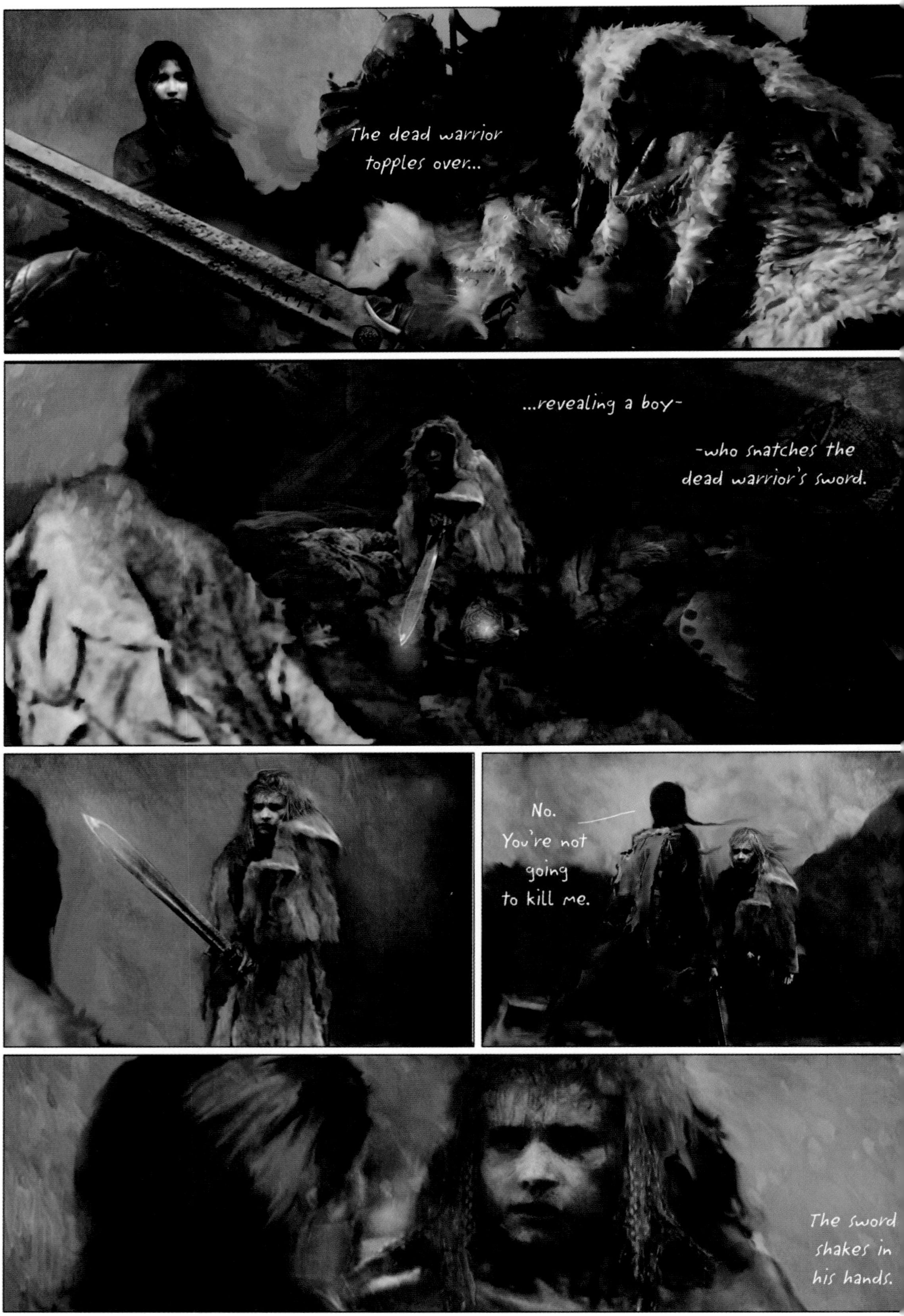
The dead warrior topples over...
...revealing a boy-
-who snatches the dead warrior's sword.
No. You're not going to kill me.
The sword shakes in his hands.

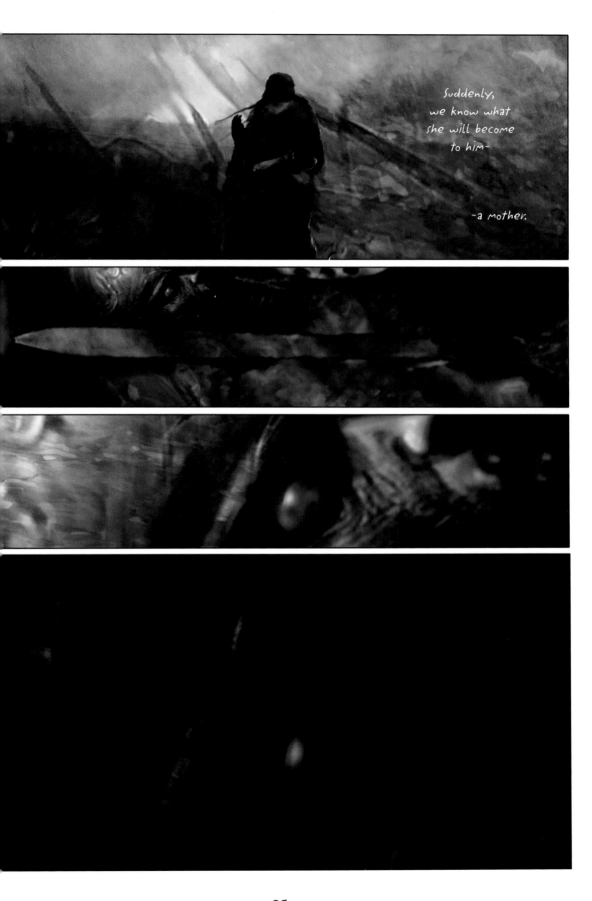

Suddenly,
we know what
she will become
to him—

—a mother.

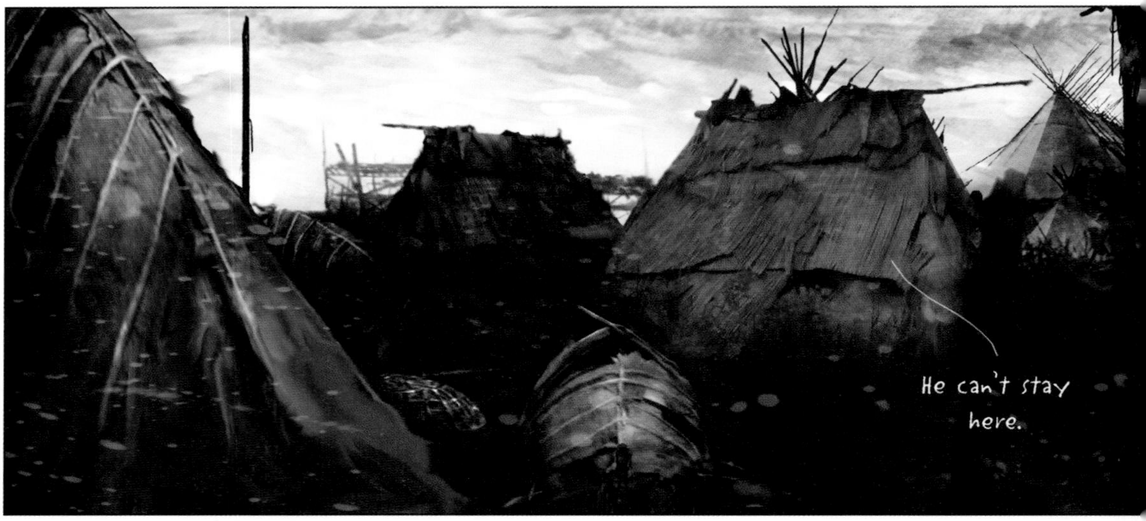
He can't stay here.

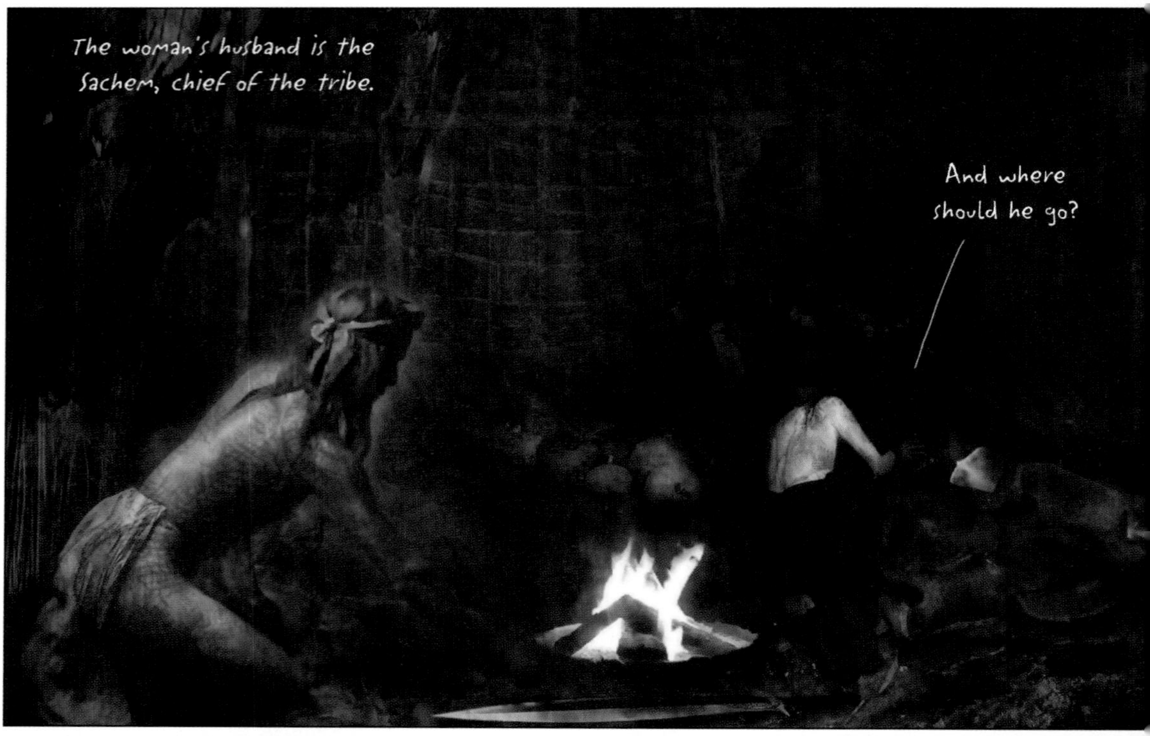
The woman's husband is the Sachem, chief of the tribe.
And where should he go?

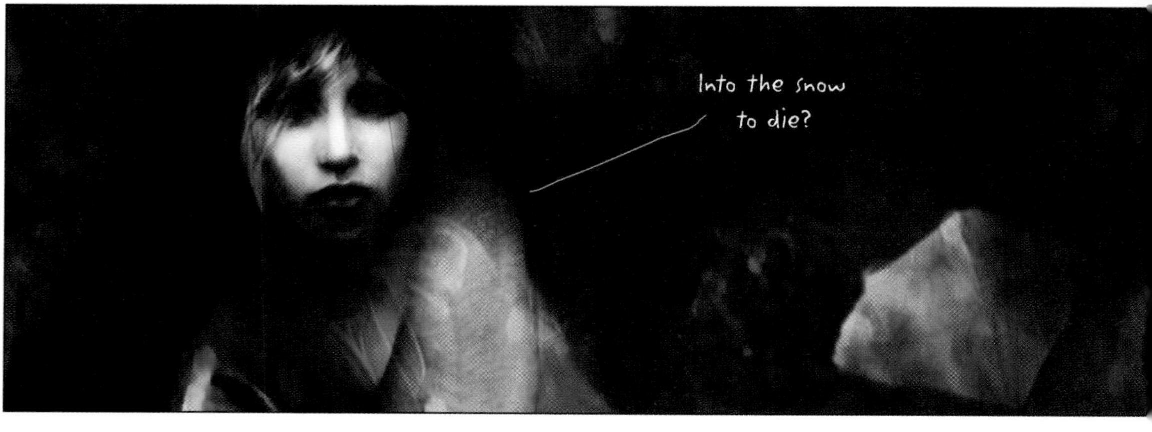
Into the snow to die?

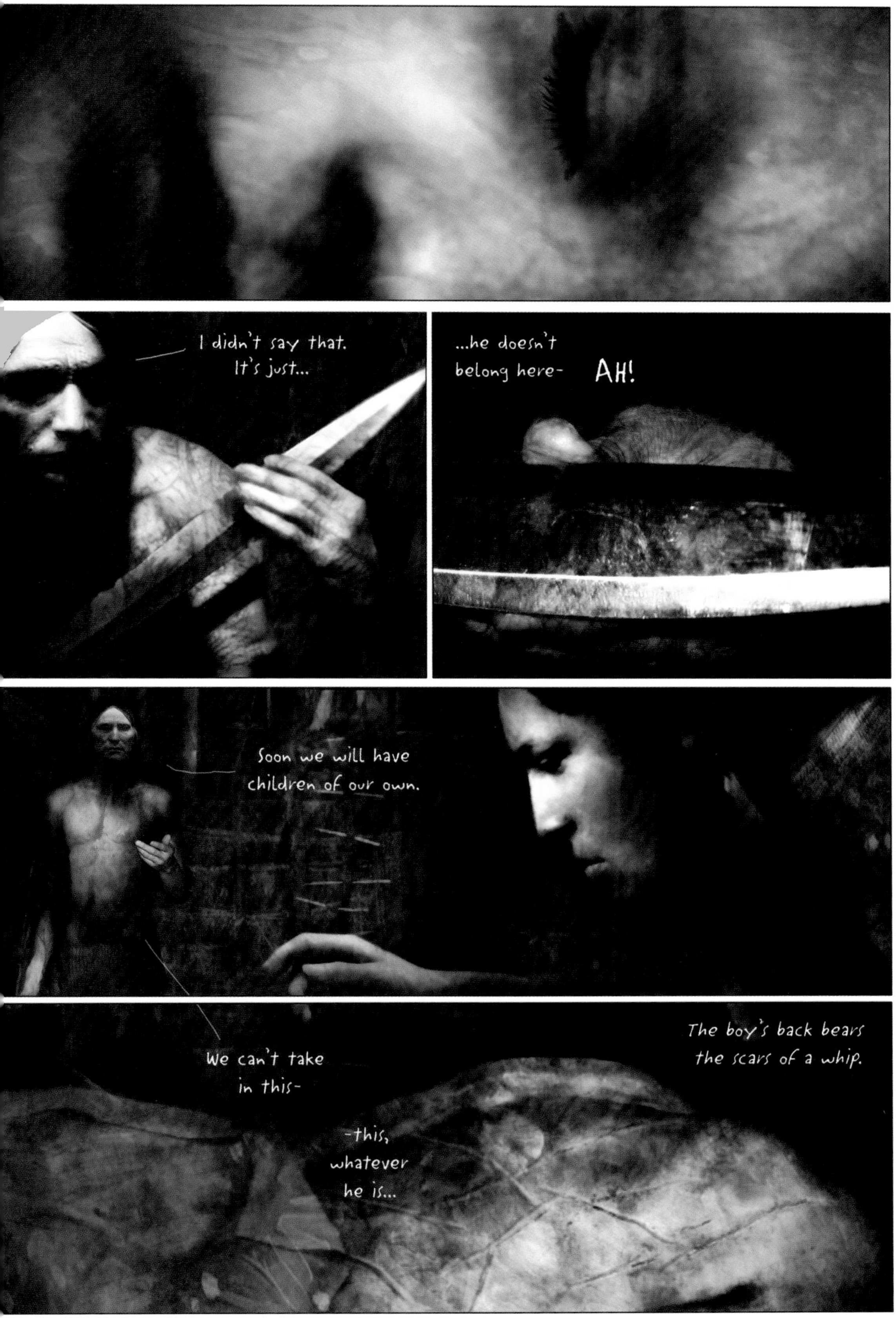

I didn't say that.
It's just...
...he doesn't
belong here-
AH!
Soon we will have
children of our own.
We can't take
in this-
The boy's back bears
the scars of a whip.
-this,
whatever
he is...

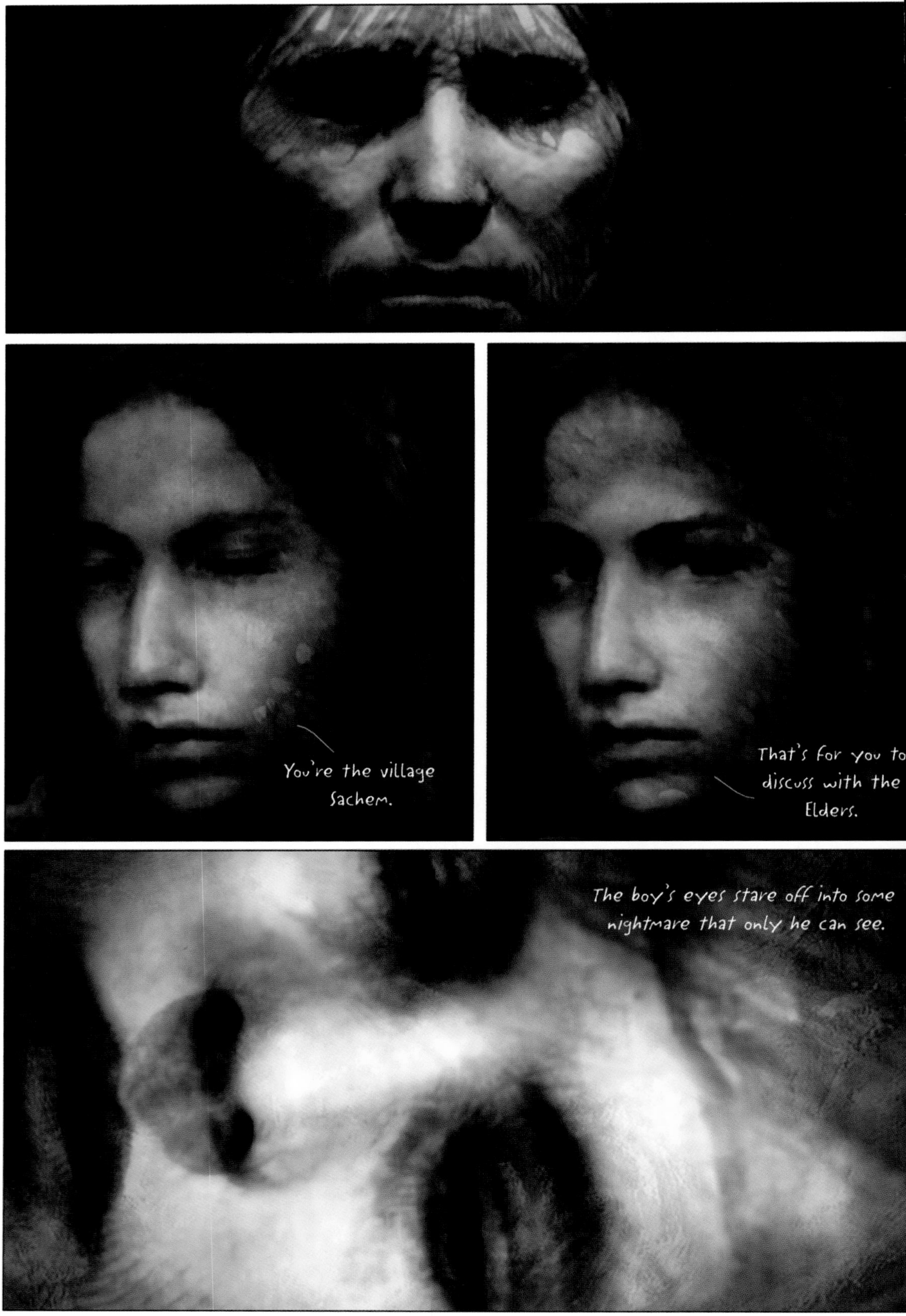
You're the village Sachem.
That's for you to discuss with the Elders.
The boy's eyes stare off into some nightmare that only he can see.

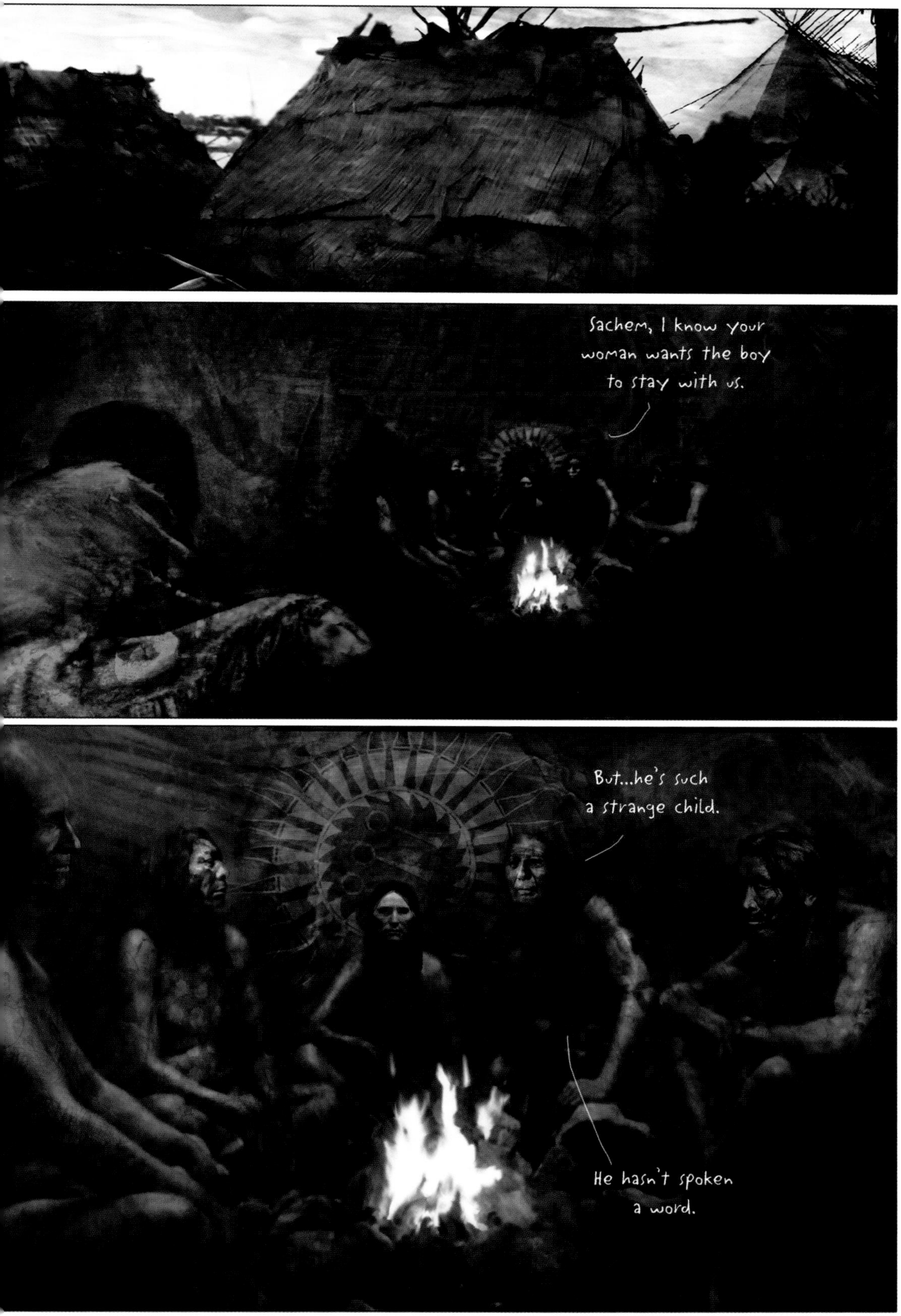
Sachem, I know your woman wants the boy to stay with us.
But...he's such a strange child.
He hasn't spoken a word.

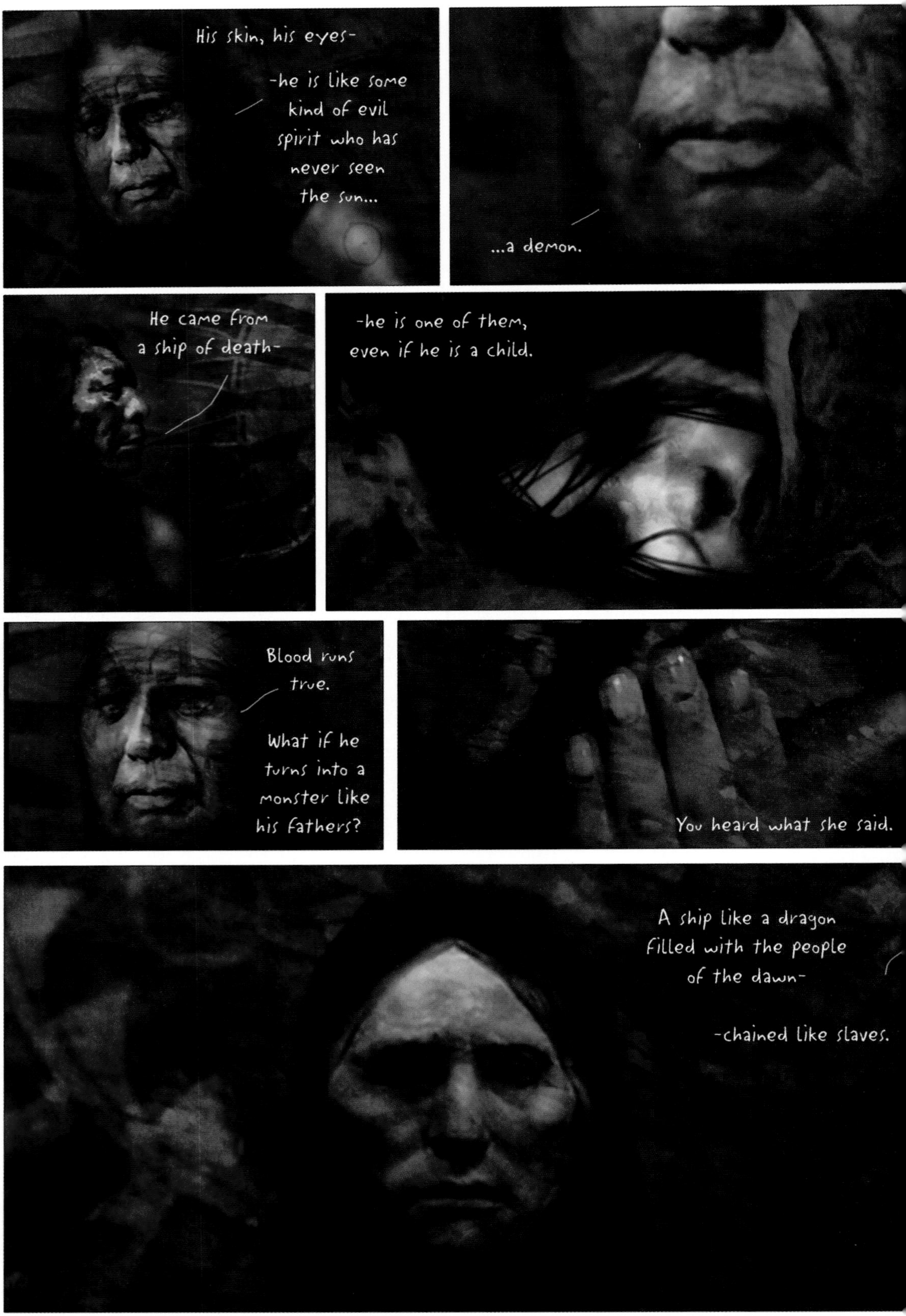
His skin, his eyes-
-he is like some kind of evil spirit who has never seen the sun...
...a demon.
He came from a ship of death-
-he is one of them, even if he is a child.
Blood runs true.
What if he turns into a monster like his fathers?
You heard what she said.
A ship like a dragon filled with the people of the dawn-
-chained like slaves.

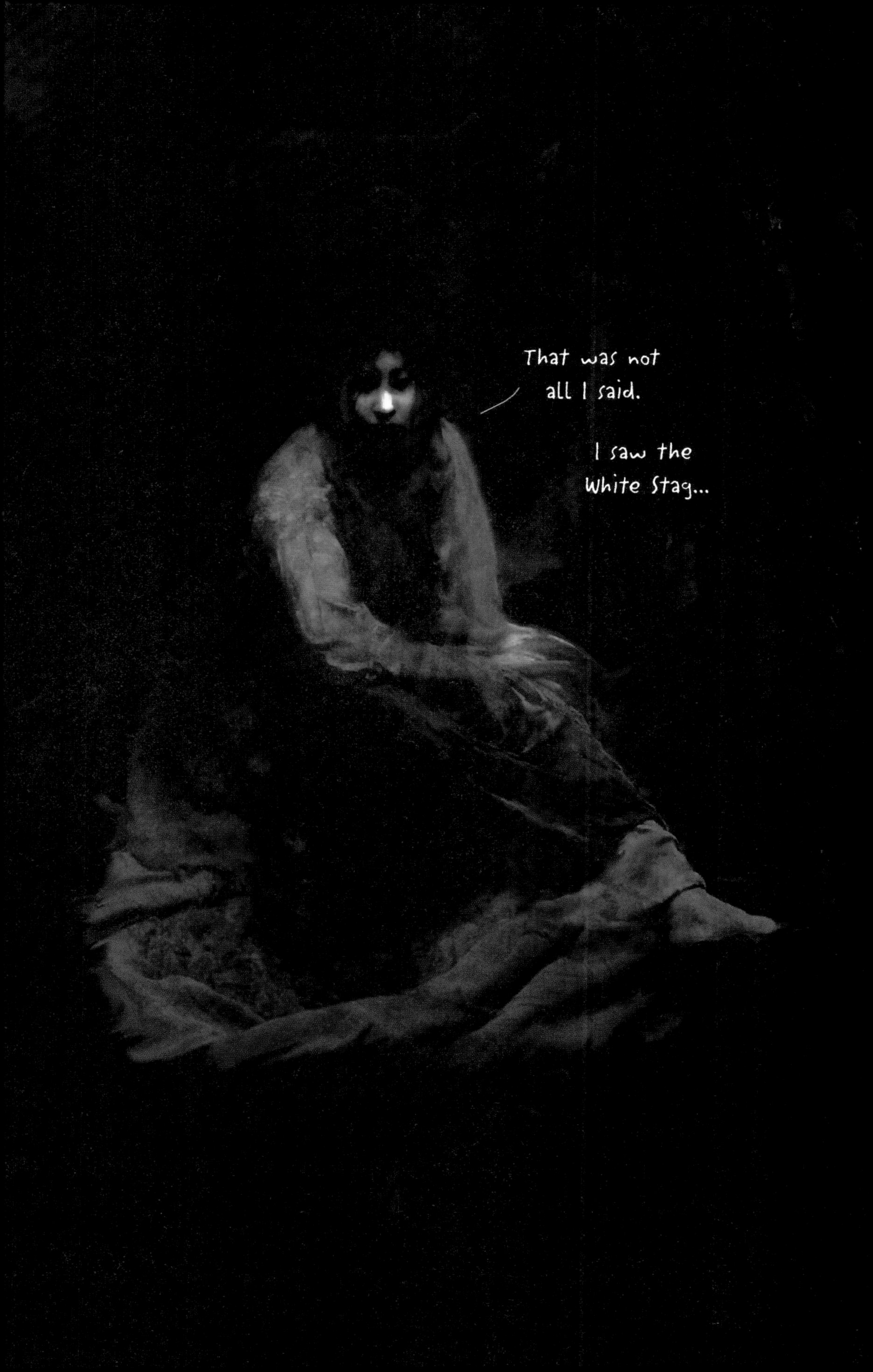
That was not all I said.
I saw the White Stag...

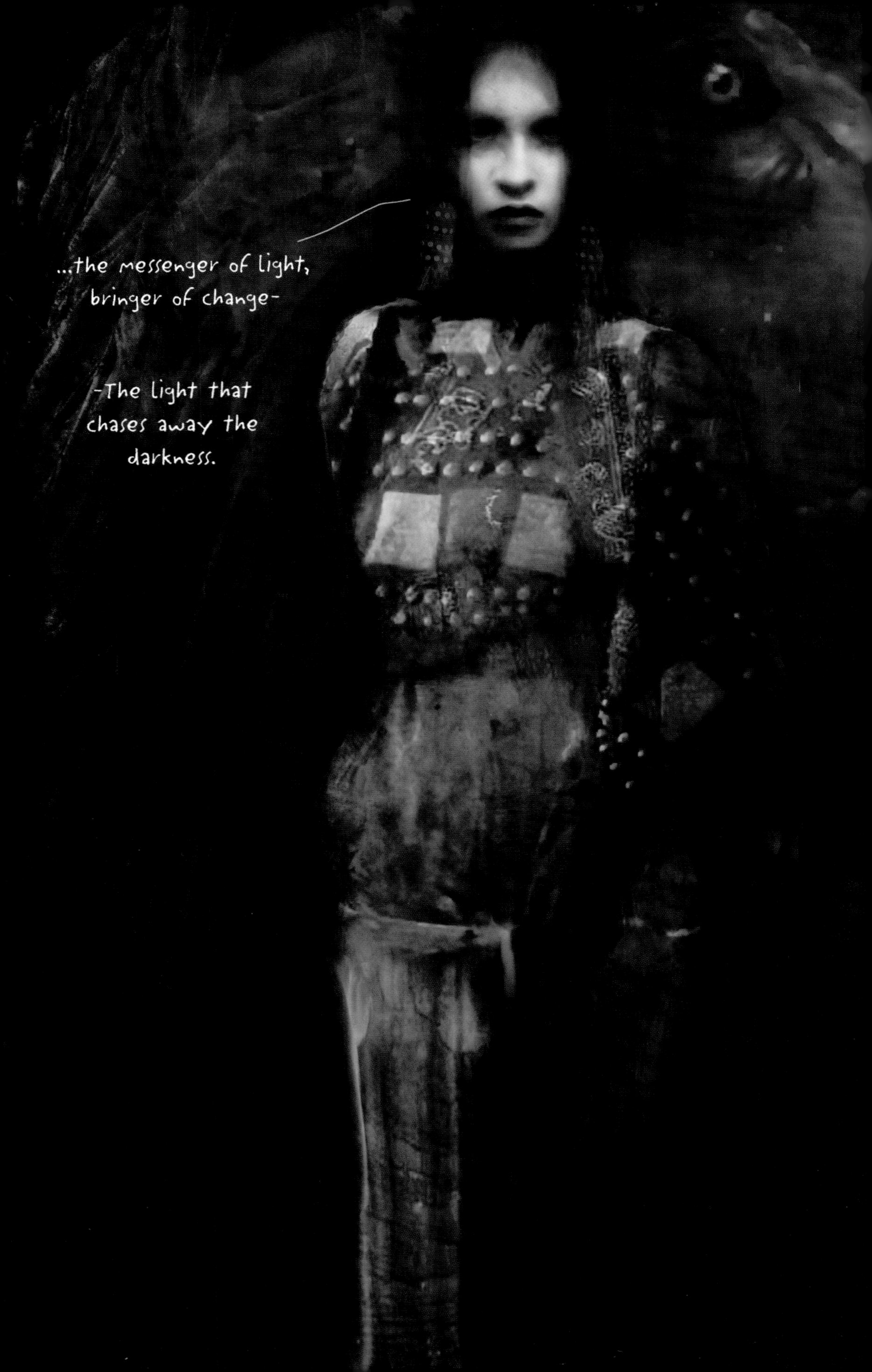
...the messenger of light, bringer of change-
-The light that chases away the darkness.

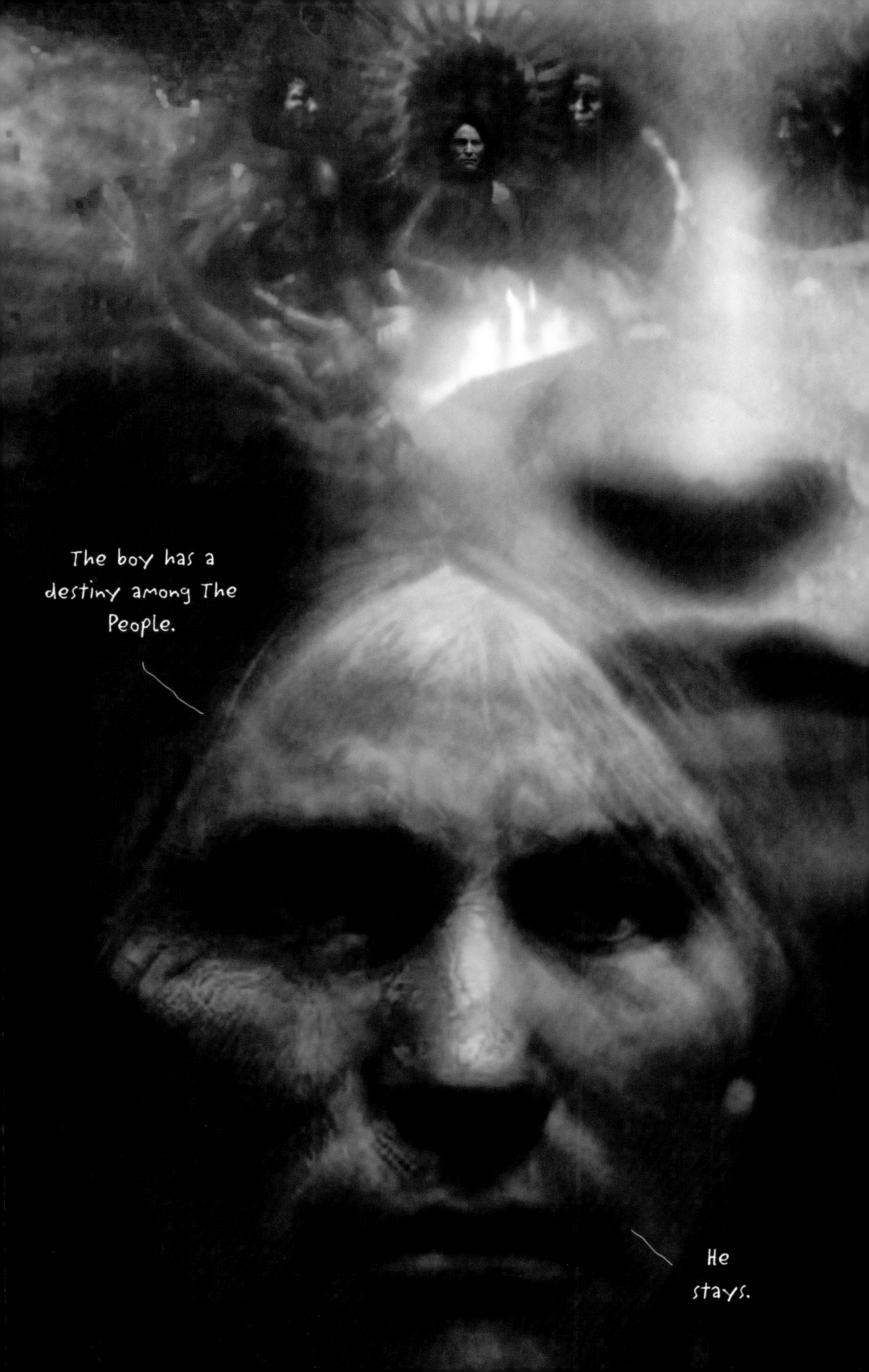
The boy has a destiny among The People.
He stays.

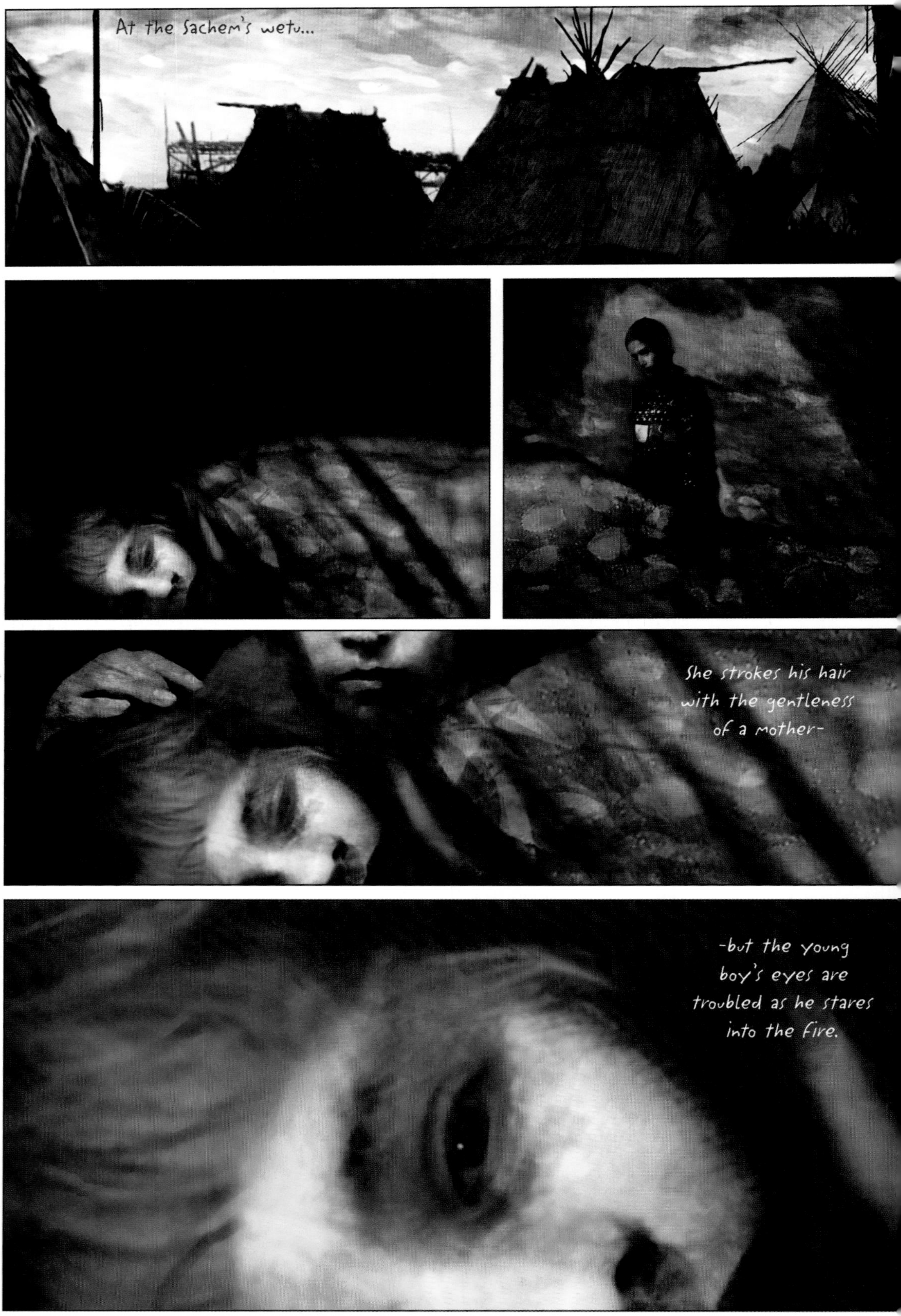
At the Sachem's wetu...
She strokes his hair with the gentleness of a mother-
-but the young boy's eyes are troubled as he stares into the fire.

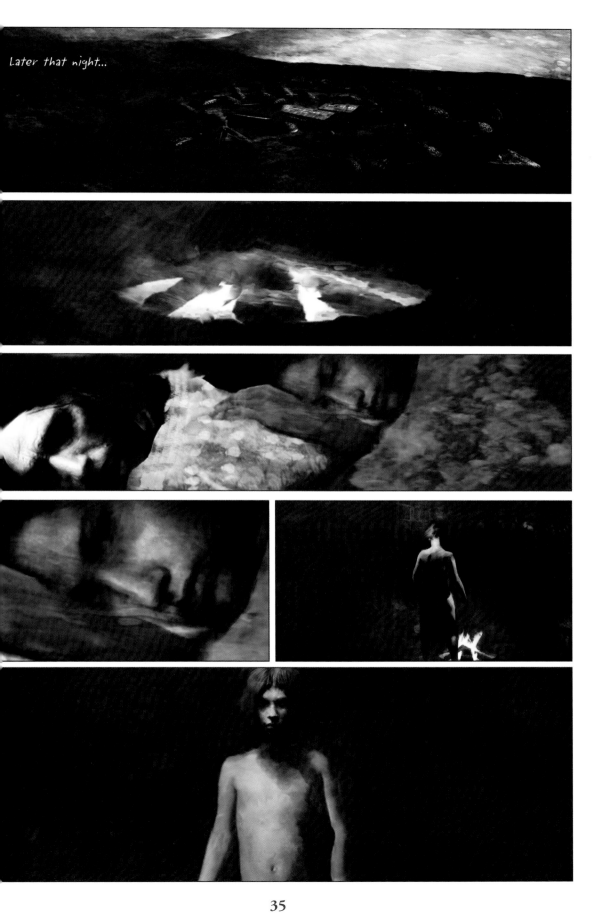

Later that night...

35

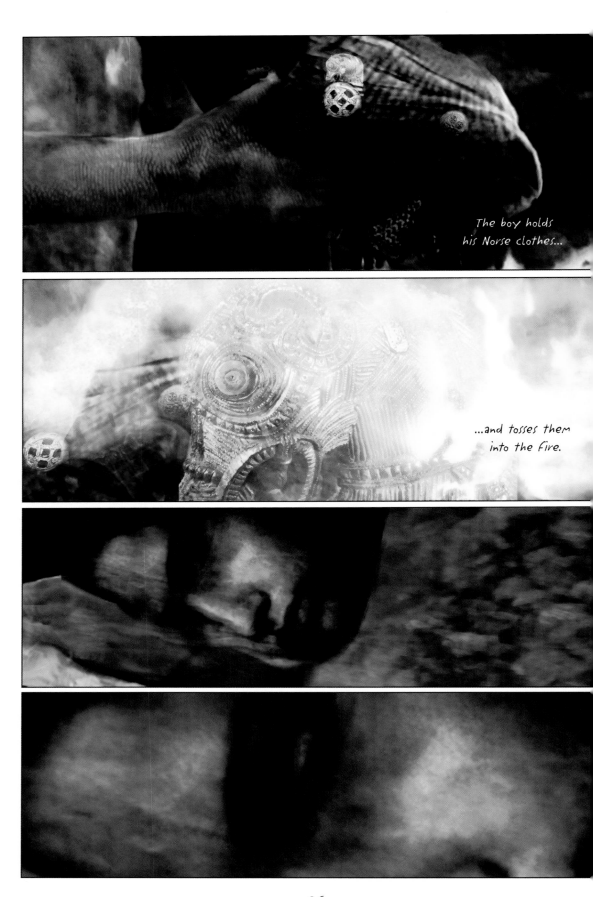

The boy holds
his Norse clothes...

...and tosses them
into the fire.

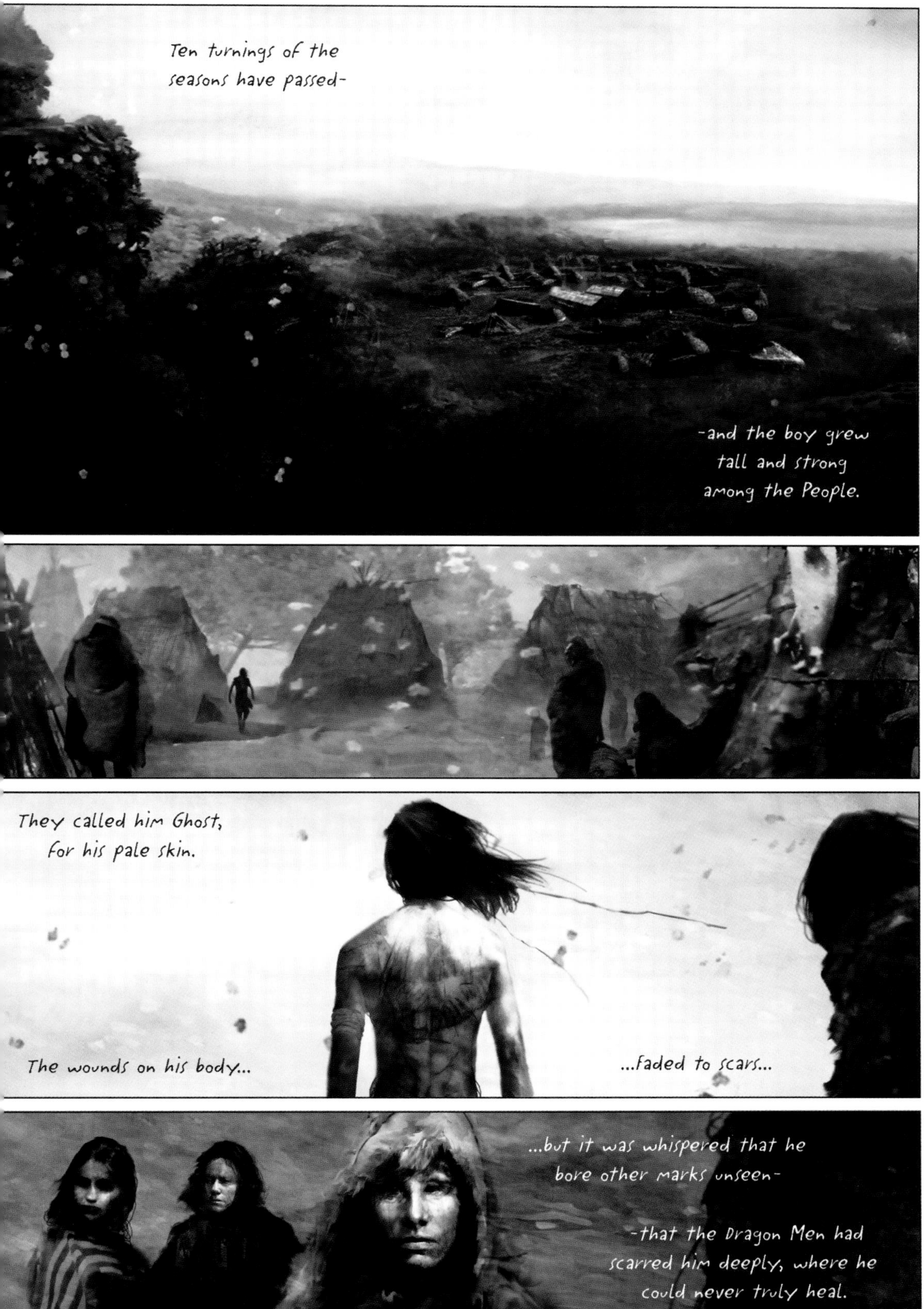
Ten turnings of the seasons have passed-
-and the boy grew tall and strong among the People.
They called him Ghost, for his pale skin.
The wounds on his body...
...faded to scars...
...but it was whispered that he bore other marks unseen-
-that the Dragon Men had scarred him deeply, where he could never truly heal.

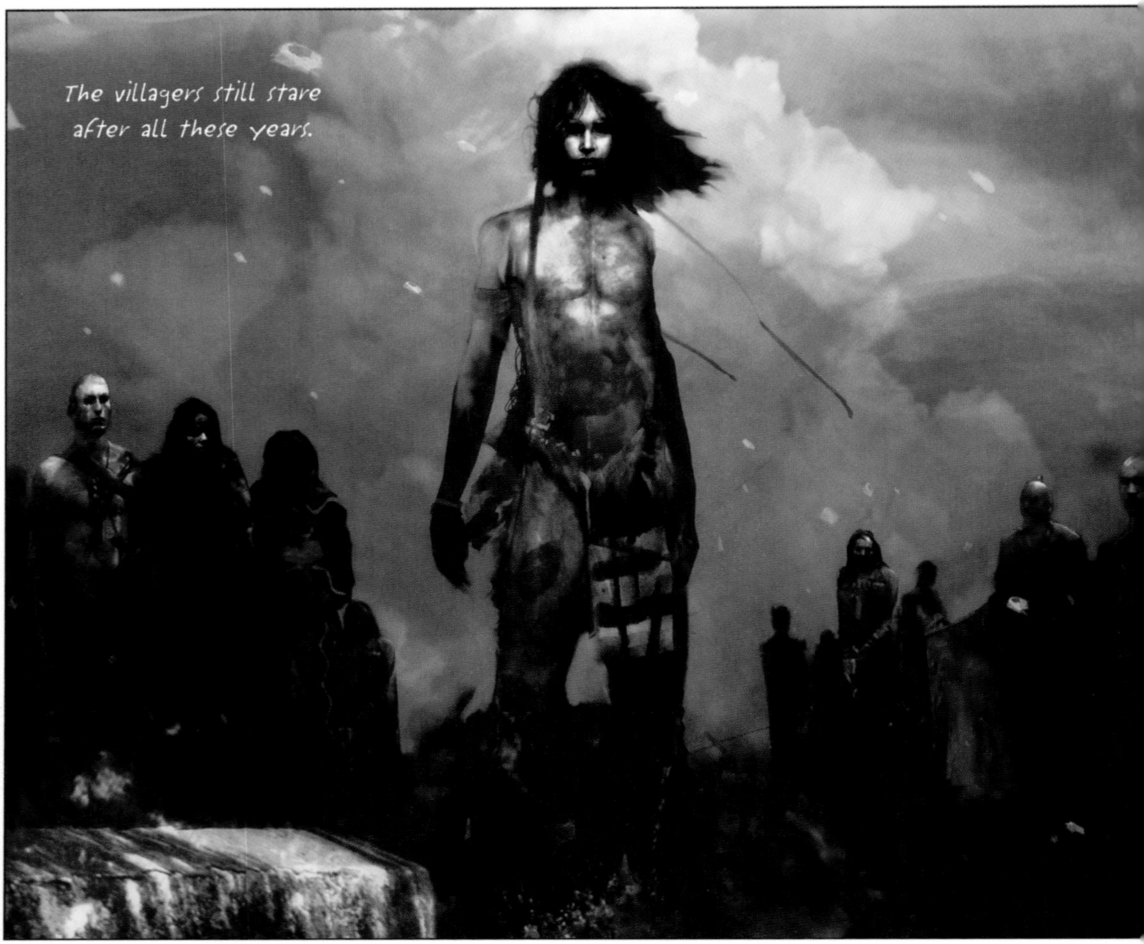
The villagers still stare after all these years.

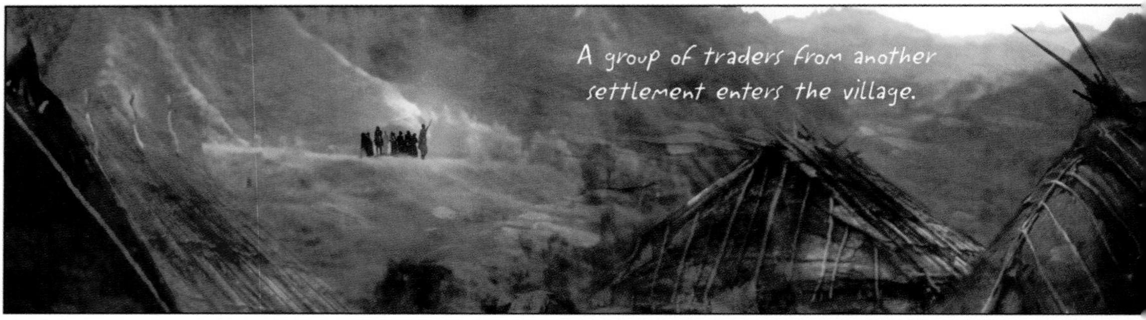
A group of traders from another settlement enters the village.

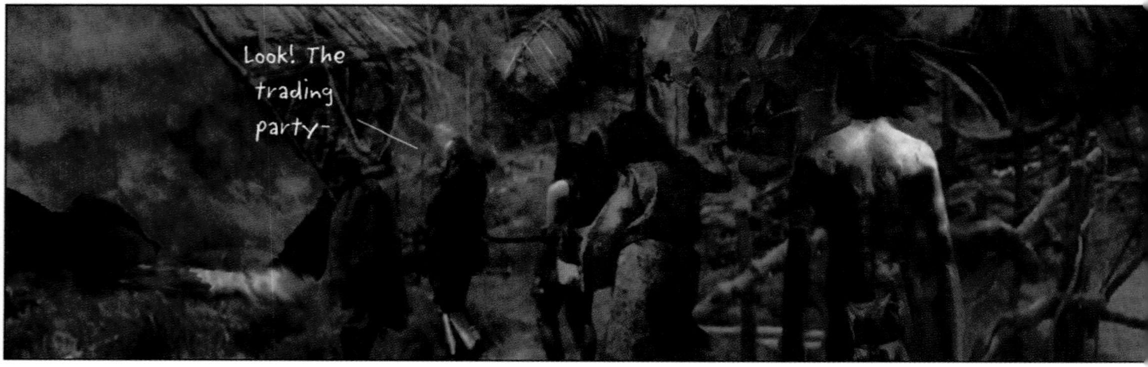
Look! The trading party-

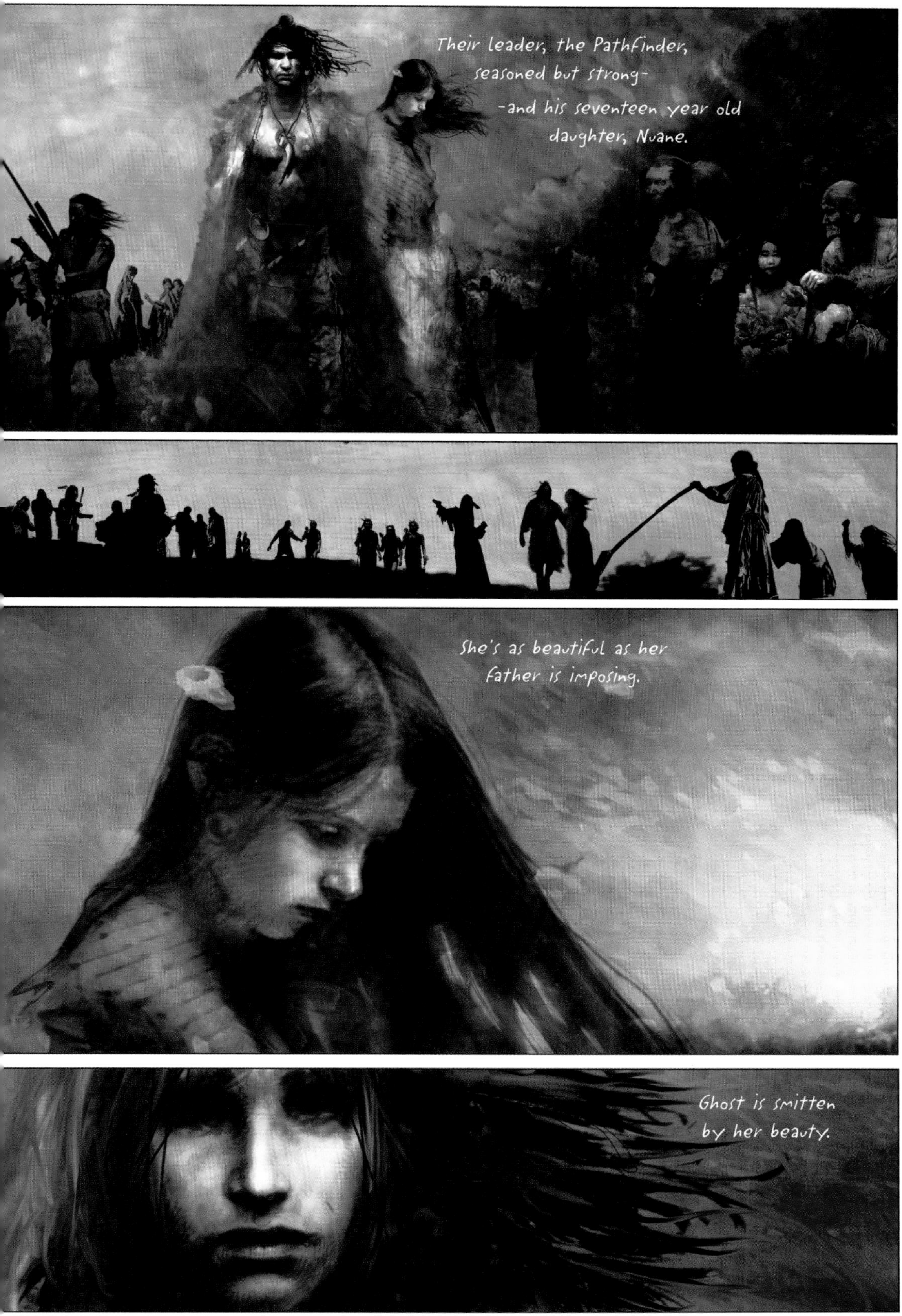
Their leader, the Pathfinder, seasoned but strong-
-and his seventeen year old daughter, Nuane.
She's as beautiful as her father is imposing.
Ghost is smitten by her beauty.

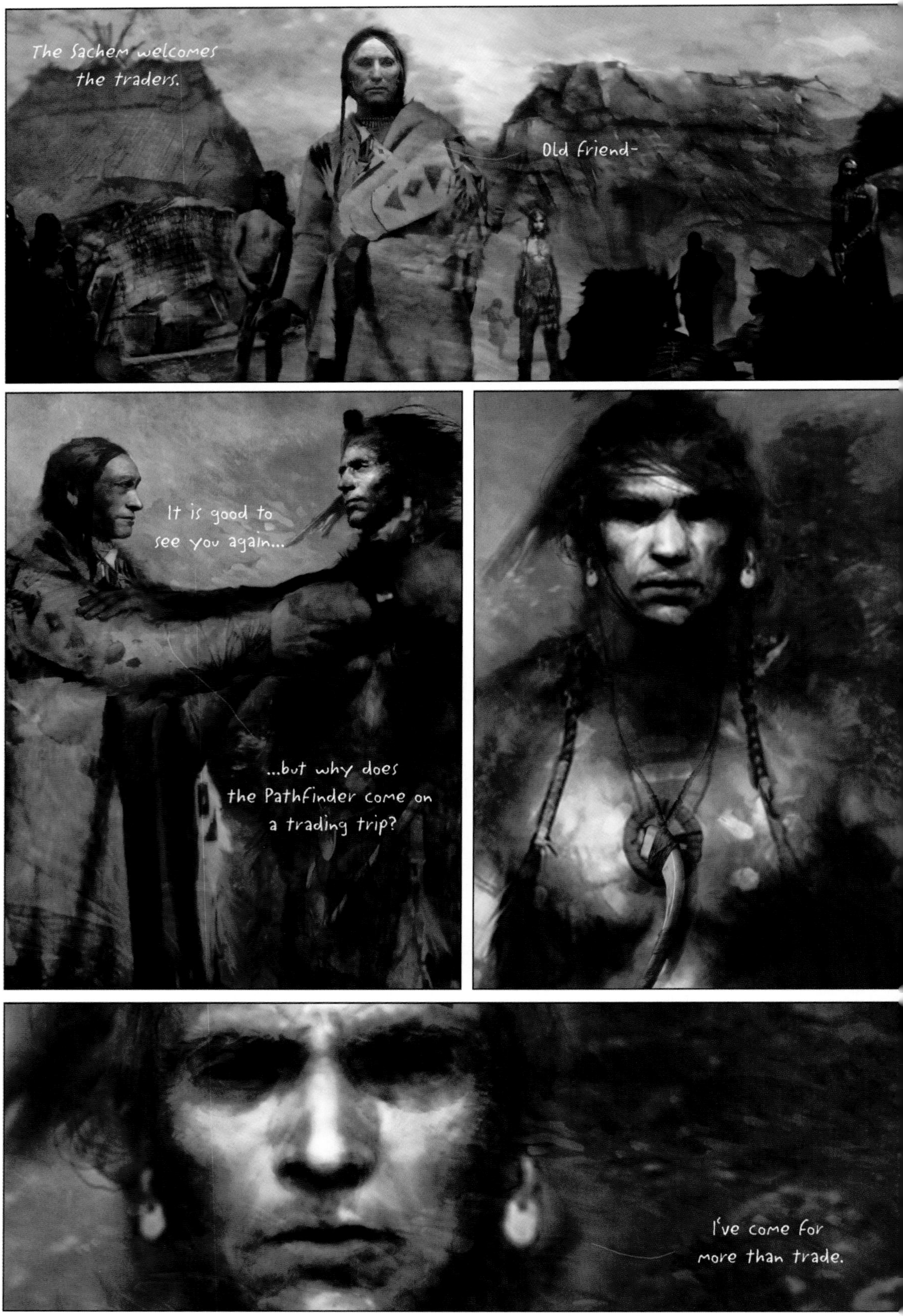
The Sachem welcomes the traders.
Old friend-
It is good to see you again...
...but why does the Pathfinder come on a trading trip?
I've come for more than trade.

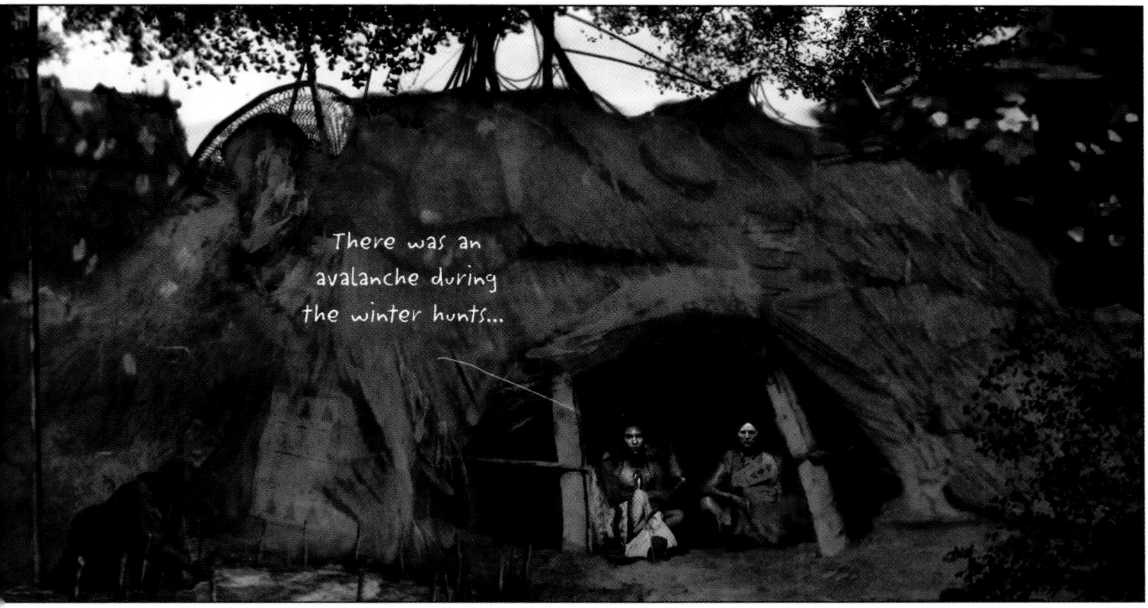
There was an avalanche during the winter hunts...

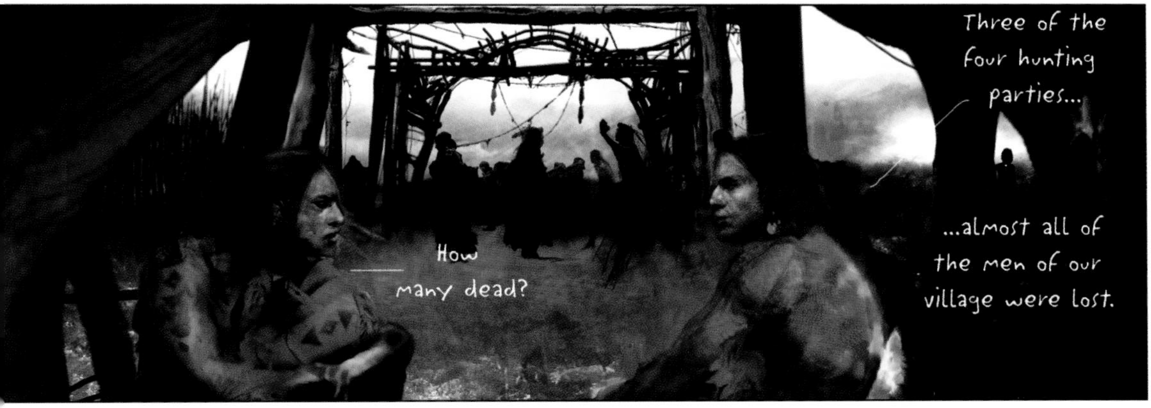
How many dead?
Three of the four hunting parties...
...almost all of the men of our village were lost.

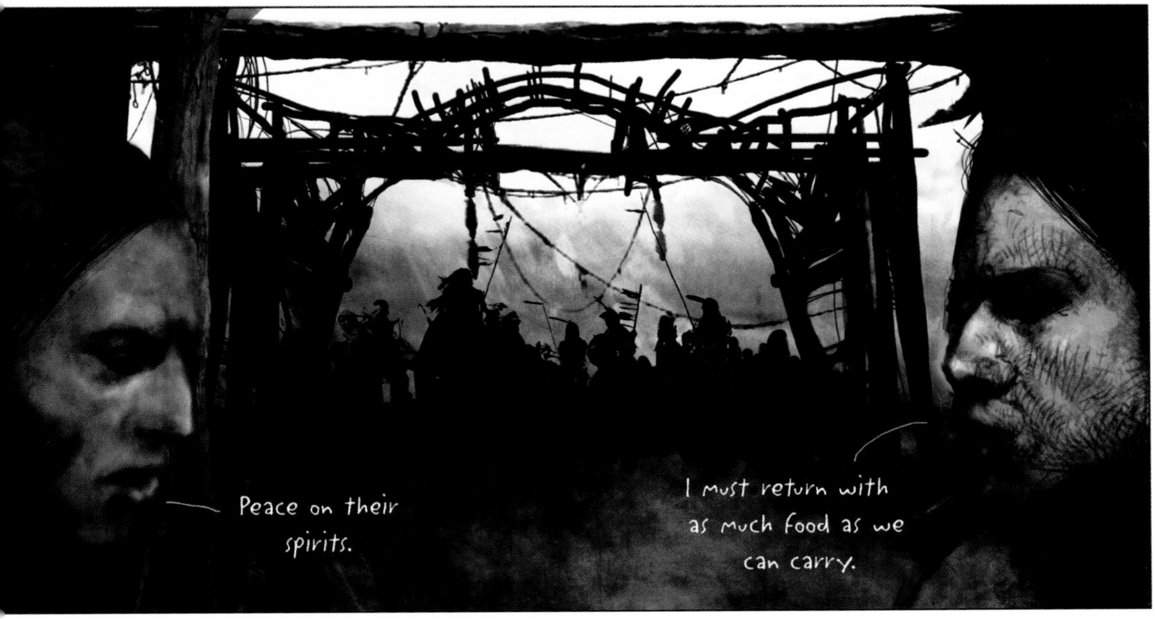
Peace on their spirits.
I must return with as much food as we can carry.

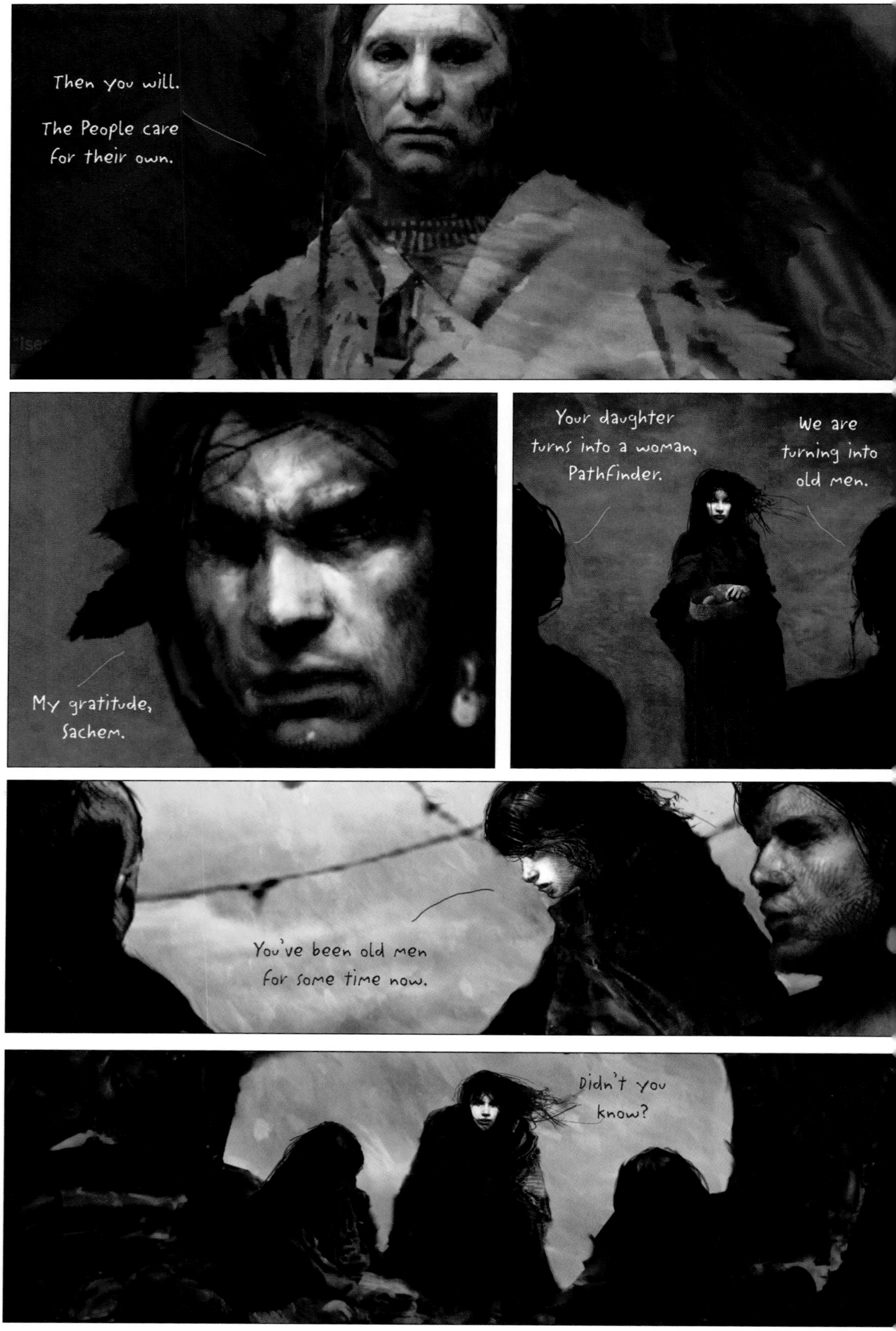
Then you will.
The People care for their own.
My gratitude, Sachem.
Your daughter turns into a woman, Pathfinder.
We are turning into old men.
You've been old men for some time now.
Didn't you know?

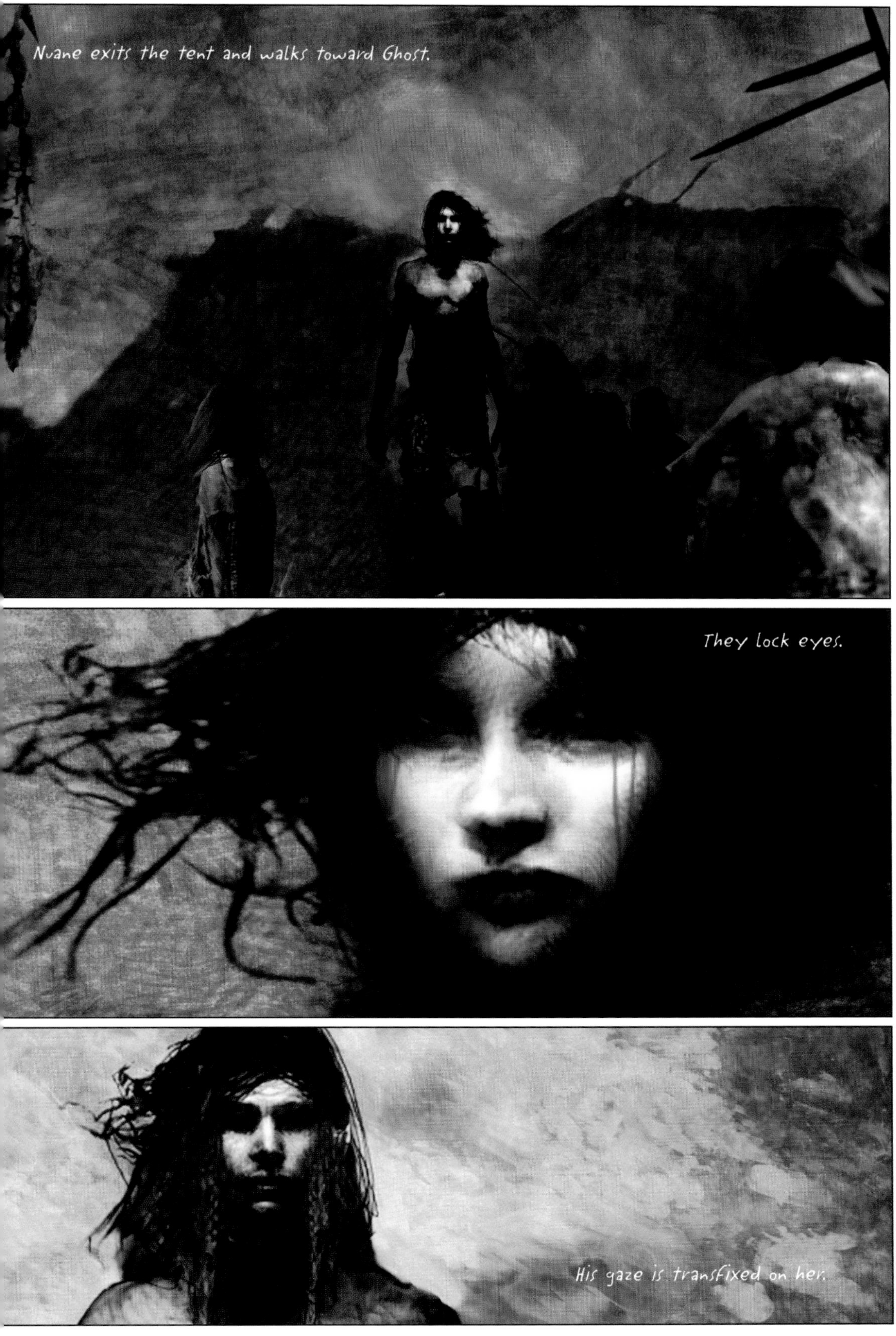
Nuane exits the tent and walks toward Ghost.
They lock eyes.
His gaze is transfixed on her.

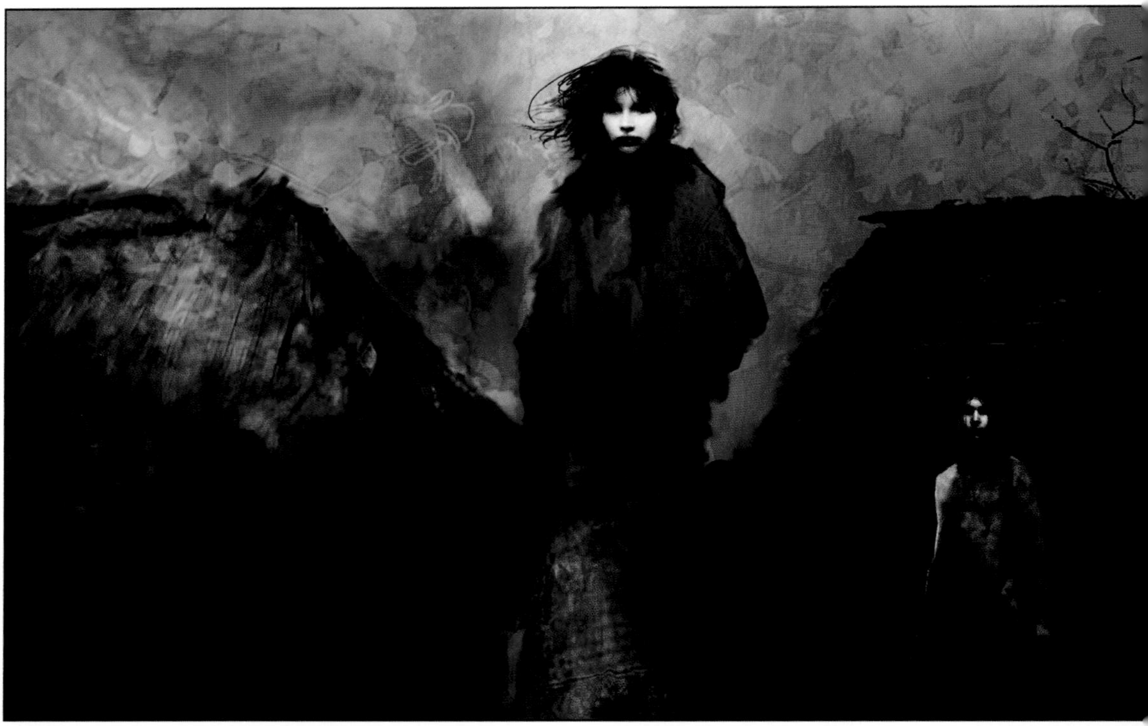

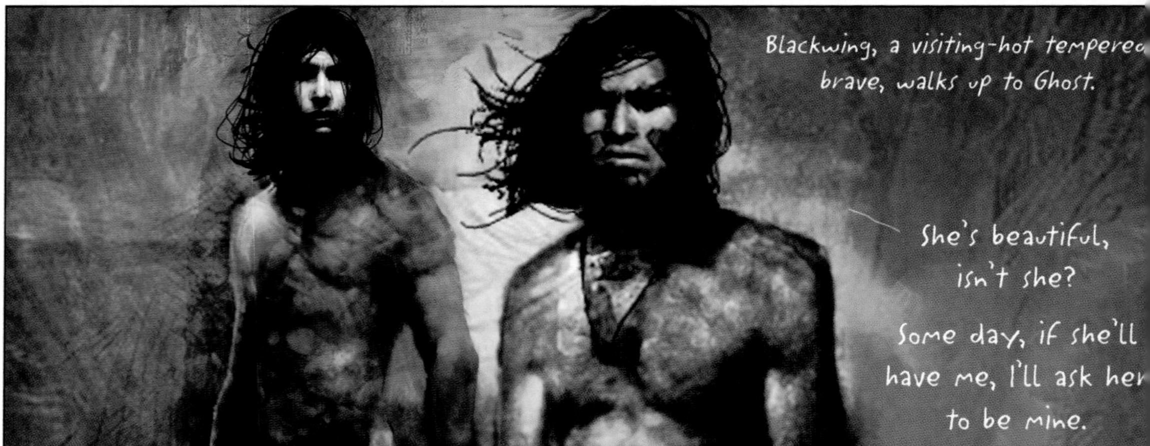
Blackwing, a visiting-hot tempere
brave, walks up to Ghost.
She's beautiful,
isn't she?
Some day, if she'll
have me, I'll ask he
to be mine.

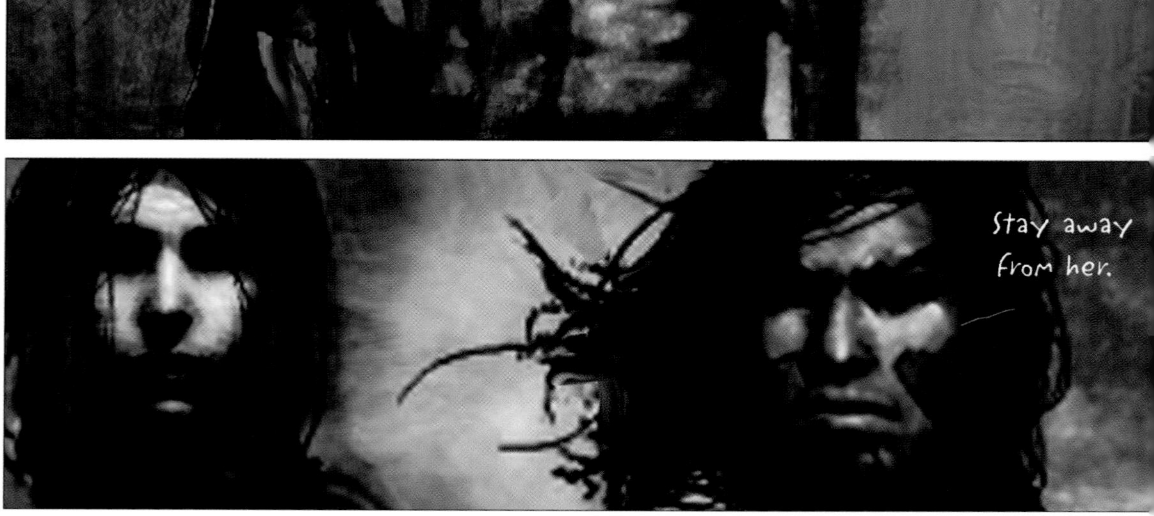
Stay away
from her.

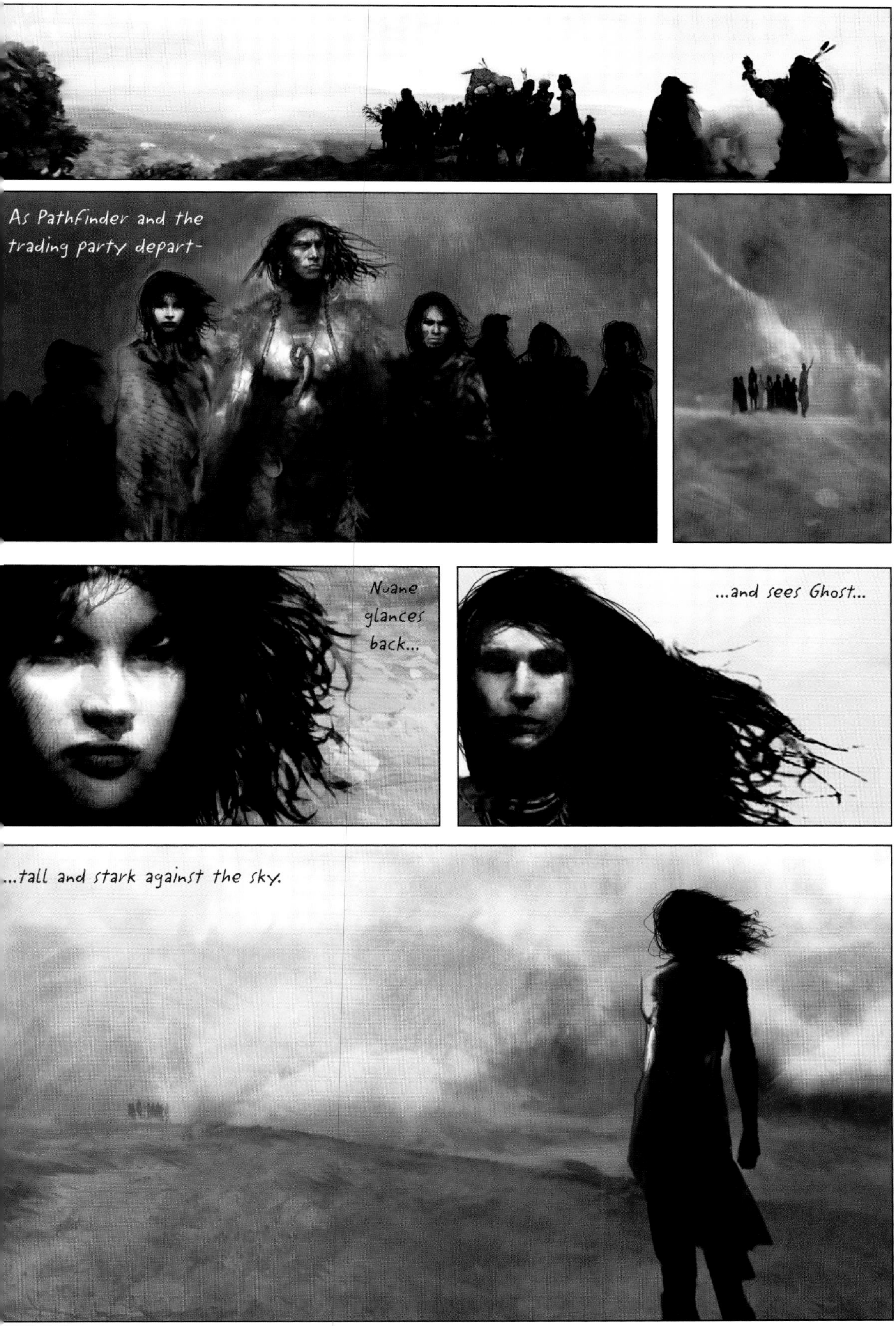
As Pathfinder and the trading party depart-
Nuane glances back...
...and sees Ghost...
...tall and stark against the sky.

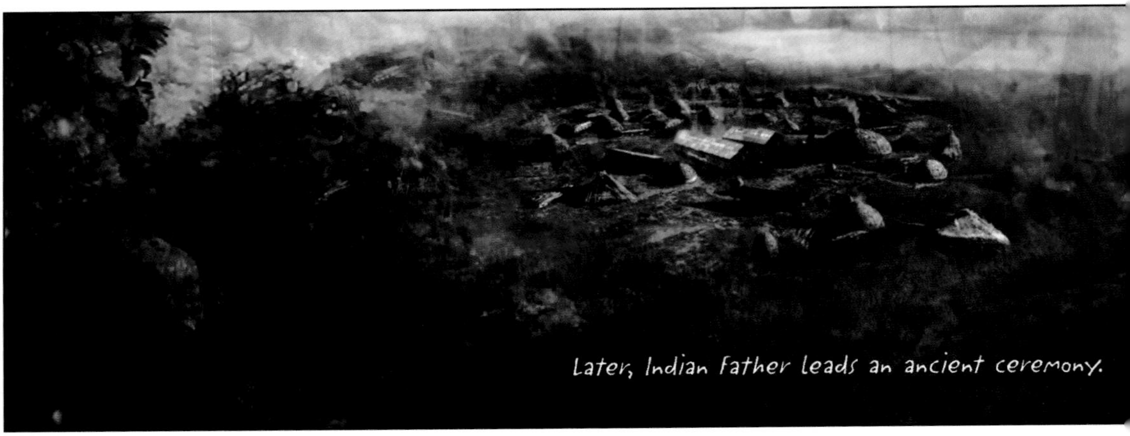
Later, Indian Father leads an ancient ceremony.

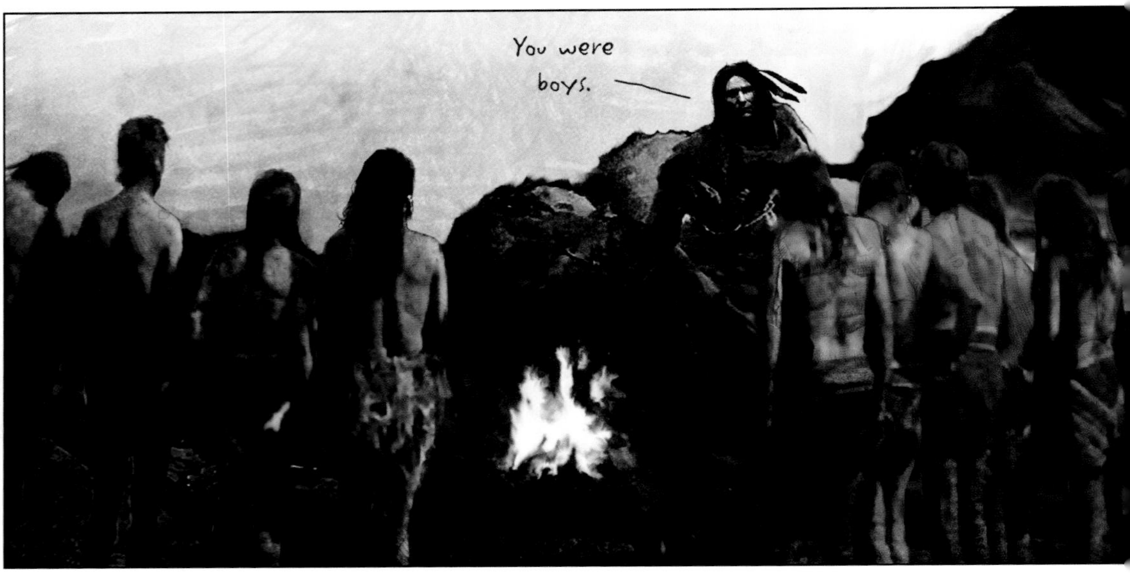
You were boys.

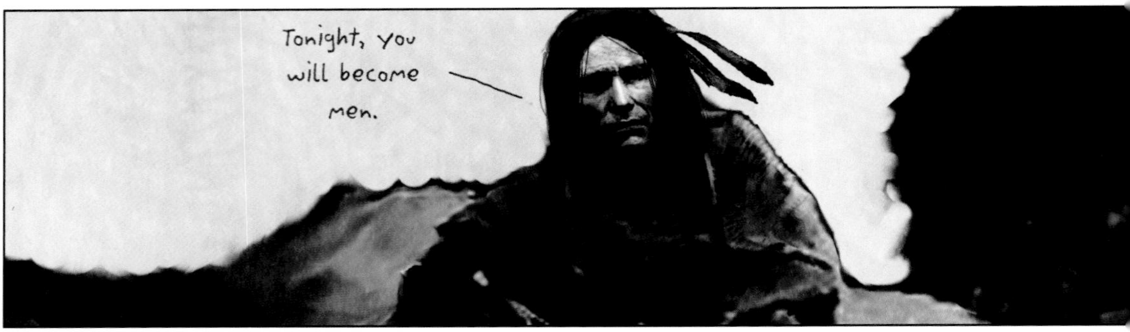
Tonight, you will become men.

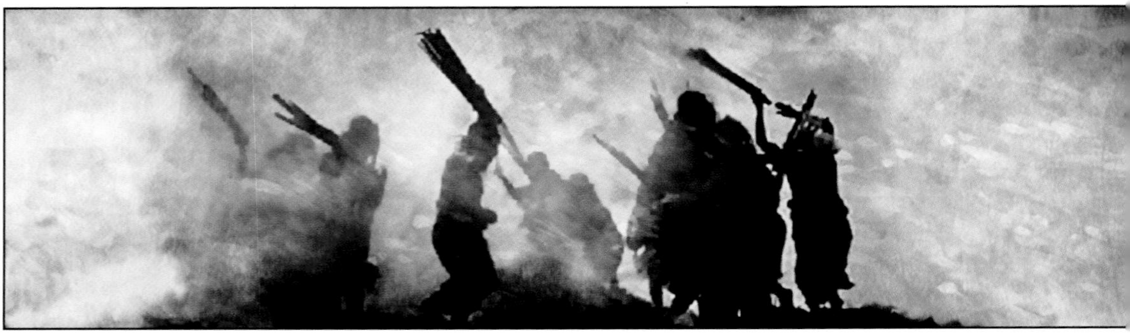

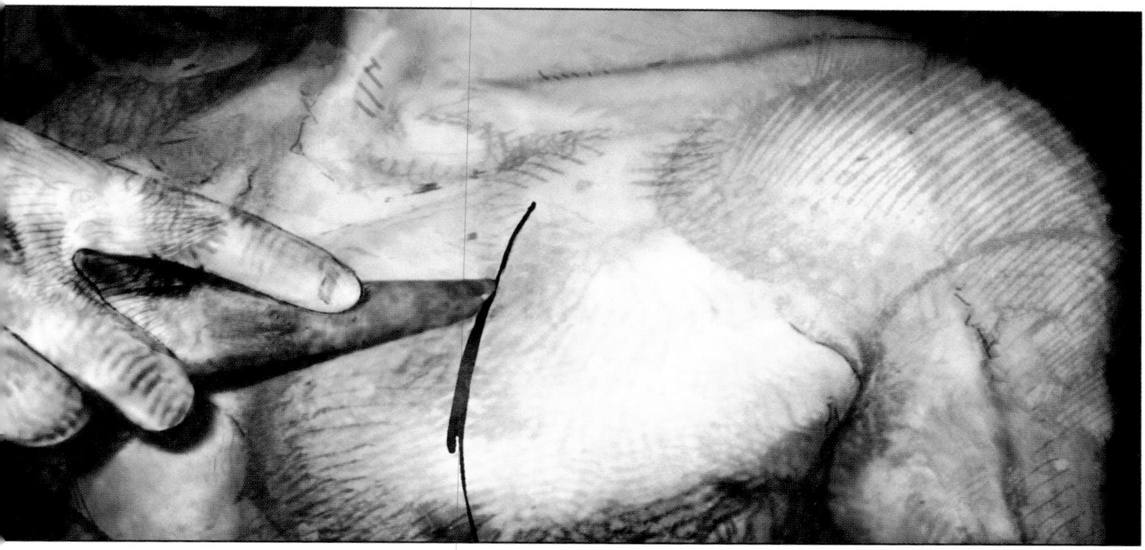

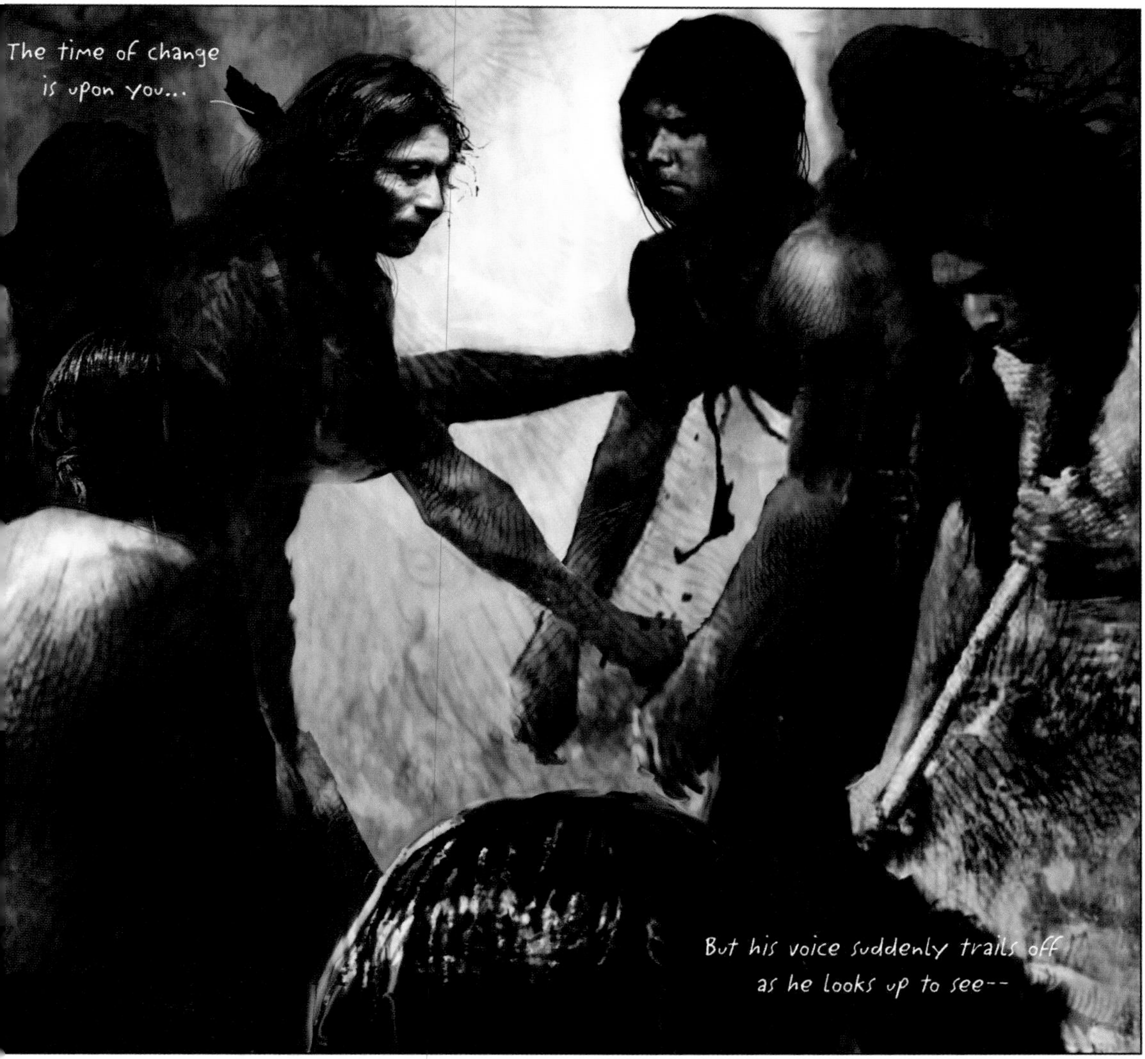
The time of change is upon you...
But his voice suddenly trails off as he looks up to see--

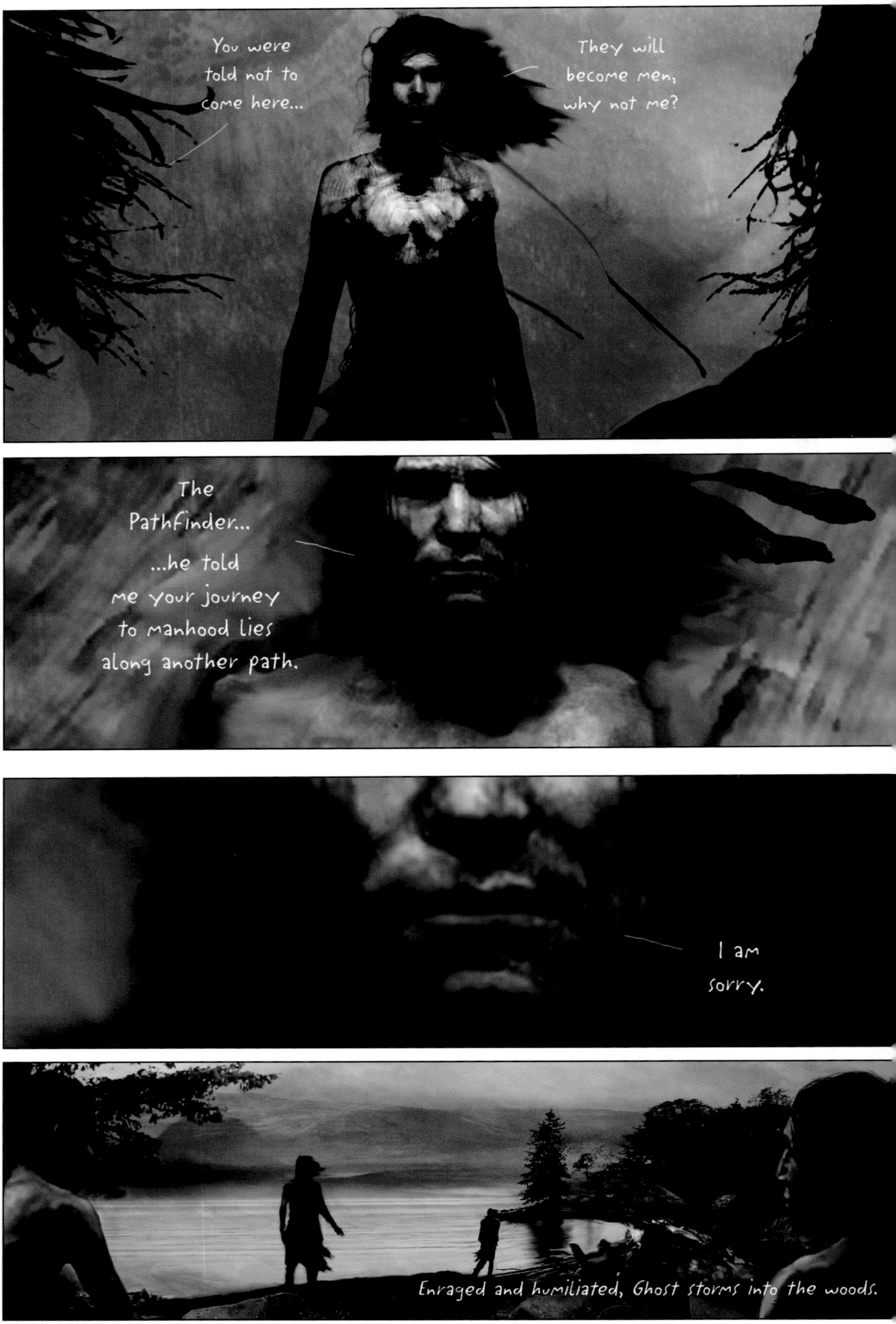
You were told not to come here...
They will become men, why not me?
The Pathfinder...
...he told me your journey to manhood lies along another path.
I am sorry.
Enraged and humiliated, Ghost storms into the woods.

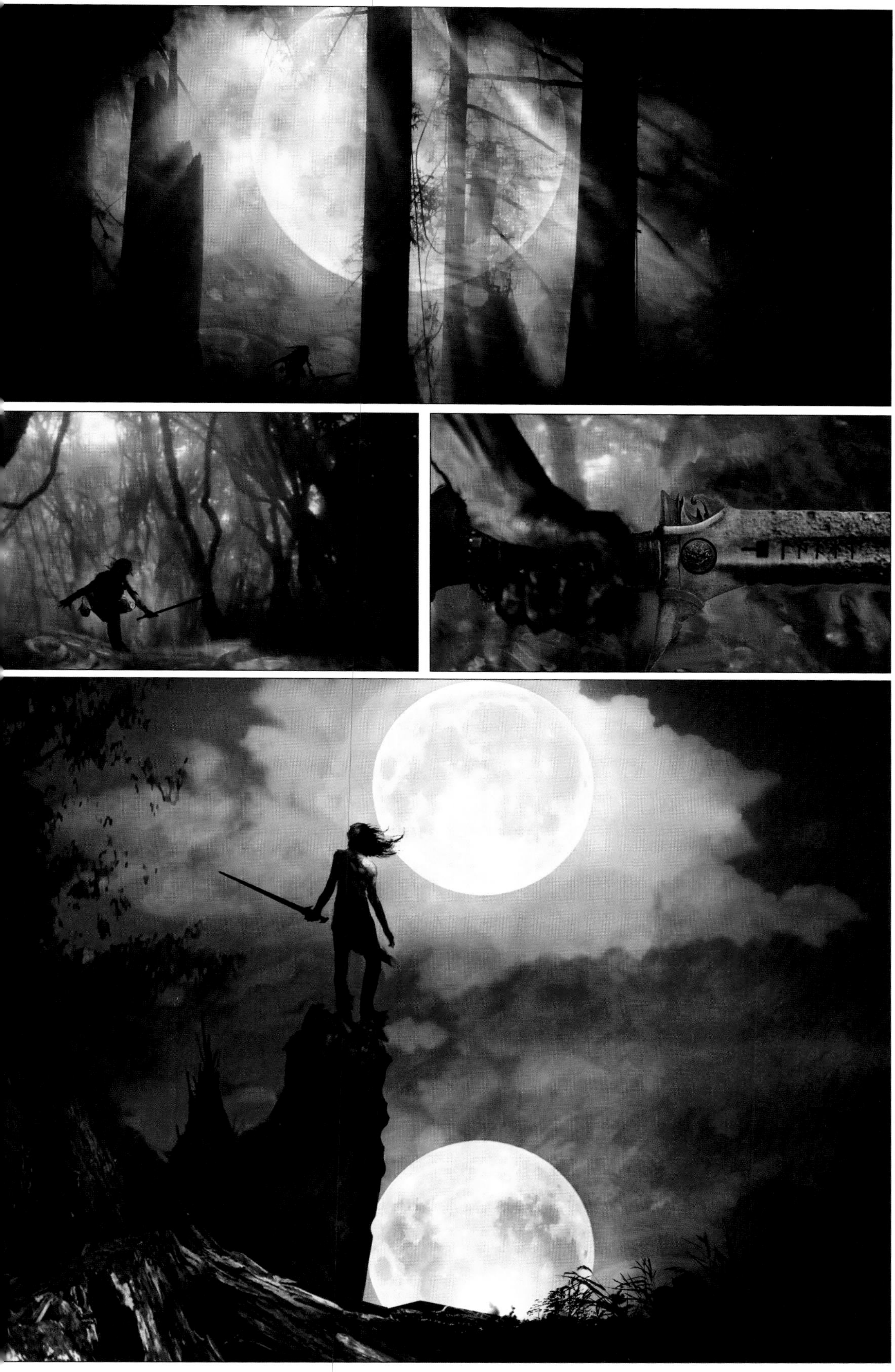

He turns the blade,
feeling its weight
and balance—

—slicing down with startling
speed and power—

—as if it has been
only hours, not years,
since he held the blade—

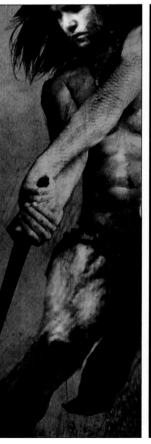

—pouring out his frustration
and anger into the wild
dance of combat.

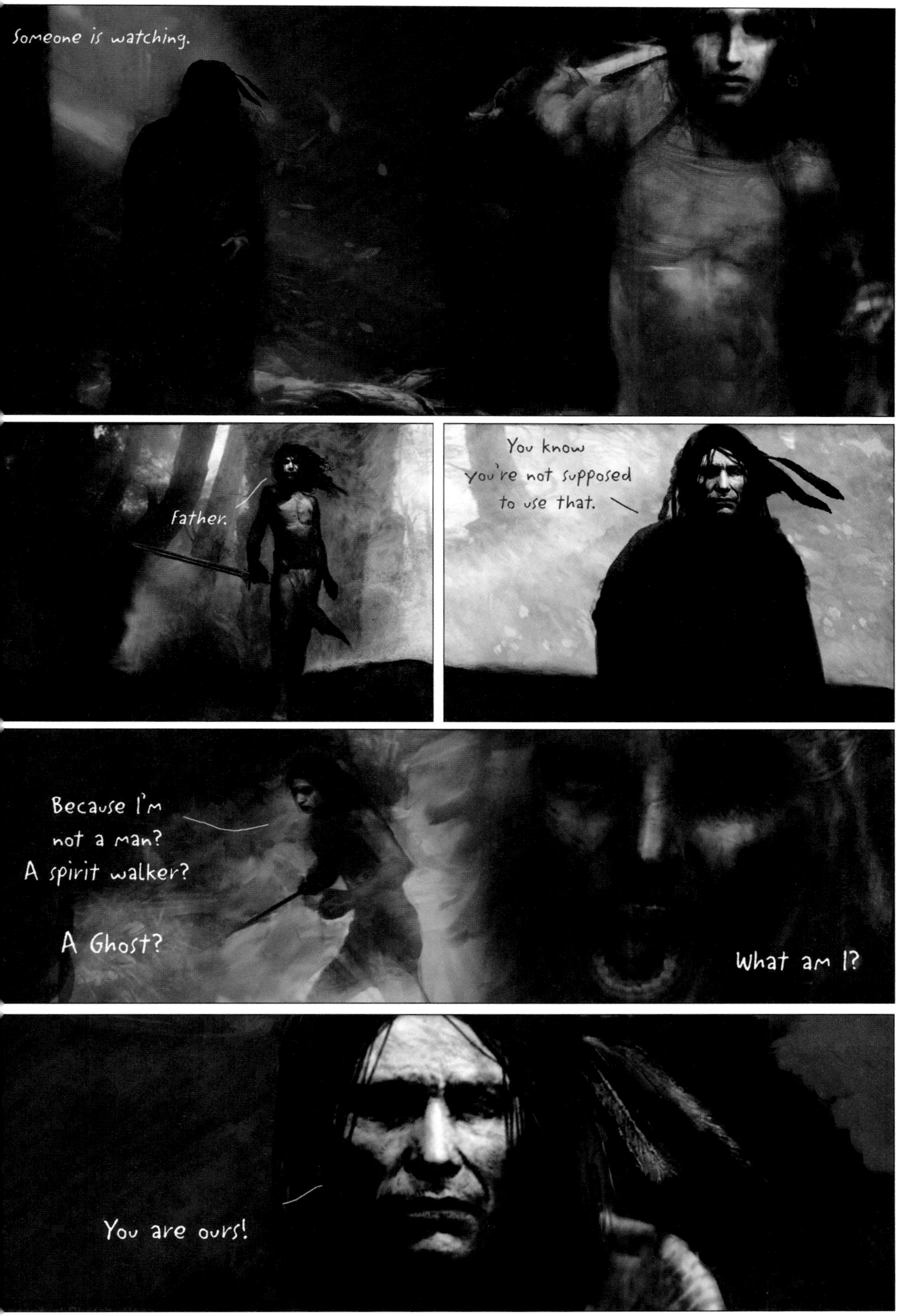
Someone is watching.
Father.
You know you're not supposed to use that.
Because I'm not a man? A spirit walker?
A Ghost?
What am I?
You are ours!

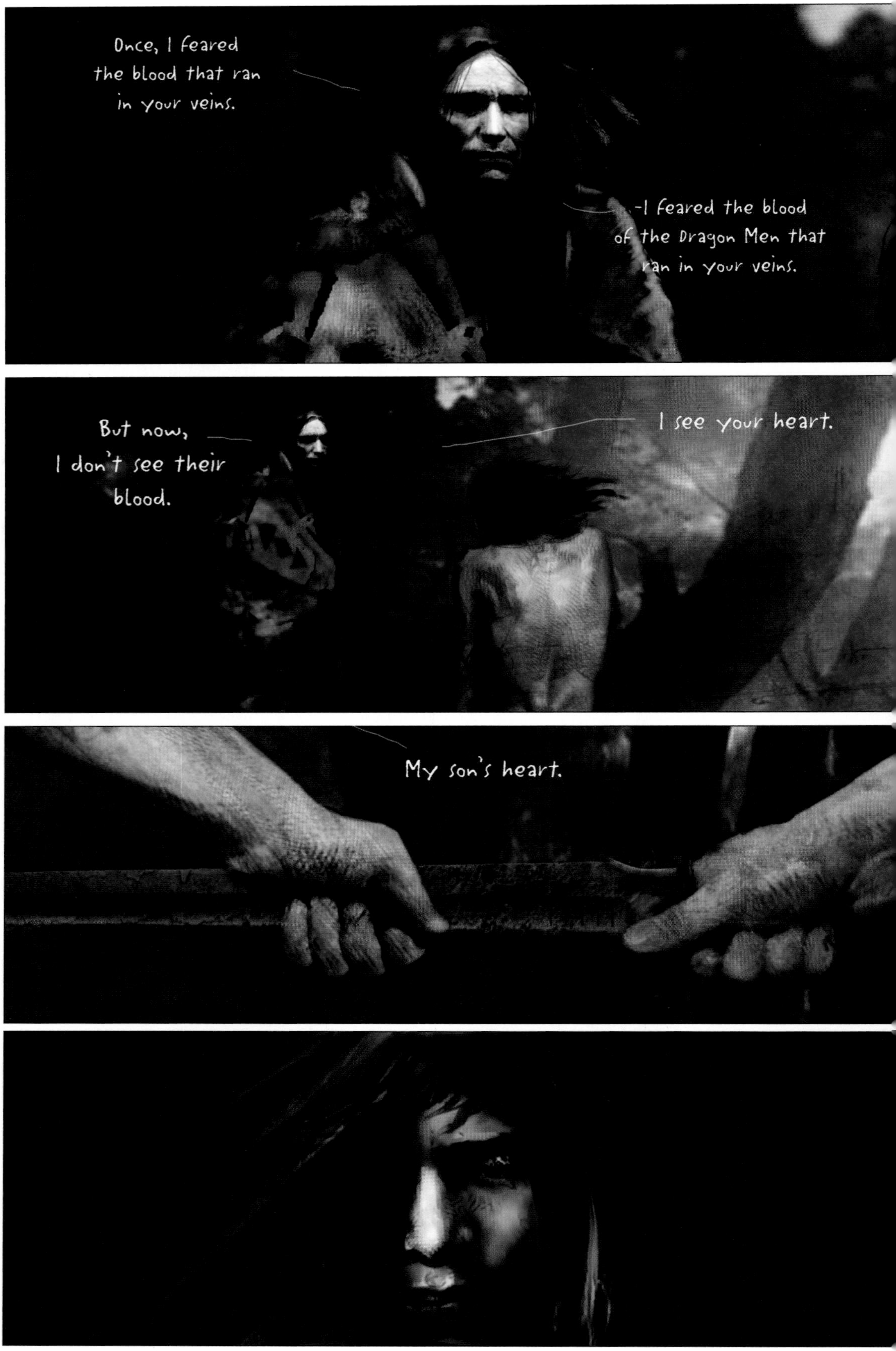

Once, I feared the blood that ran in your veins.
-I feared the blood of the Dragon Men that ran in your veins.
But now, I don't see their blood.
I see your heart.
My son's heart.

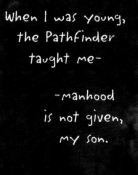

When I was young,
the Pathfinder
taught me—

—manhood
is not given,
my son.

It is earned.

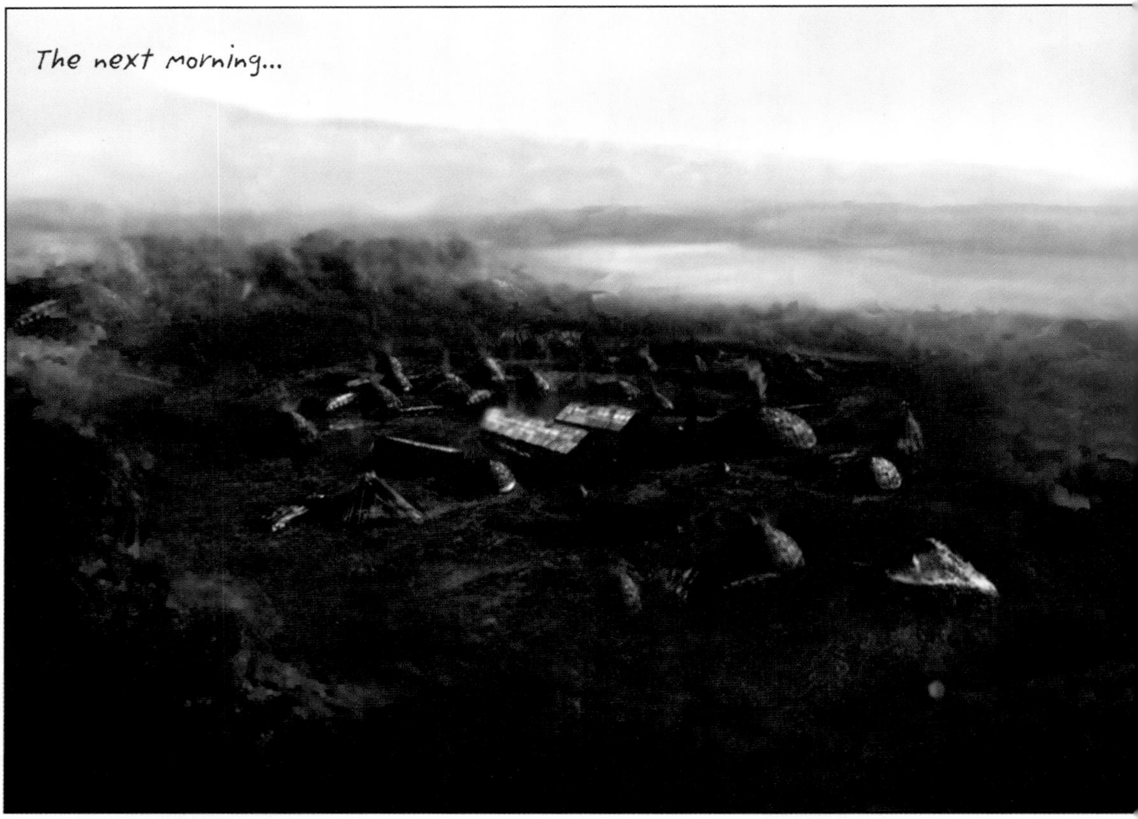
The next morning...

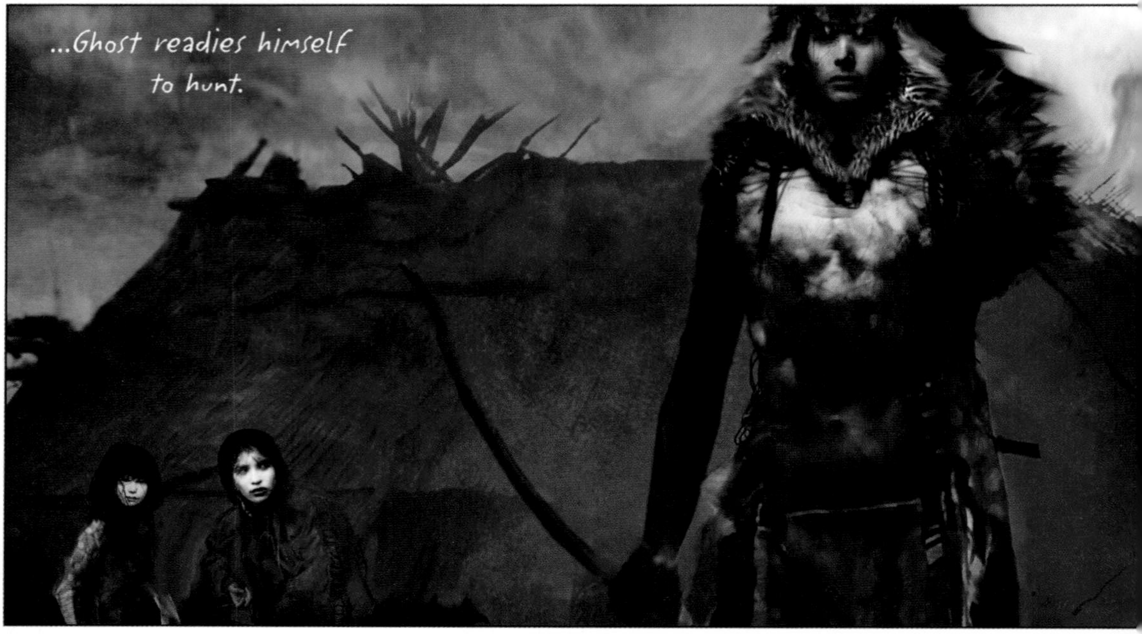
...Ghost readies himself to hunt.

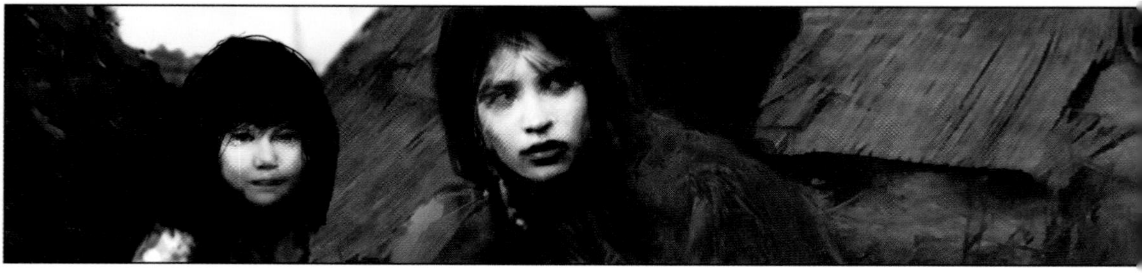

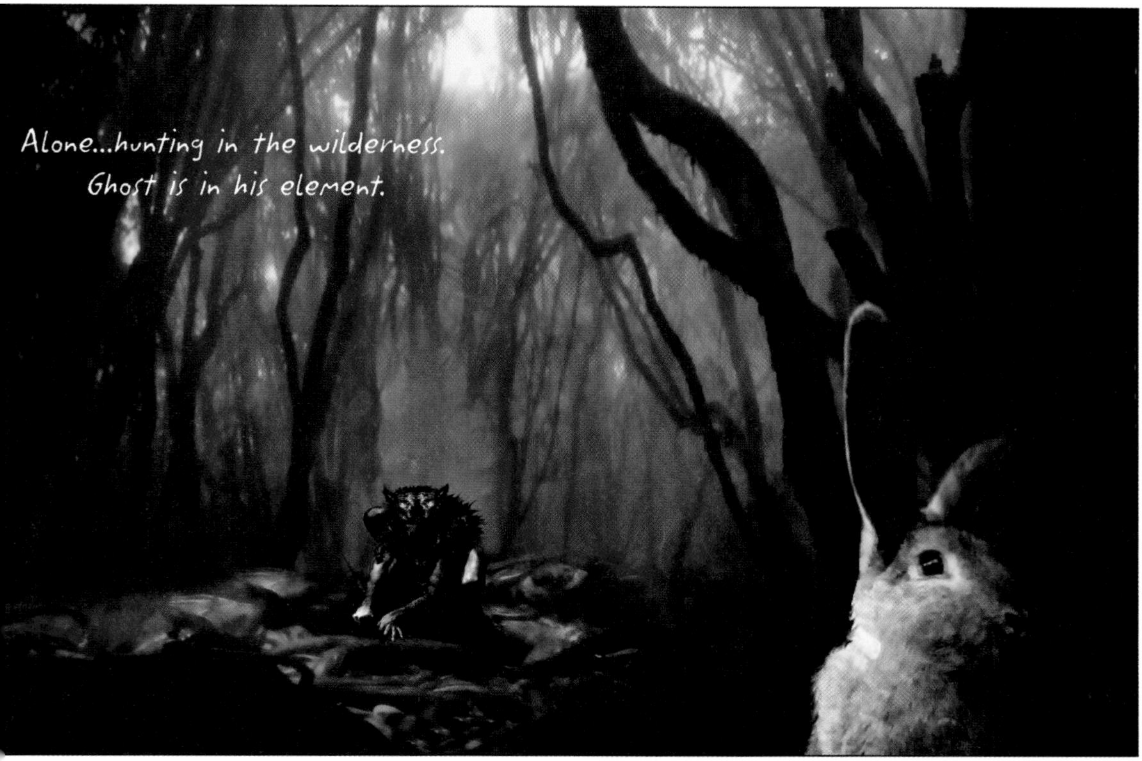
Alone...hunting in the wilderness.
Ghost is in his element.

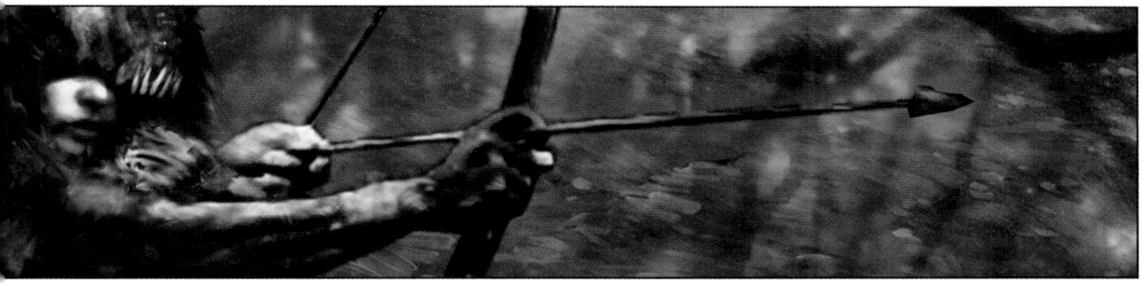

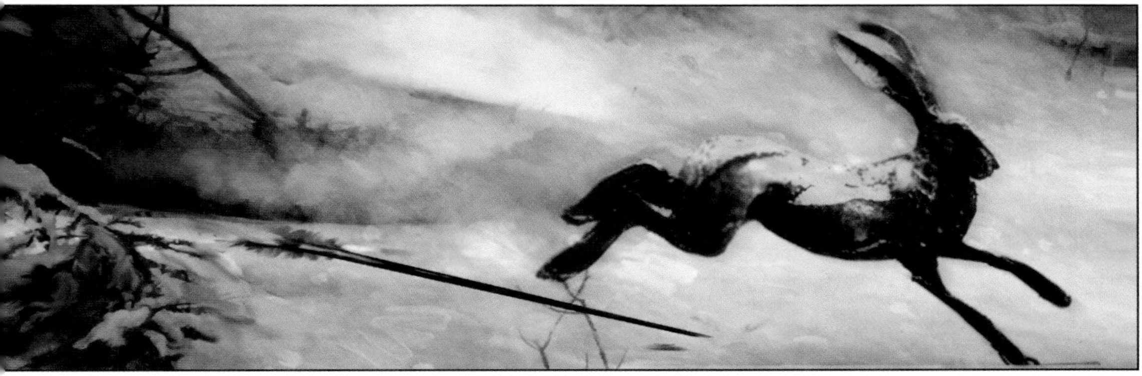

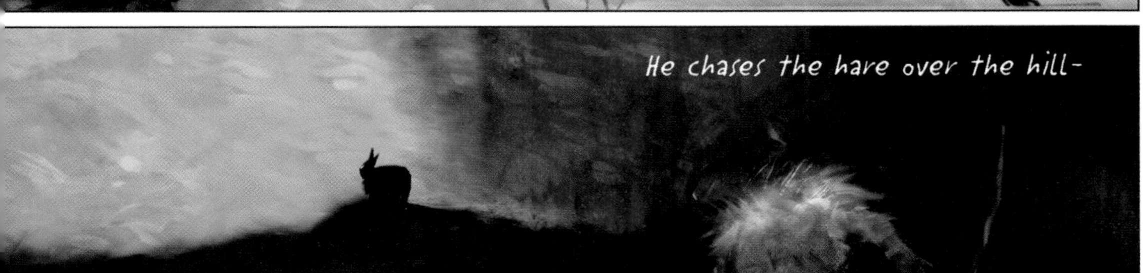
He chases the hare over the hill-

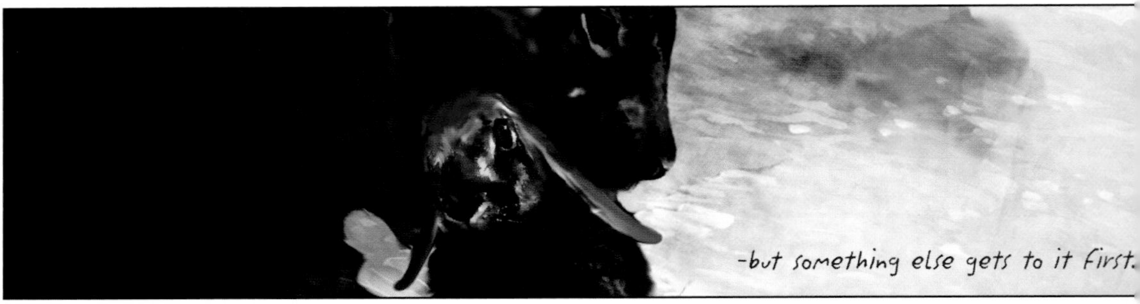
-but something else gets to it first.

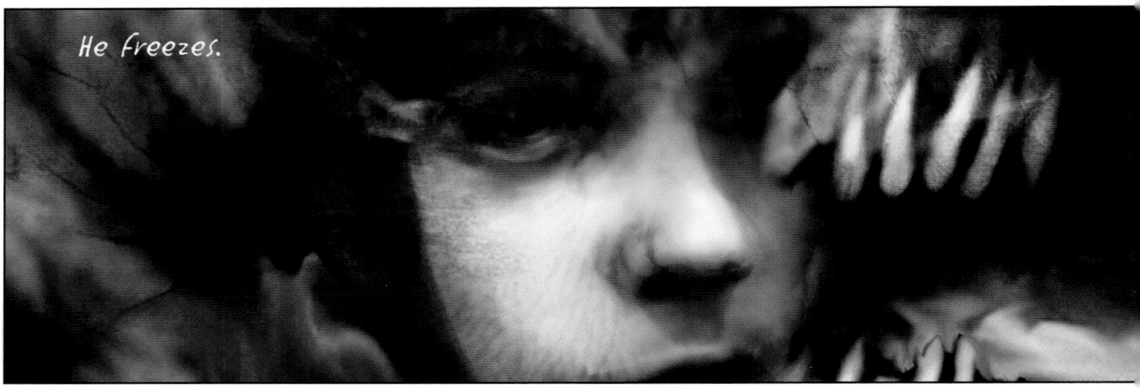
He freezes.

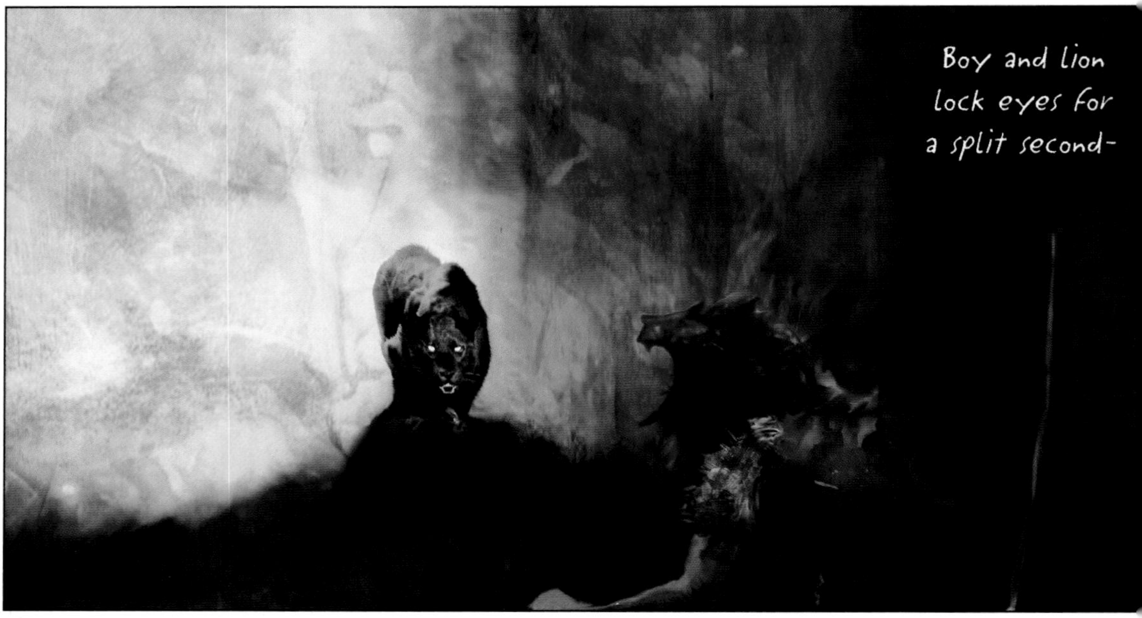
Boy and lion
lock eyes for
a split second-

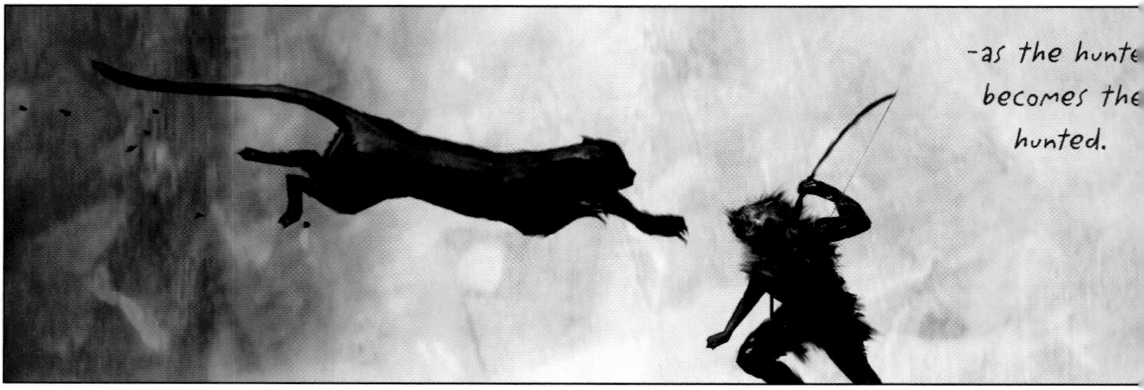
-as the hunte
becomes the
hunted.

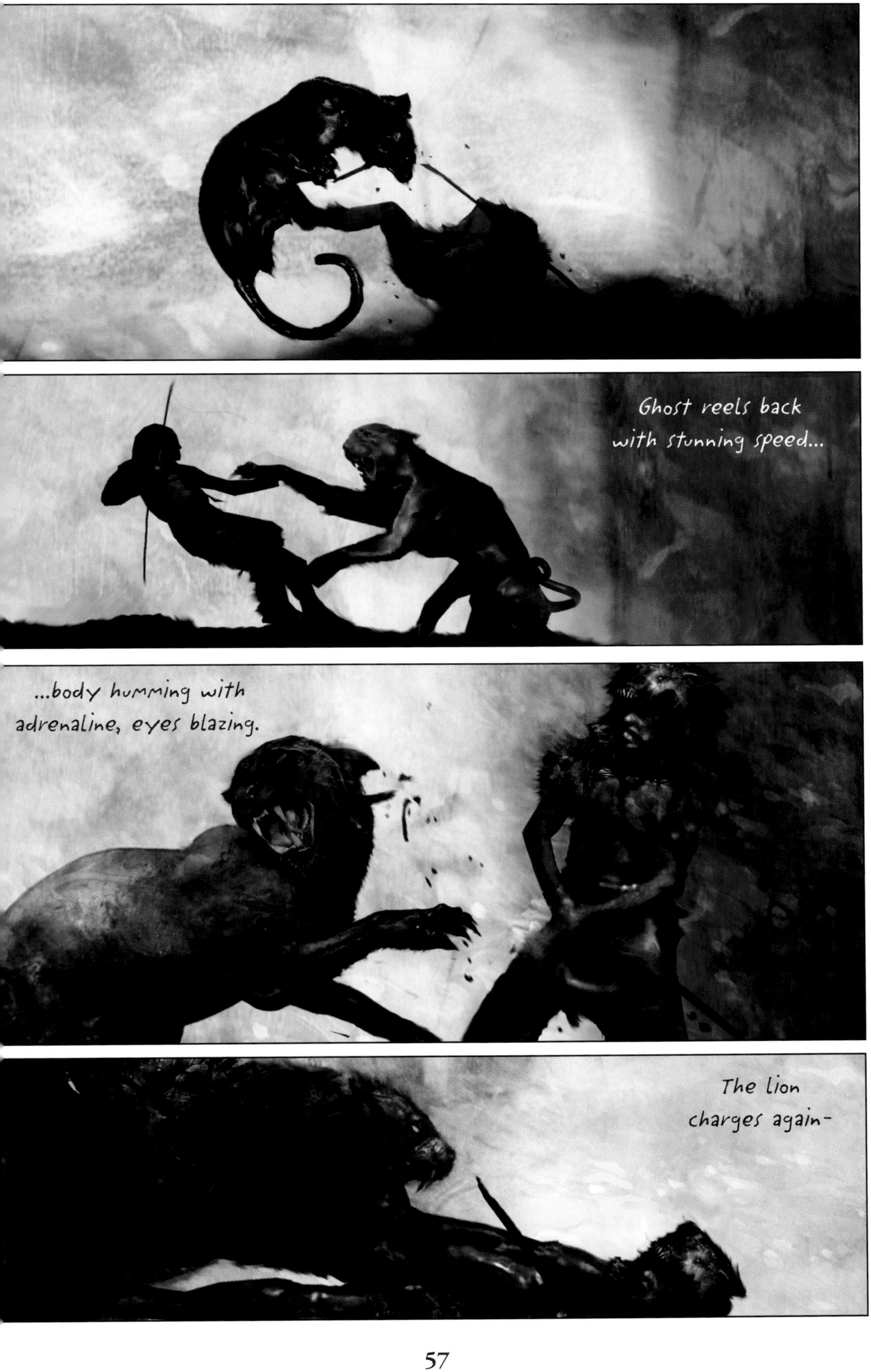
Ghost reels back with stunning speed...
...body humming with adrenaline, eyes blazing.
The lion charges again-

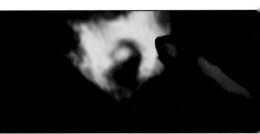
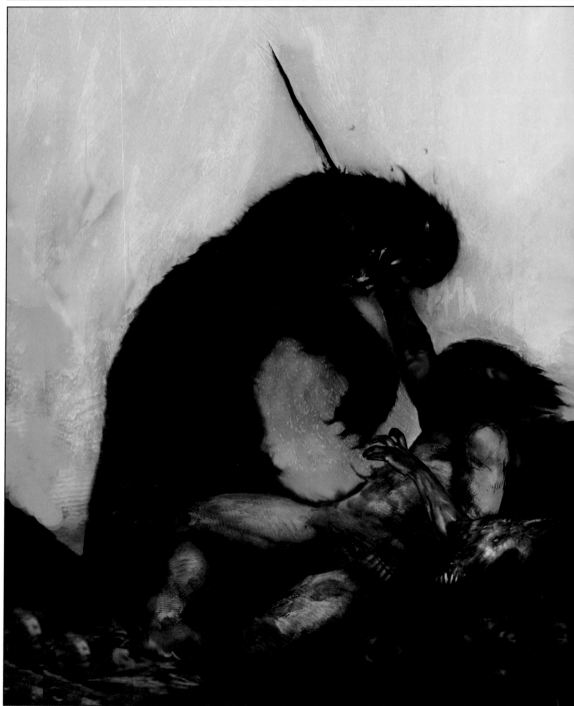

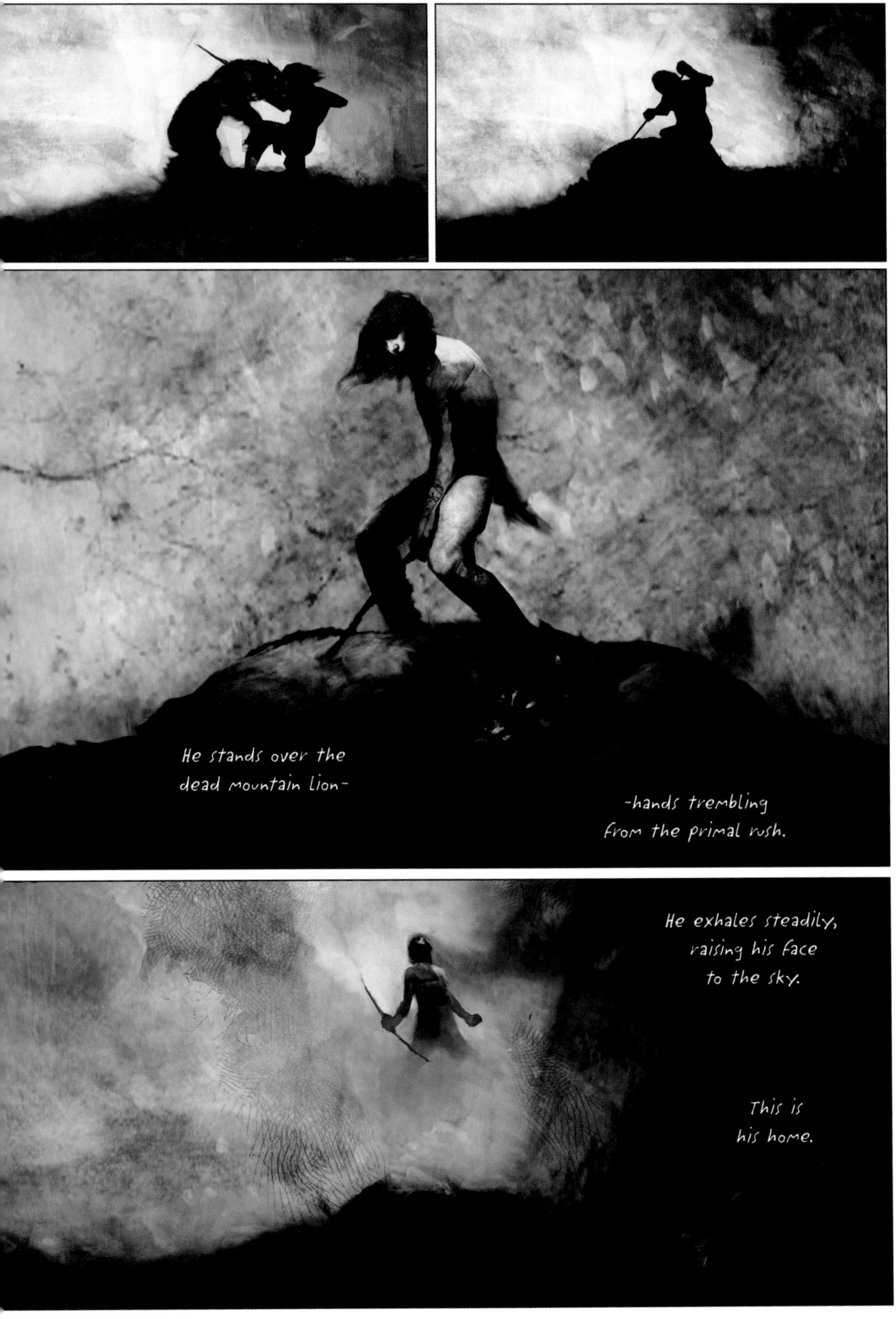
He stands over the
dead mountain lion-
-hands trembling
from the primal rush.
He exhales steadily,
raising his face
to the sky.
This is
his home.

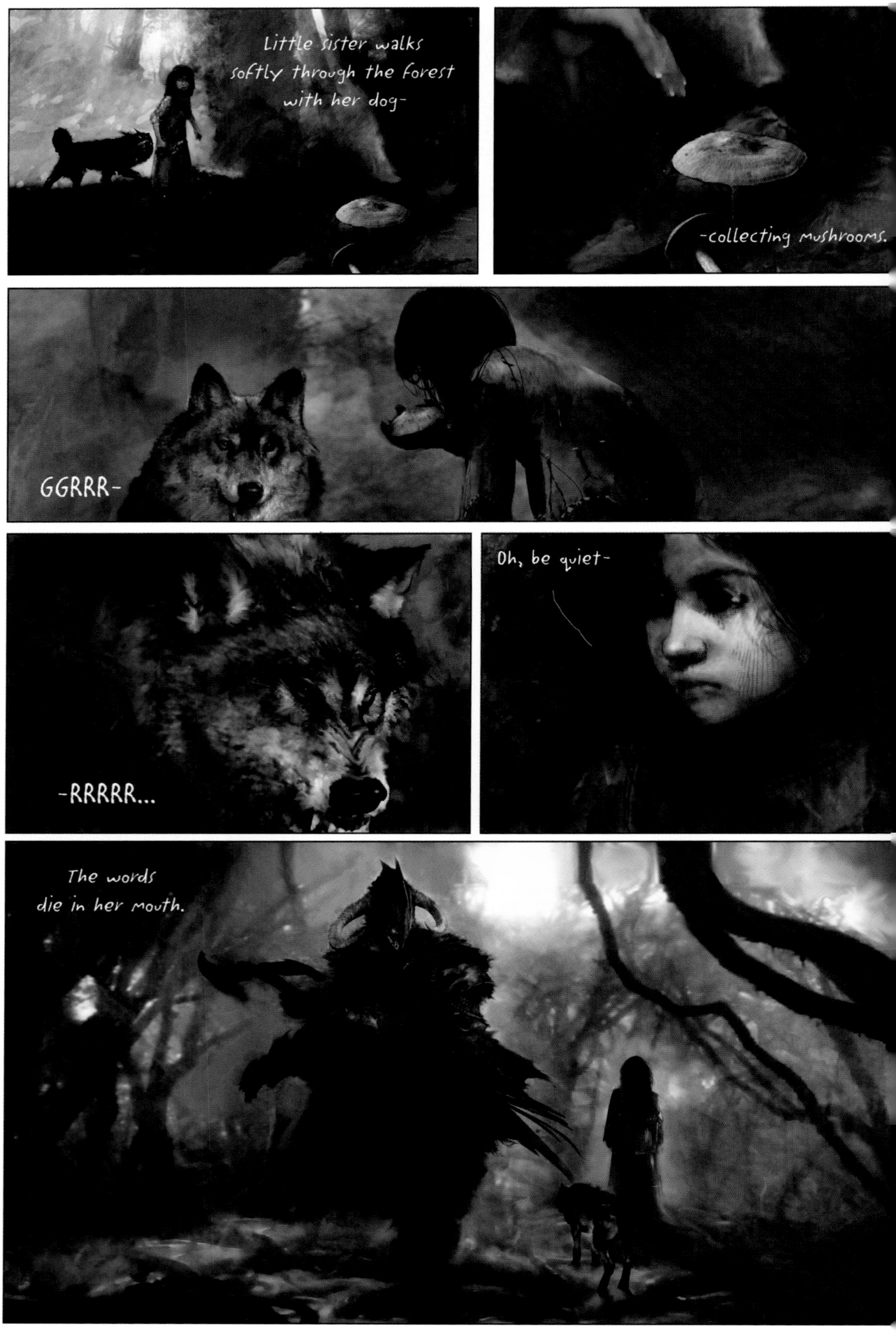
Little sister walks softly through the forest with her dog-
-collecting mushrooms.
GGRRR-
-RRRRR...
Oh, be quiet-
The words die in her mouth.

Still hunting, Ghost stops at a small ravine.

Little Sister's doll is on the ground beside the dead dog.

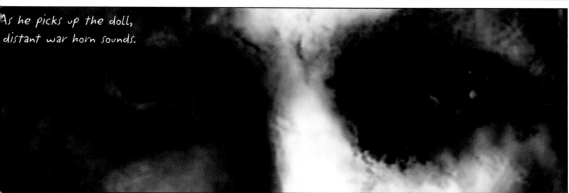

As he picks up the doll, distant war horn sounds.

He's heard that sound before and it strikes fear in his heart.

He scrambles desperately to get home.

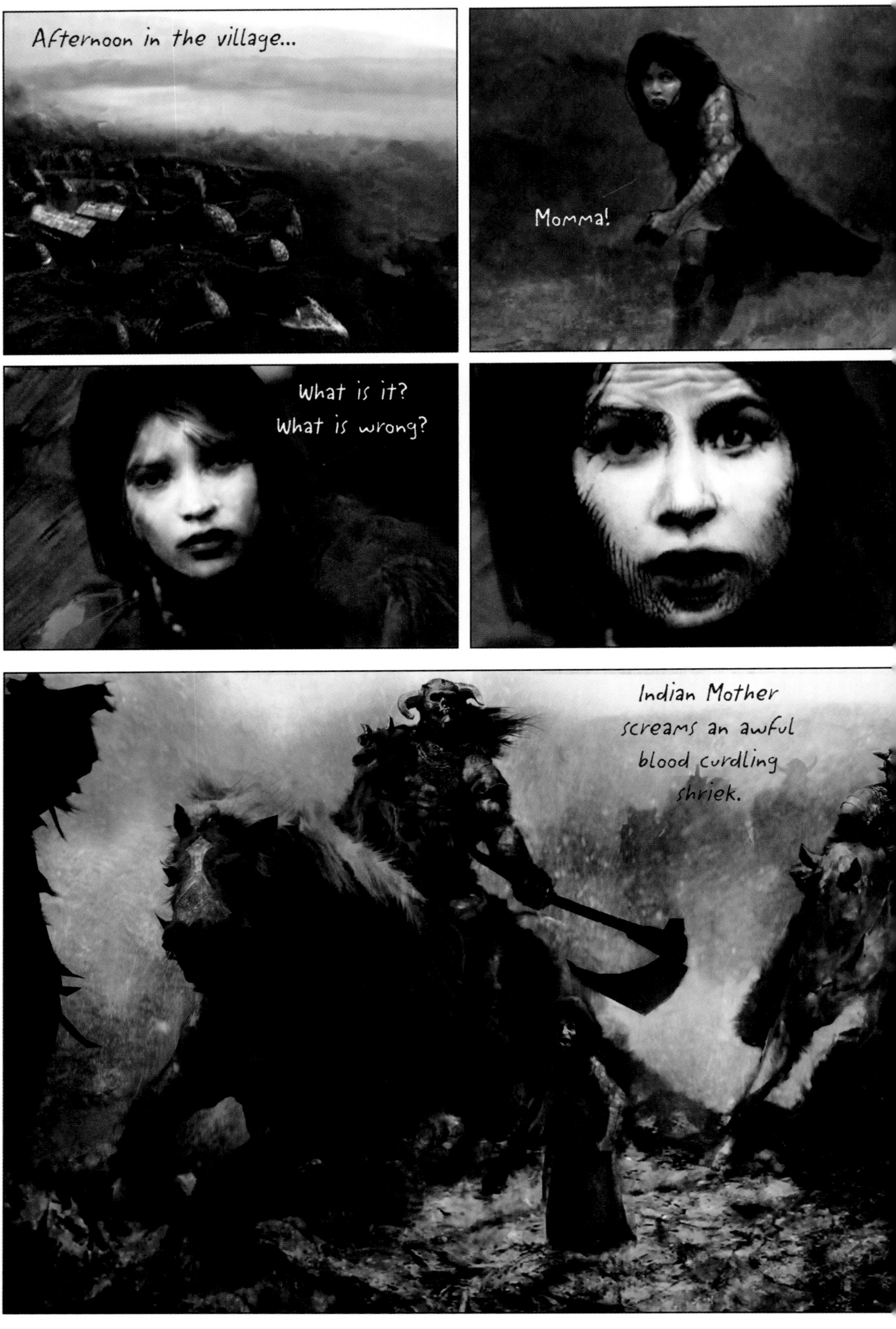
Afternoon in the village...
Momma!
What is it?
What is wrong?
Indian Mother screams an awful blood curdling shriek.

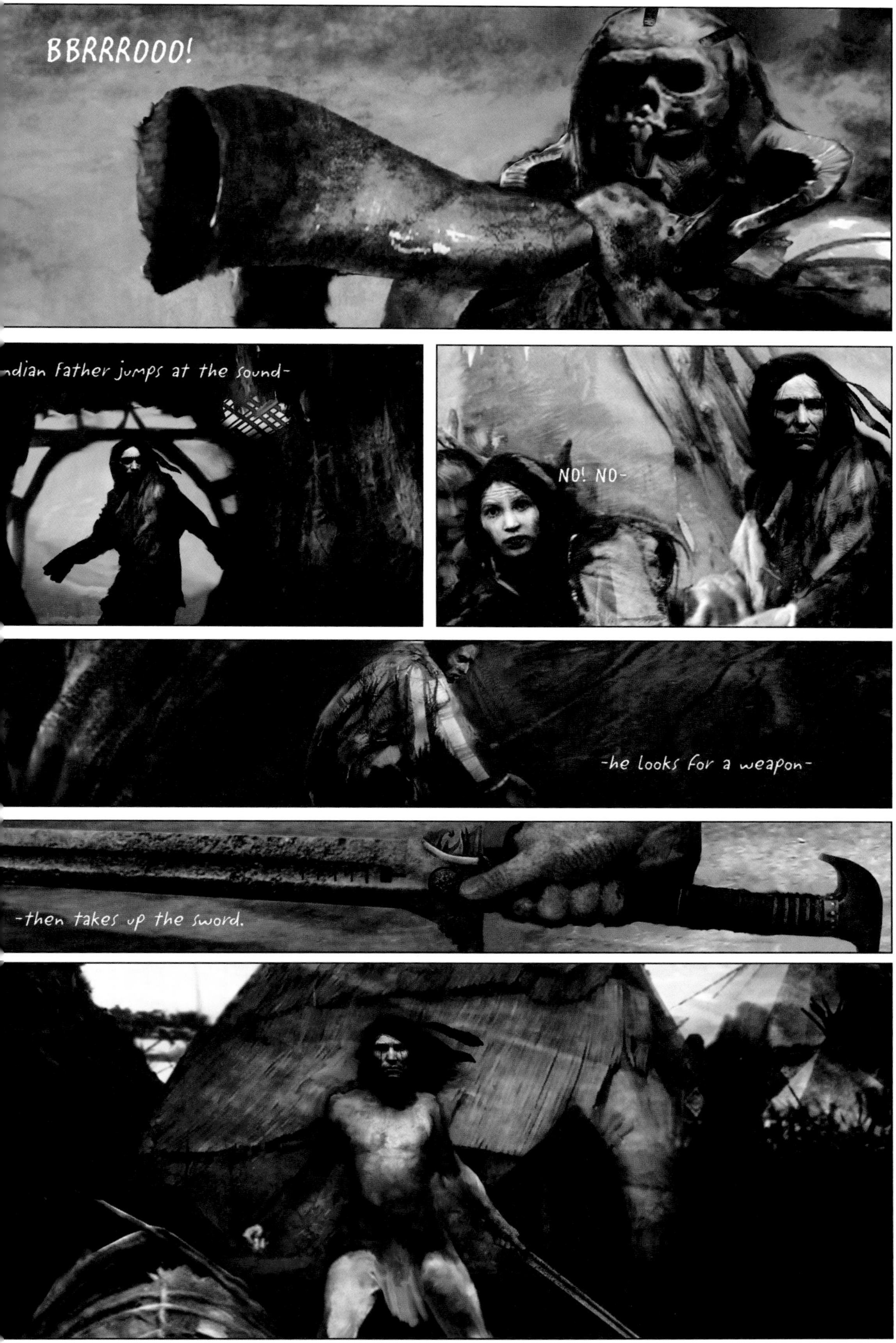
BBRRROOO!
ndian father jumps at the sound-
NO! NO-
-he looks for a weapon-
-then takes up the sword.

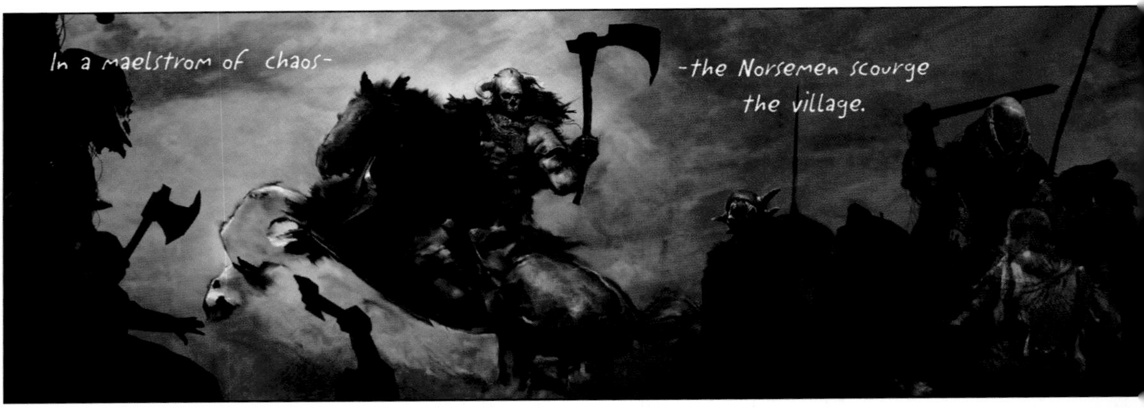
In a maelstrom of chaos-
-the Norsemen scourge the village.

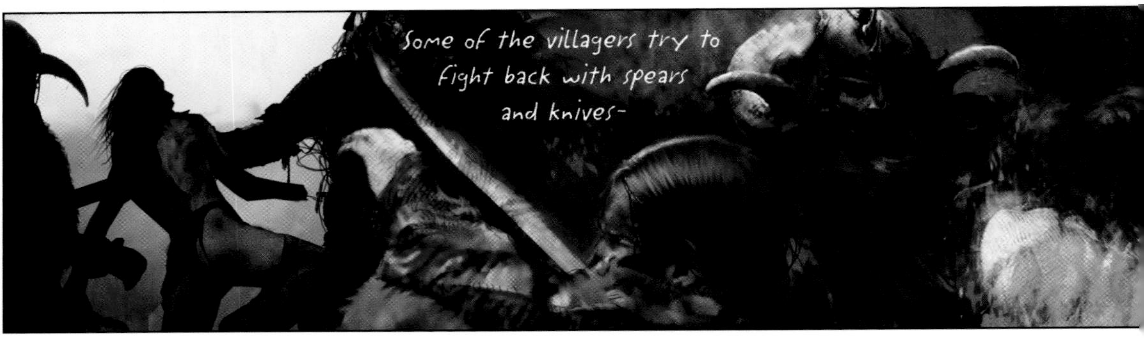
Some of the villagers try to fight back with spears and knives-

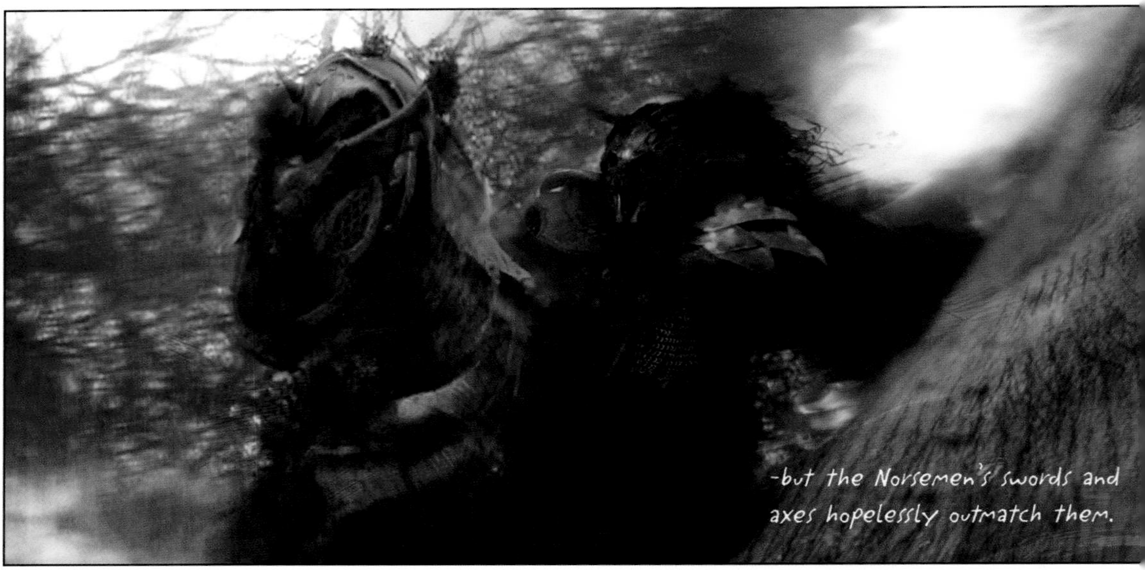
-but the Norsemen's swords and axes hopelessly outmatch them.

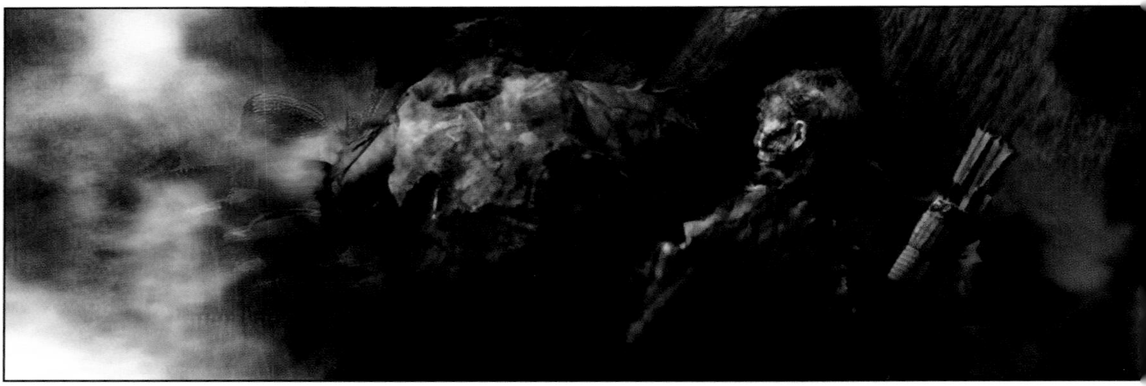

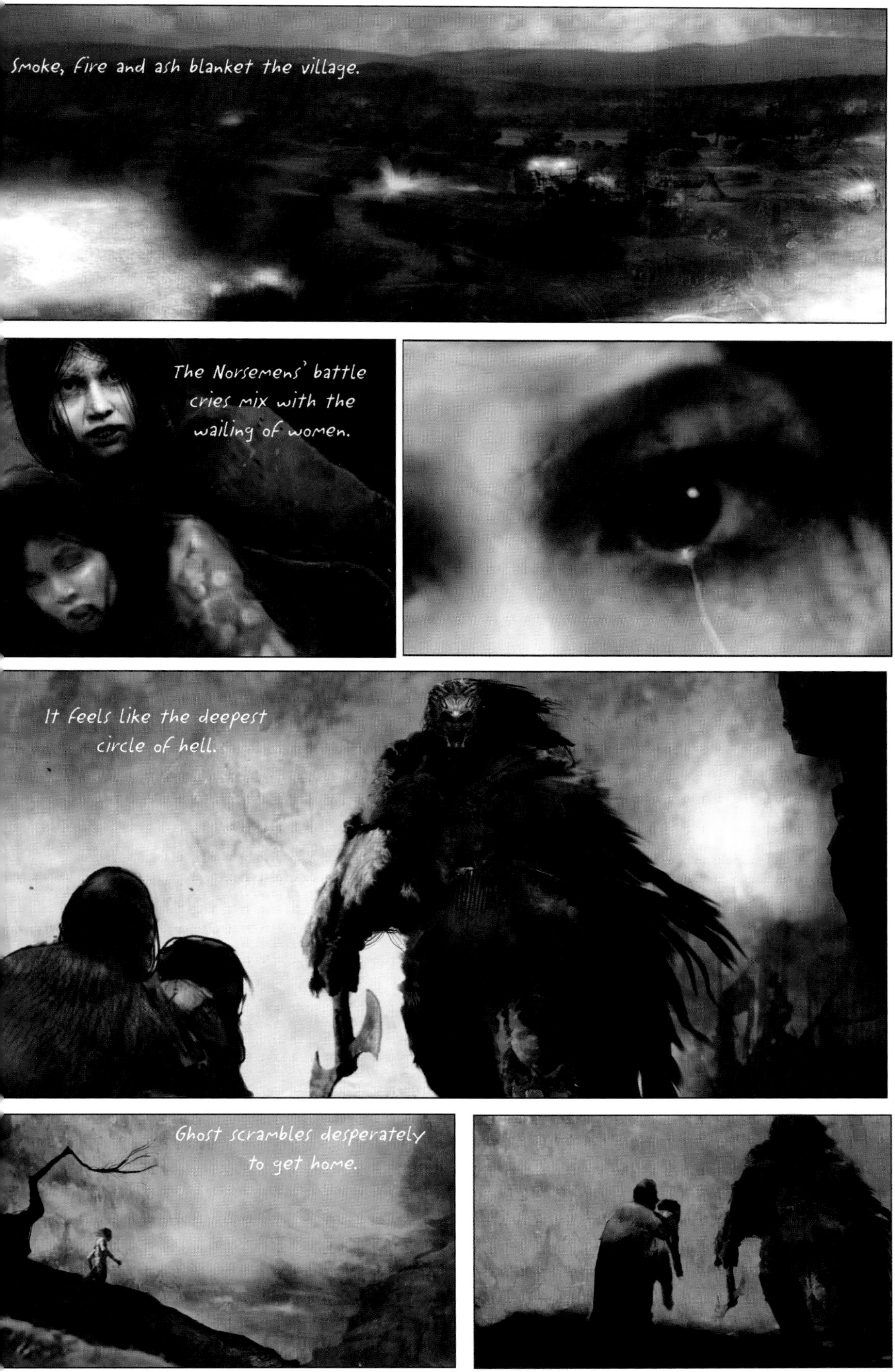
Smoke, fire and ash blanket the village.
The Norsemens' battle cries mix with the wailing of women.
It feels like the deepest circle of hell.
Ghost scrambles desperately to get home.

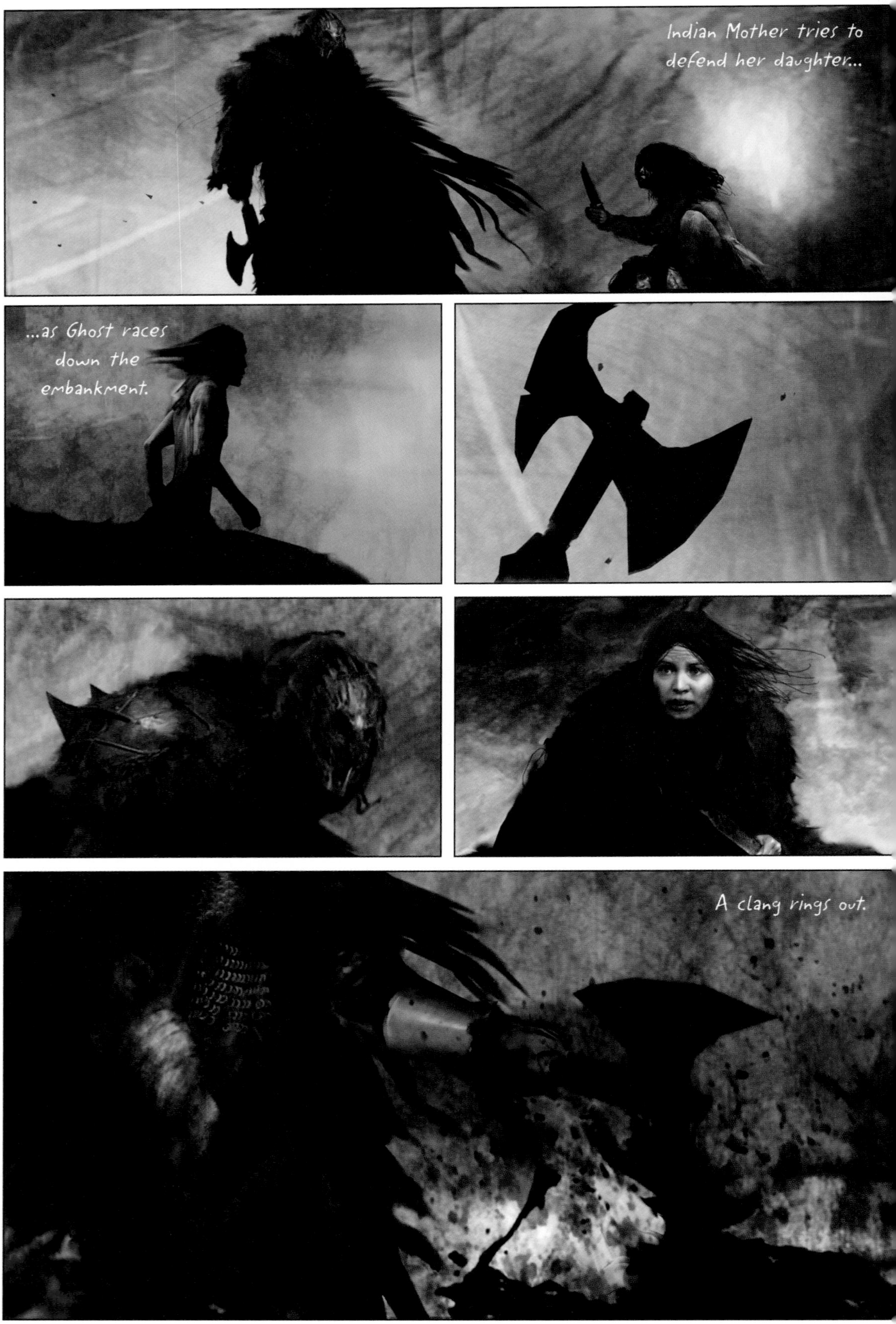
Indian Mother tries to defend her daughter...
...as Ghost races down the embankment.
A clang rings out.

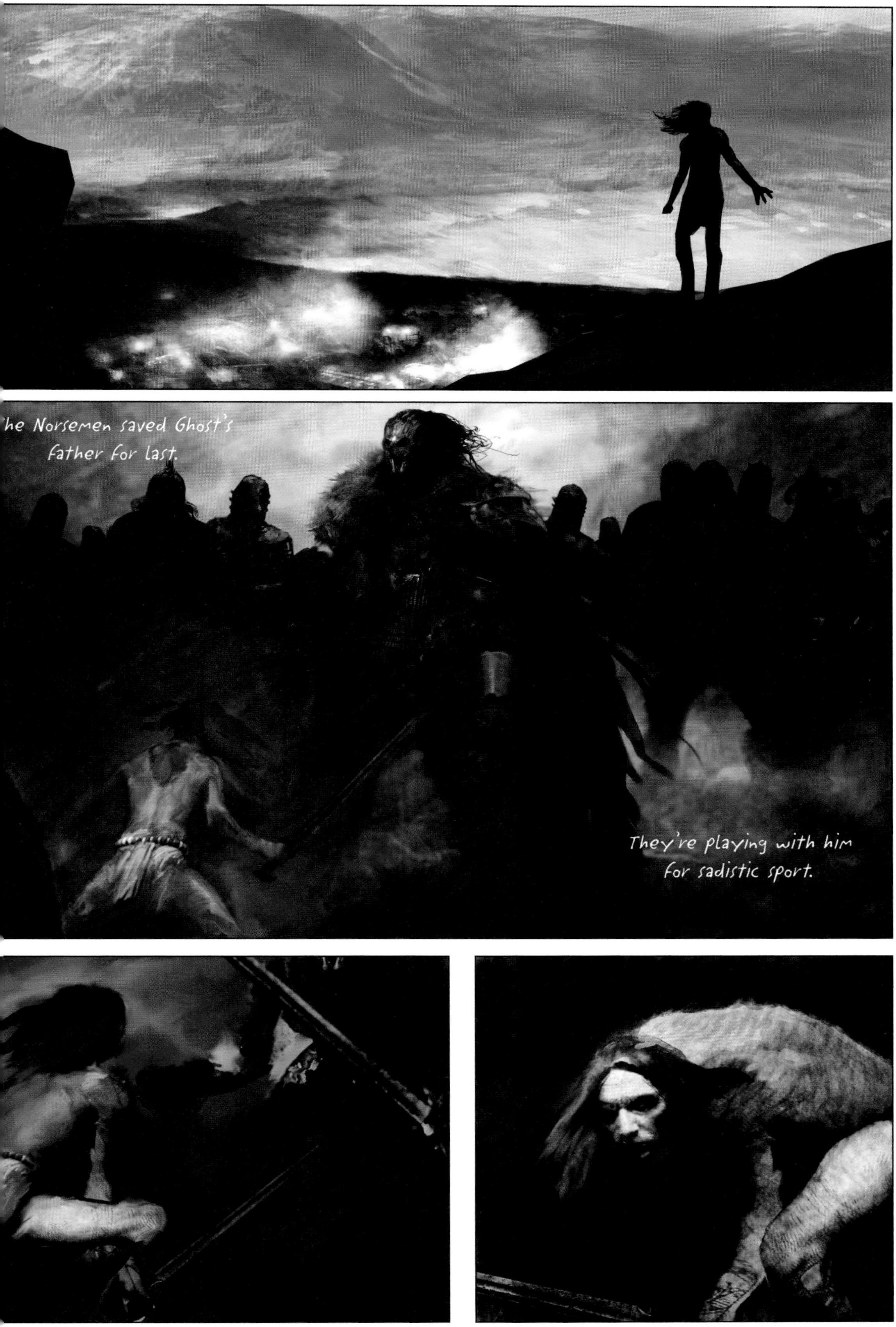
he Norsemen saved Ghost's
father for last.
They're playing with him
for sadistic sport.

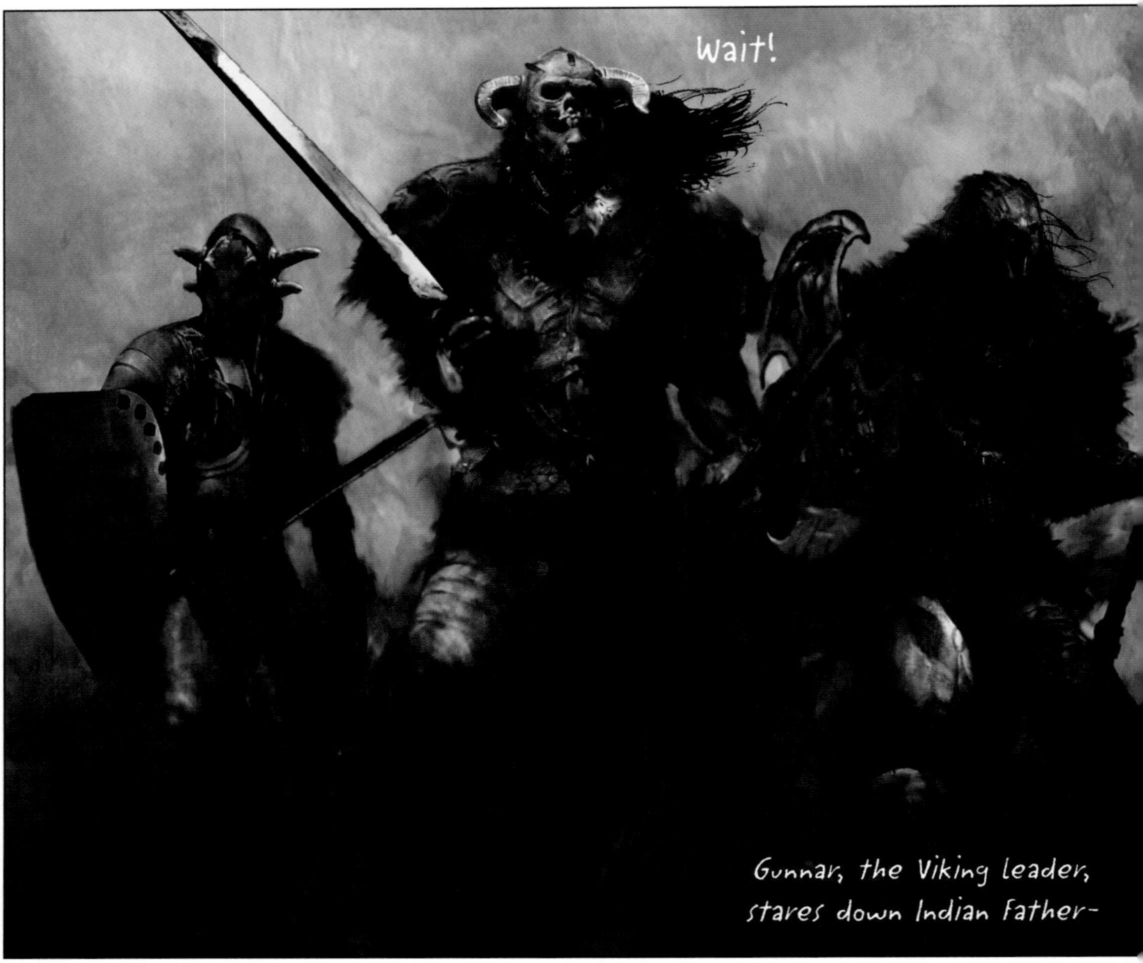
Wait!
Gunnar, the Viking leader, stares down Indian Father-

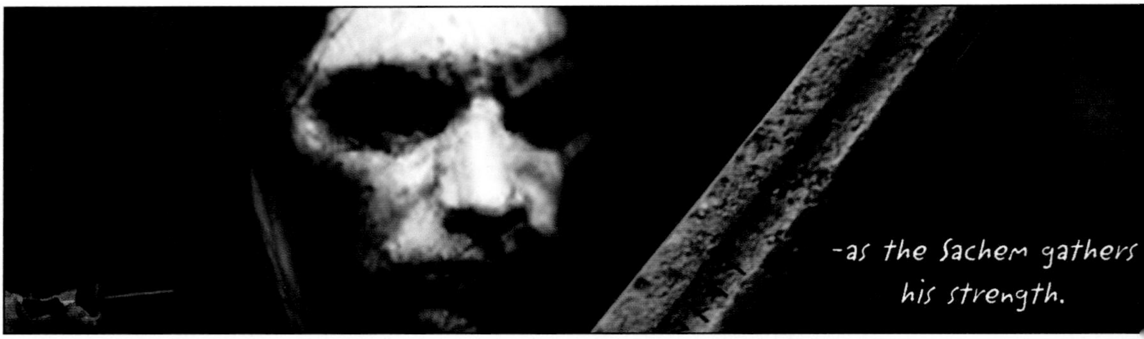
-as the Sachem gathers his strength.

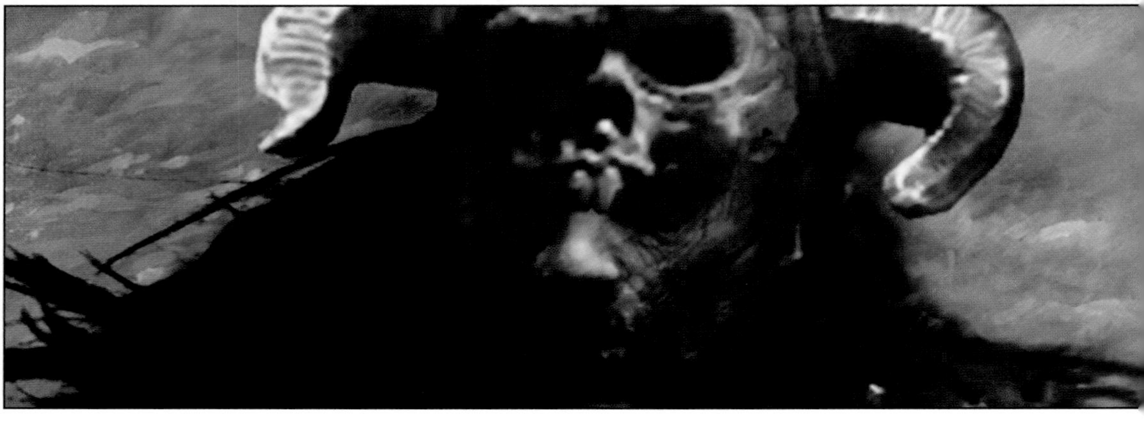

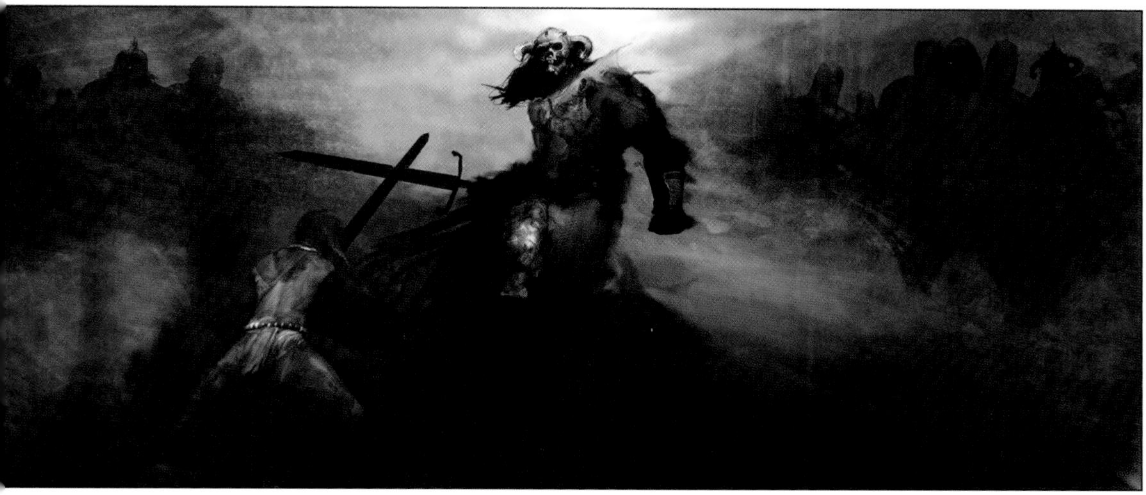

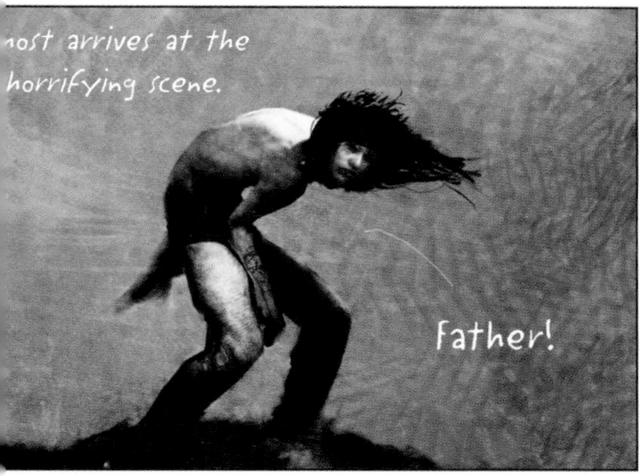

ost arrives at the
horrifying scene.
Father!

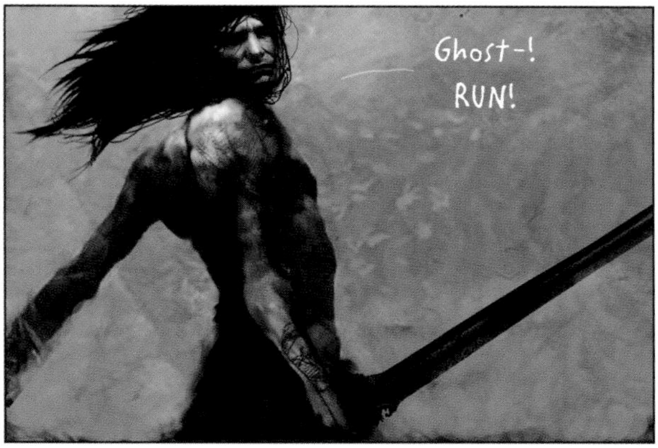

Ghost-!
RUN!

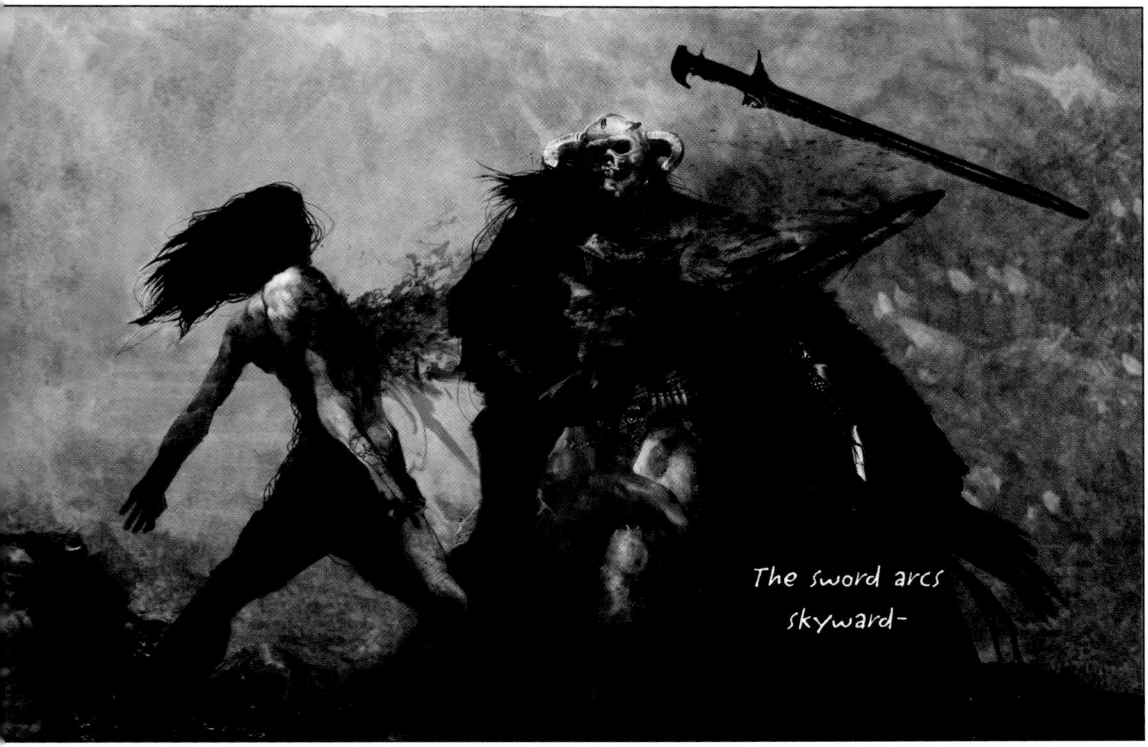

The sword arcs
skyward-

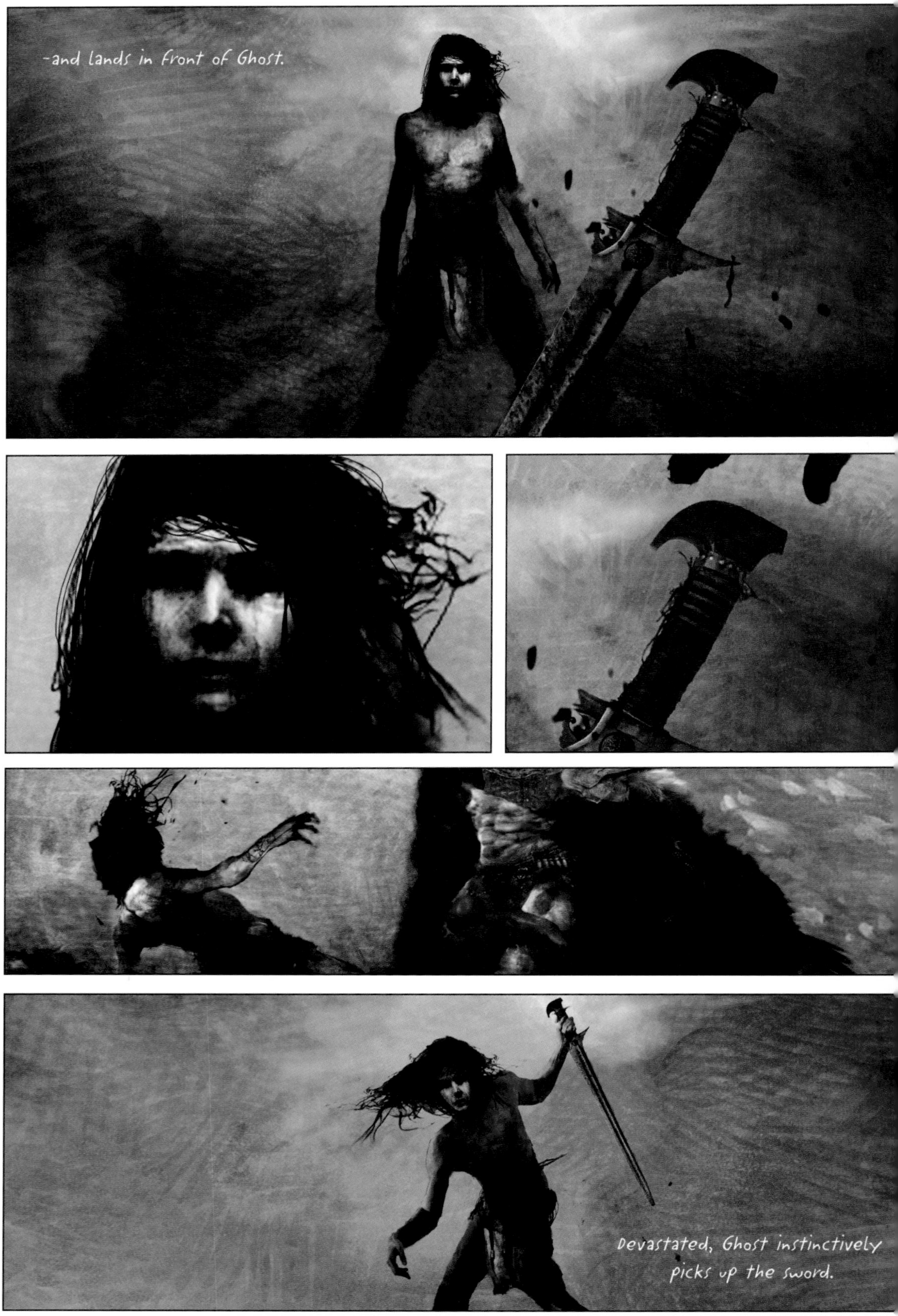
-and lands in front of Ghost.
Devastated, Ghost instinctively picks up the sword.

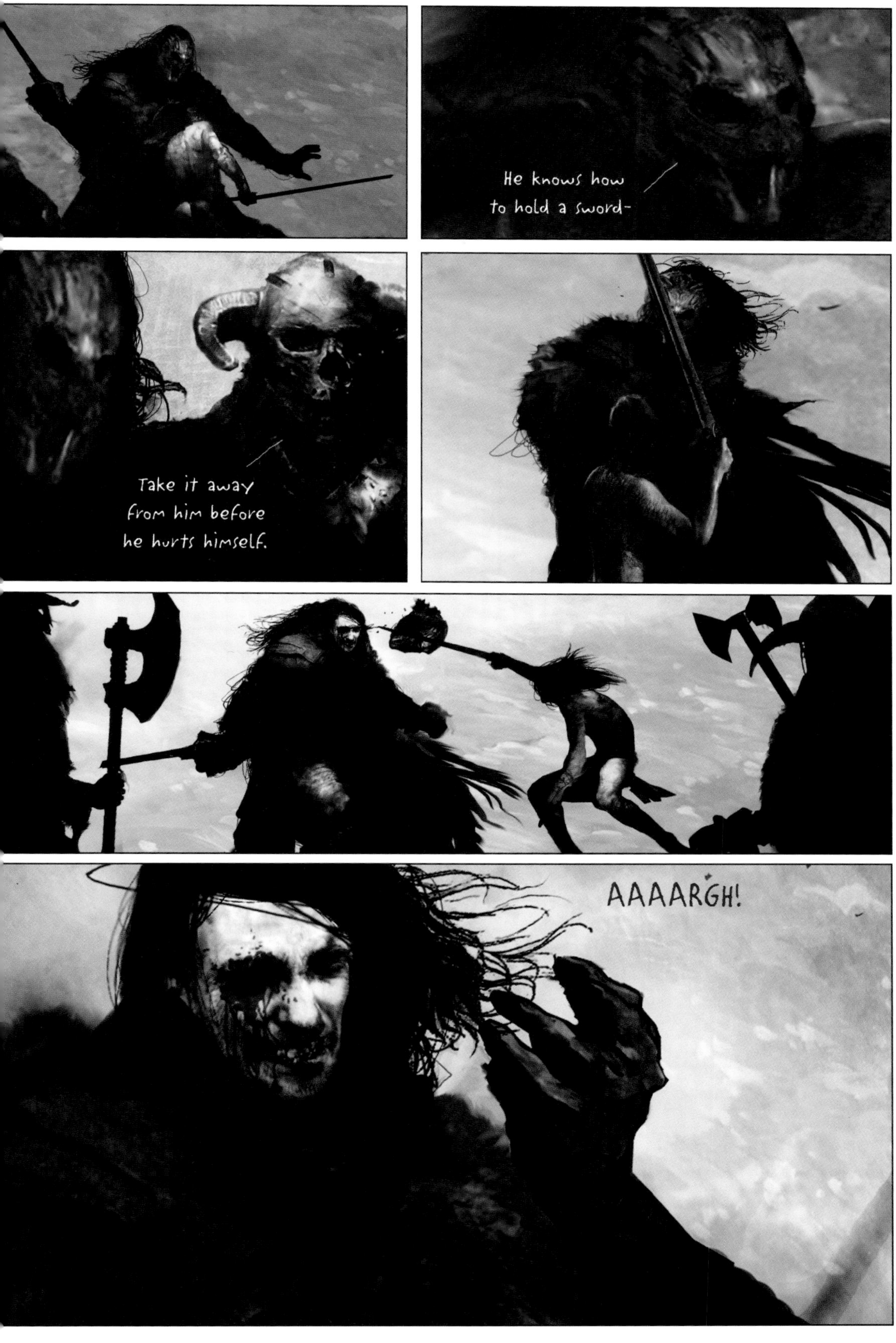
He knows how to hold a sword-
Take it away from him before he hurts himself.
AAAARGH!

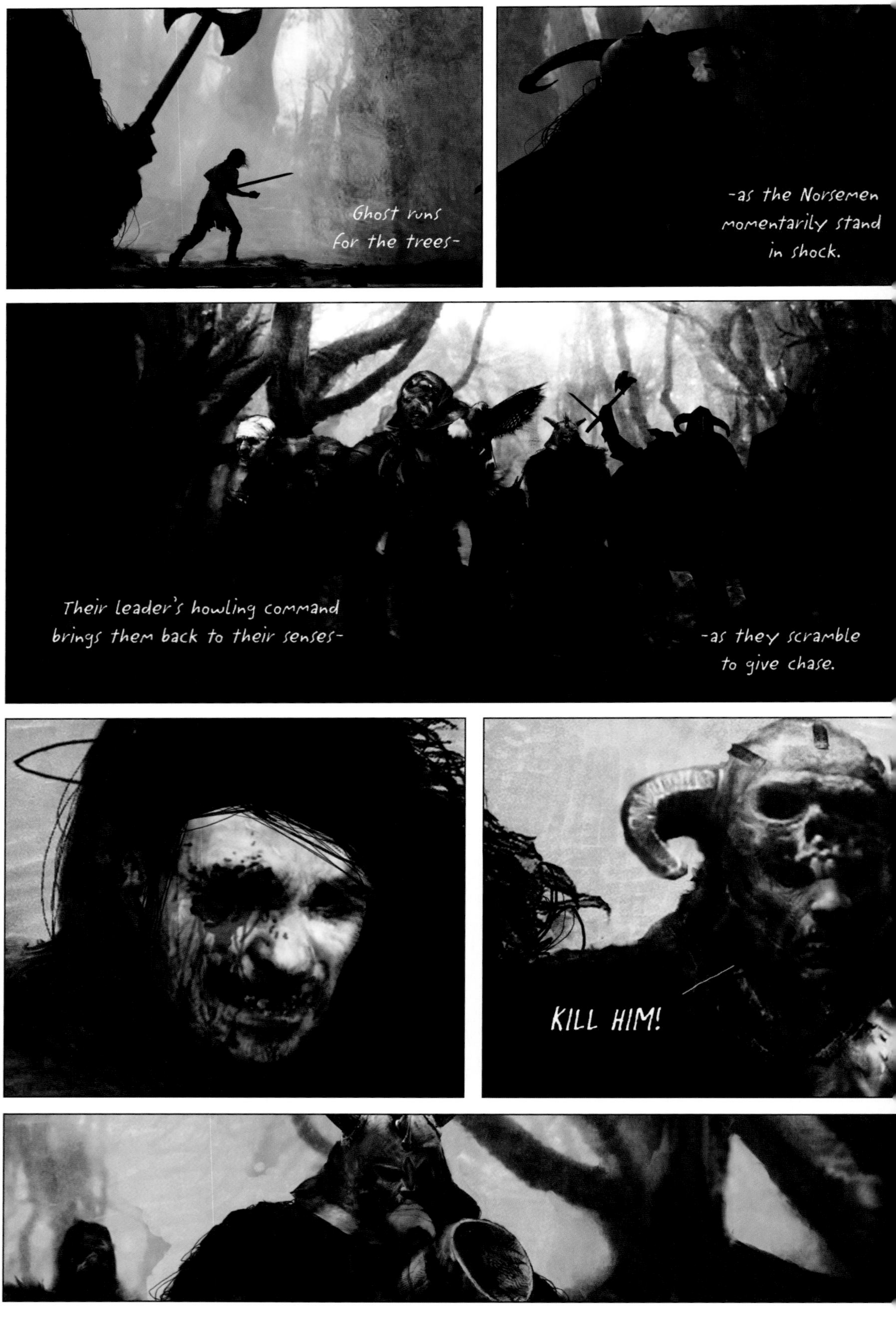
Ghost runs
for the trees-
-as the Norsemen
momentarily stand
in shock.
Their leader's howling command
brings them back to their senses-
-as they scramble
to give chase.
KILL HIM!

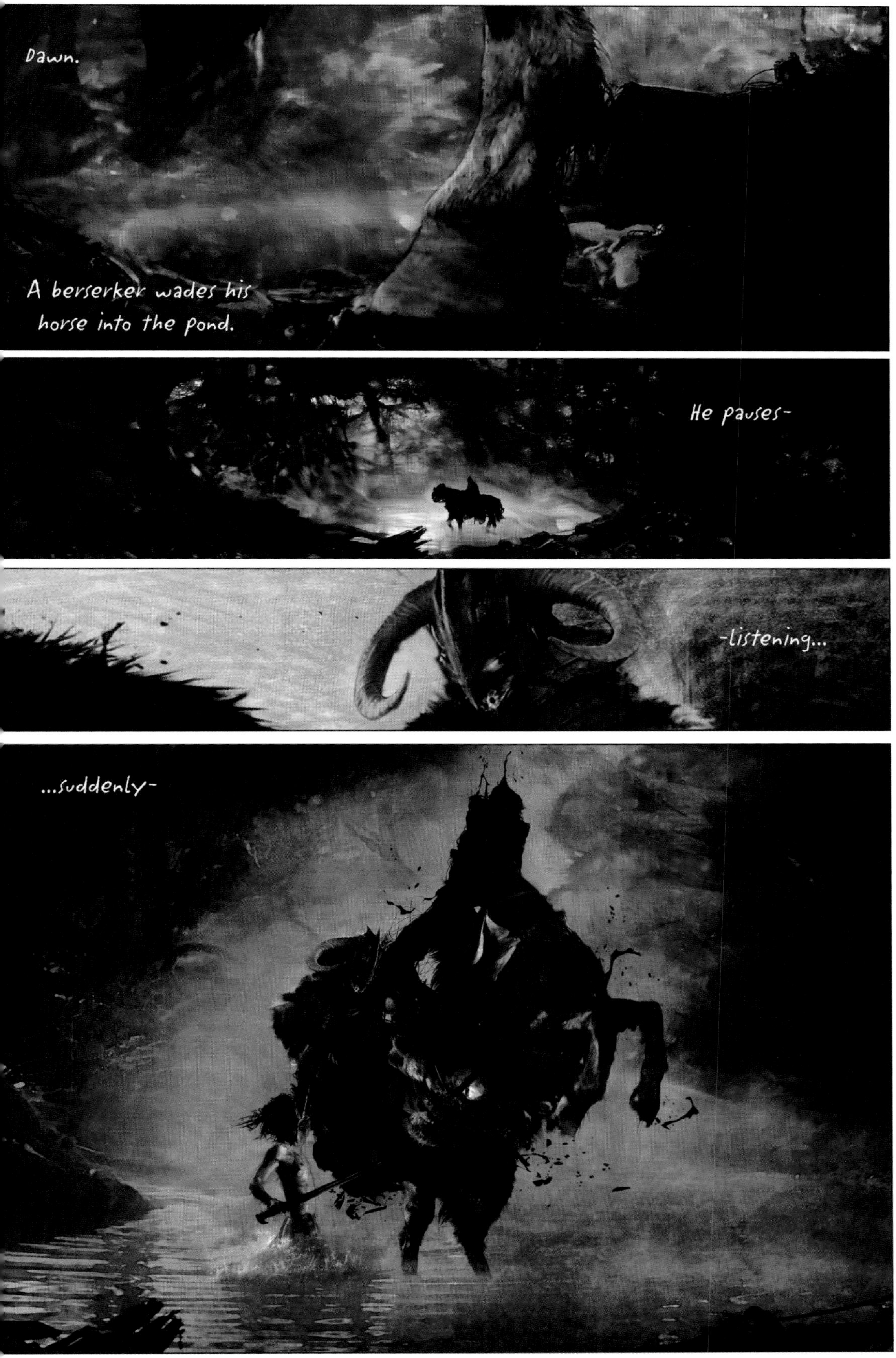
Dawn.
A berserker wades his horse into the pond.
He pauses-
-listening...
...suddenly-

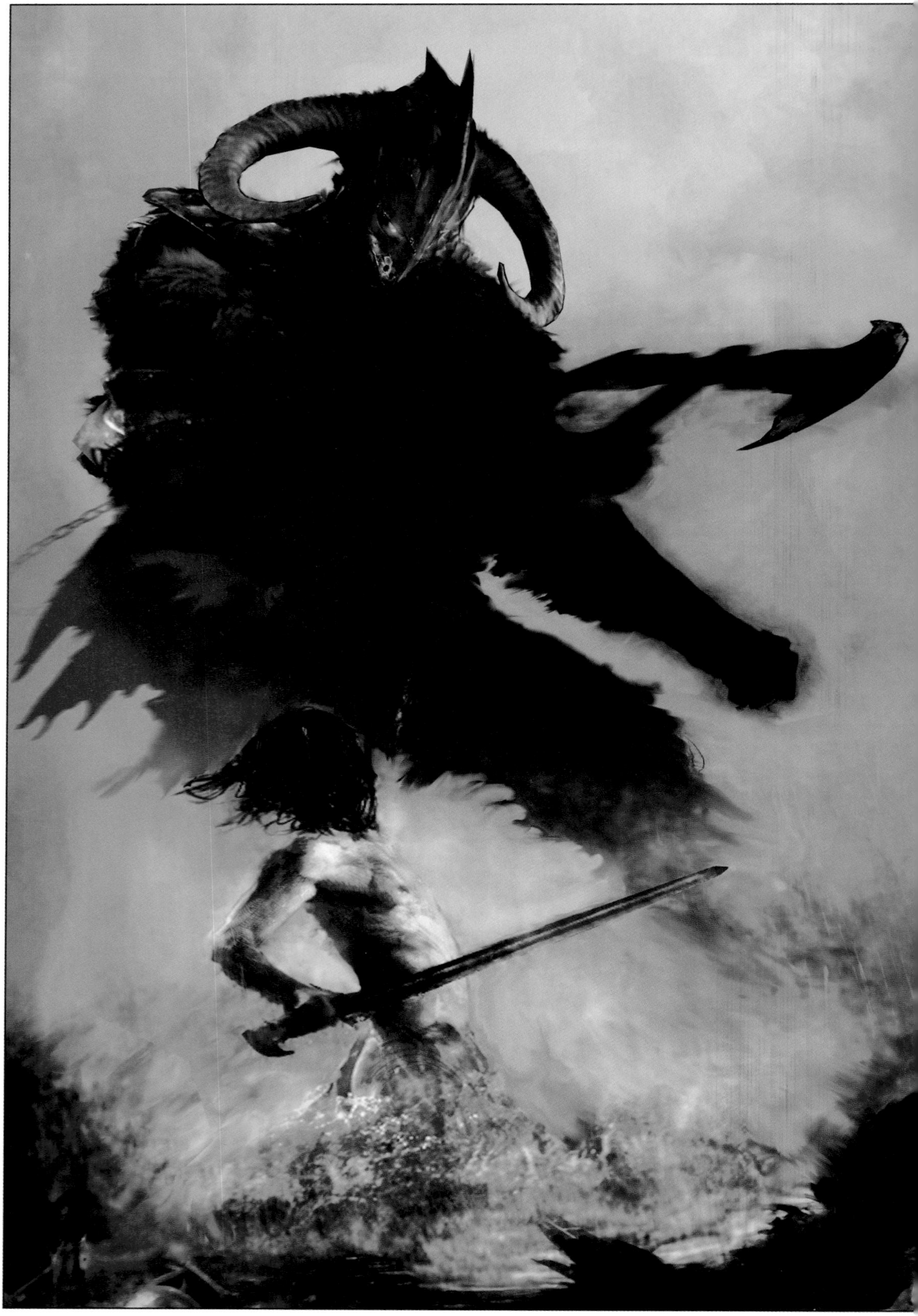

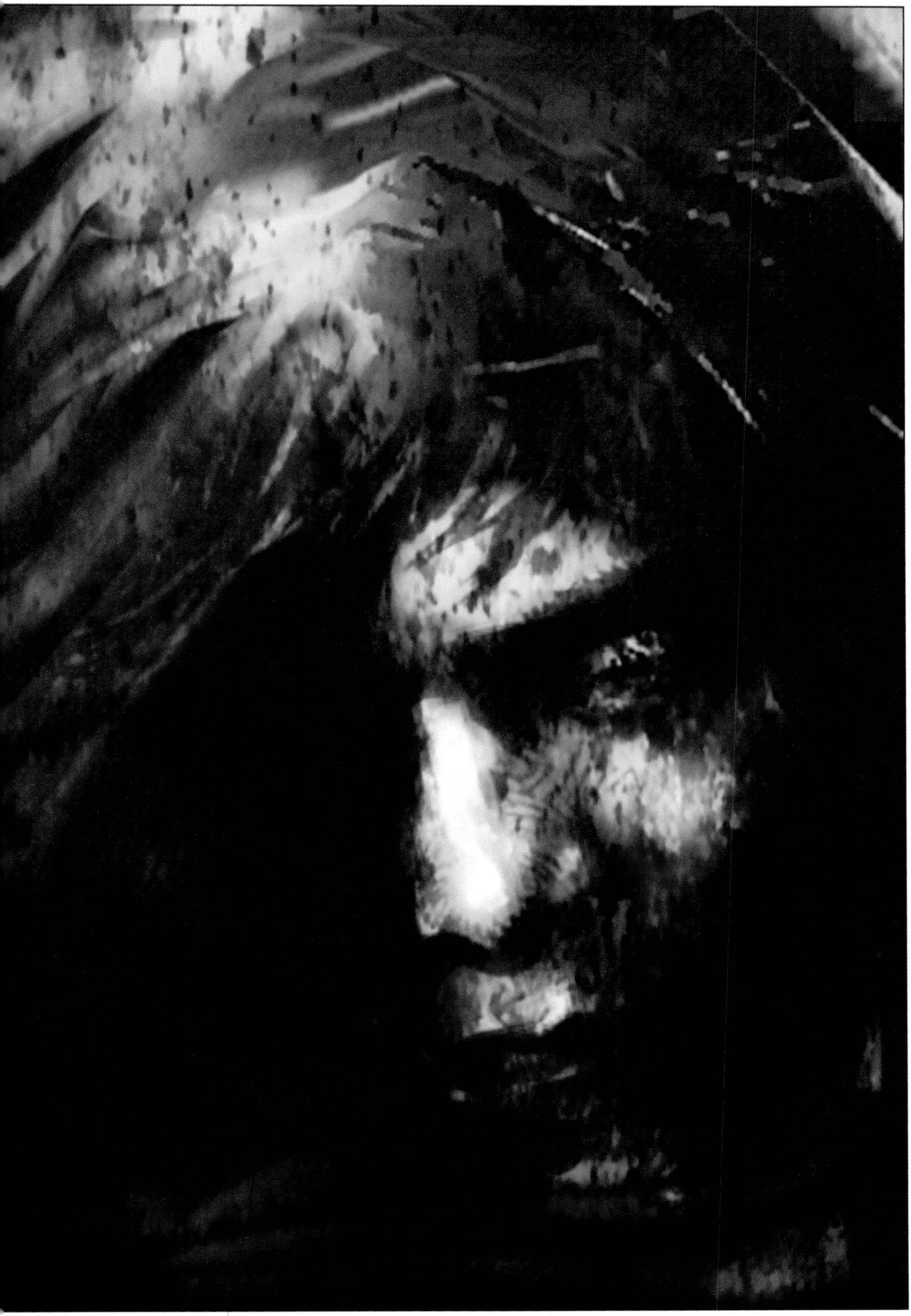

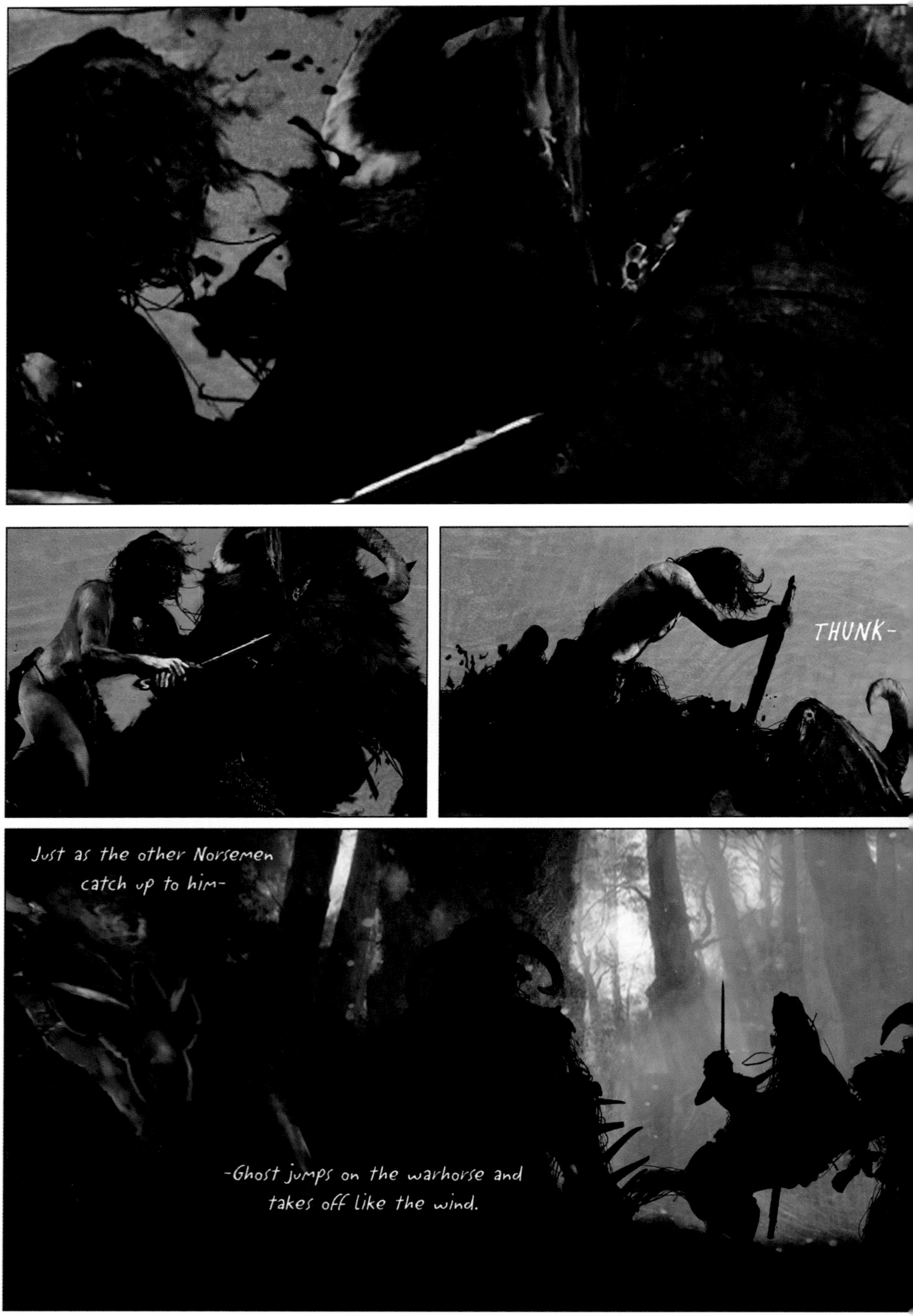
THUNK-
Just as the other Norsemen catch up to him-
-Ghost jumps on the warhorse and takes off like the wind.

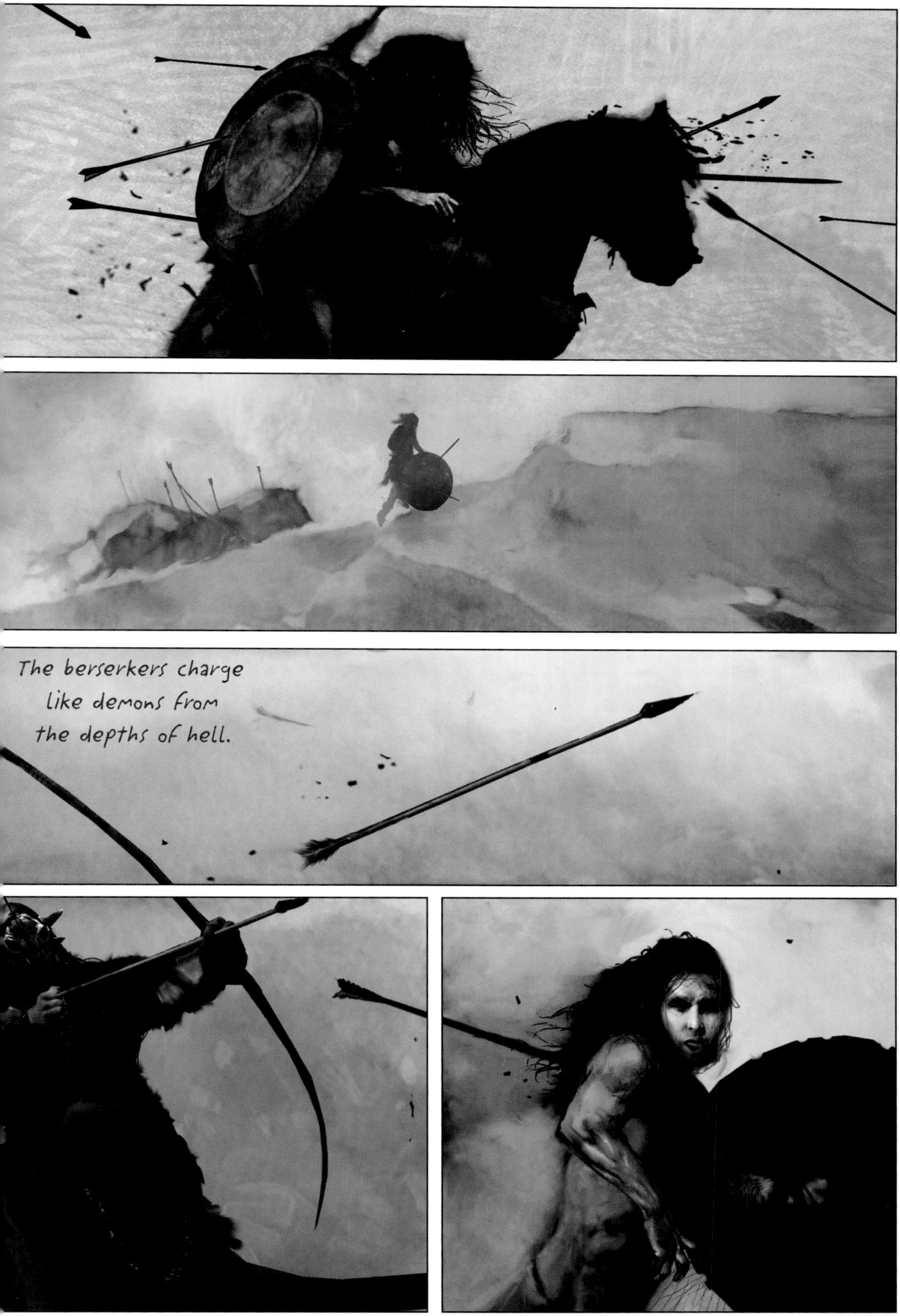
The berserkers charge like demons from the depths of hell.

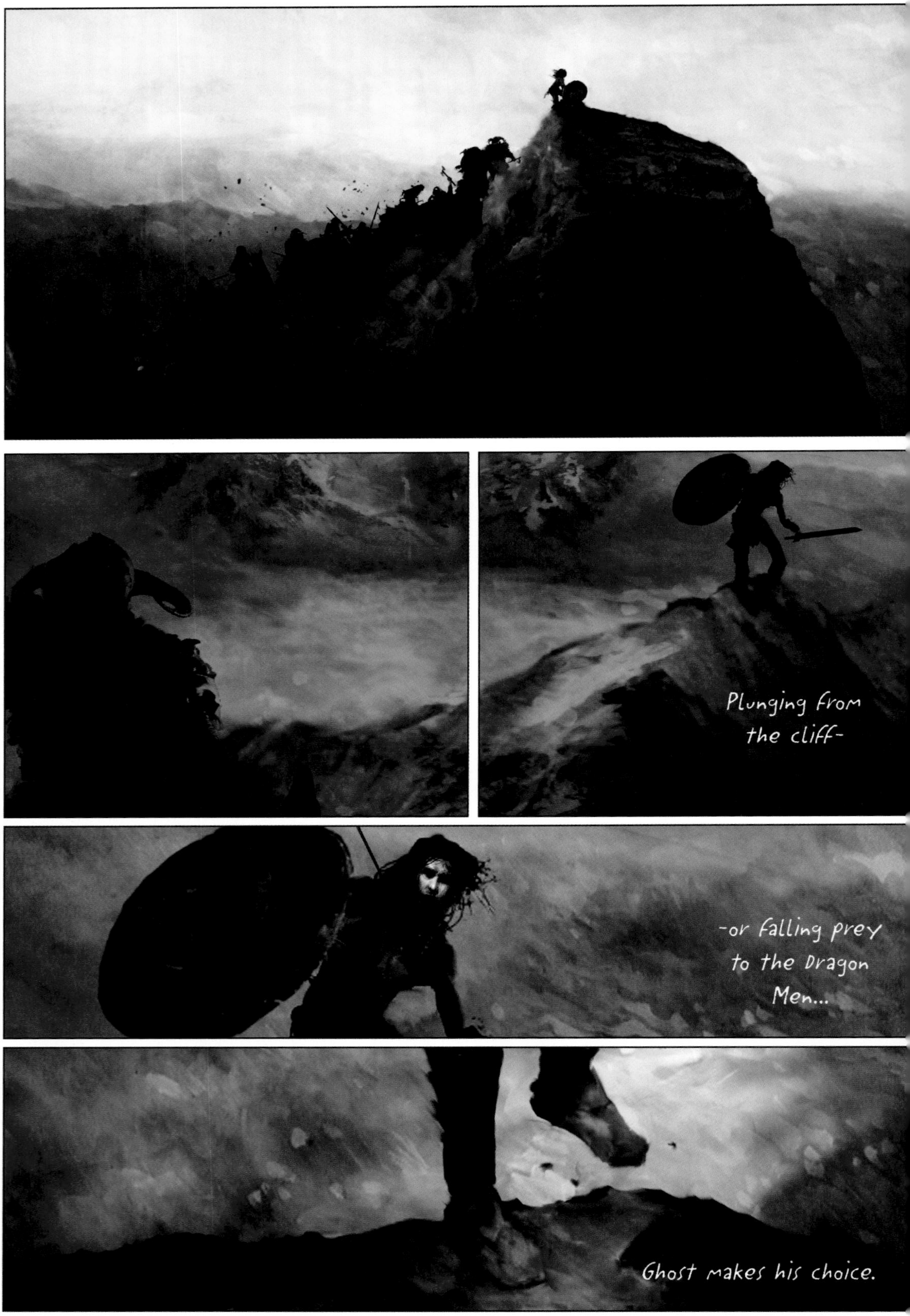
Plunging from the cliff-
-or falling prey to the Dragon Men...
Ghost makes his choice.

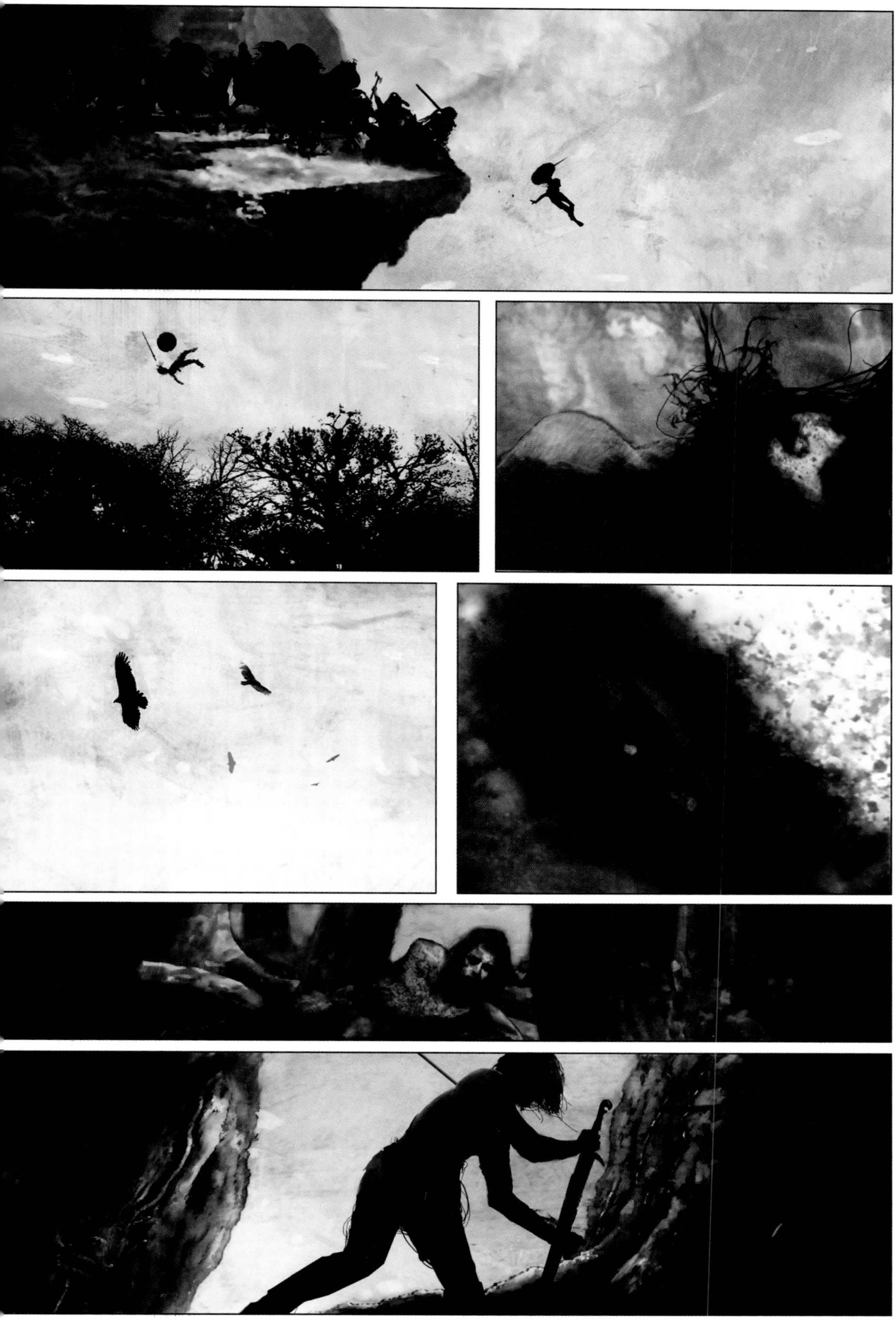

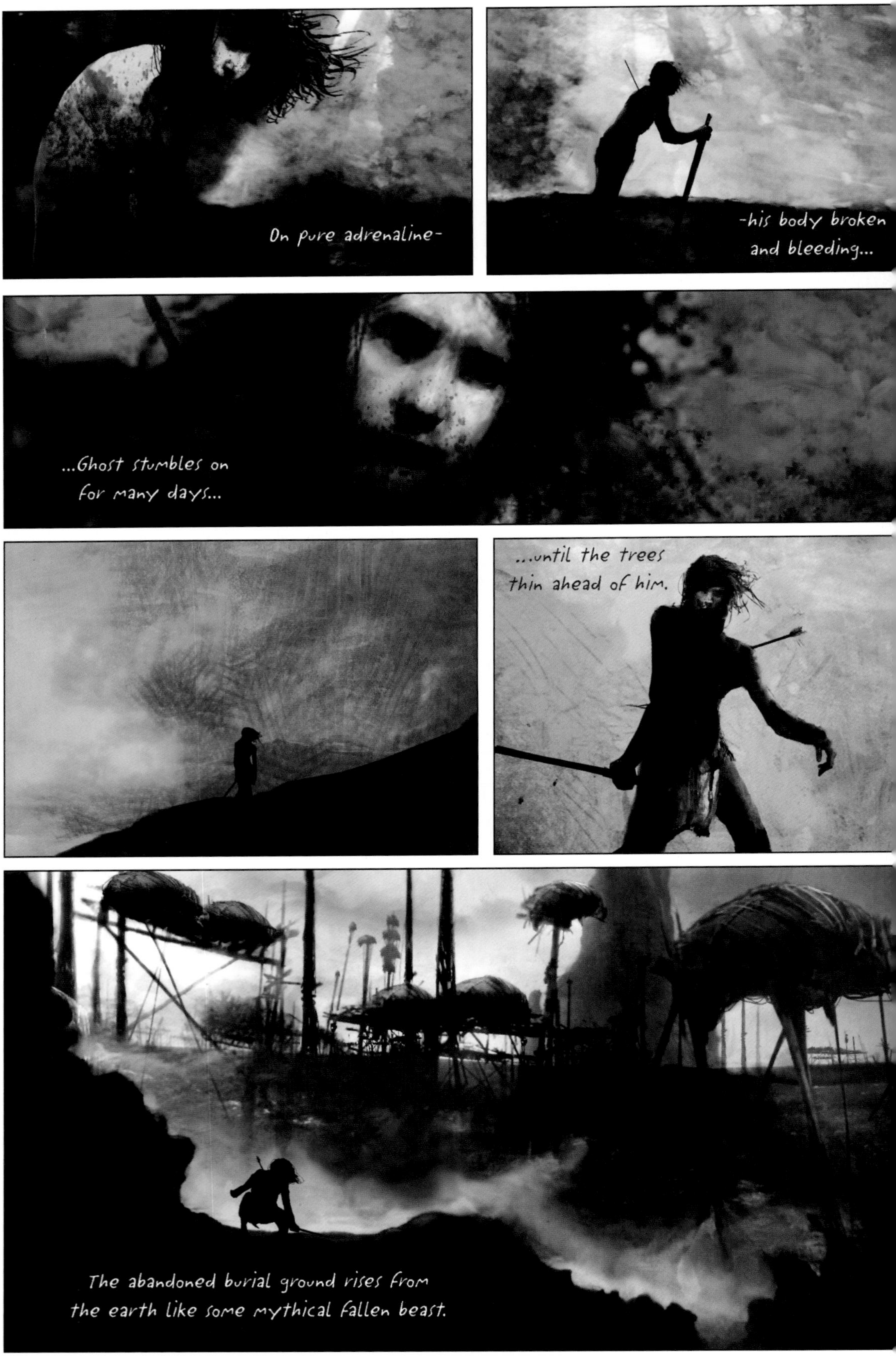
On pure adrenaline-
-his body broken and bleeding...
...Ghost stumbles on for many days...
...until the trees thin ahead of him.
The abandoned burial ground rises from the earth like some mythical fallen beast.

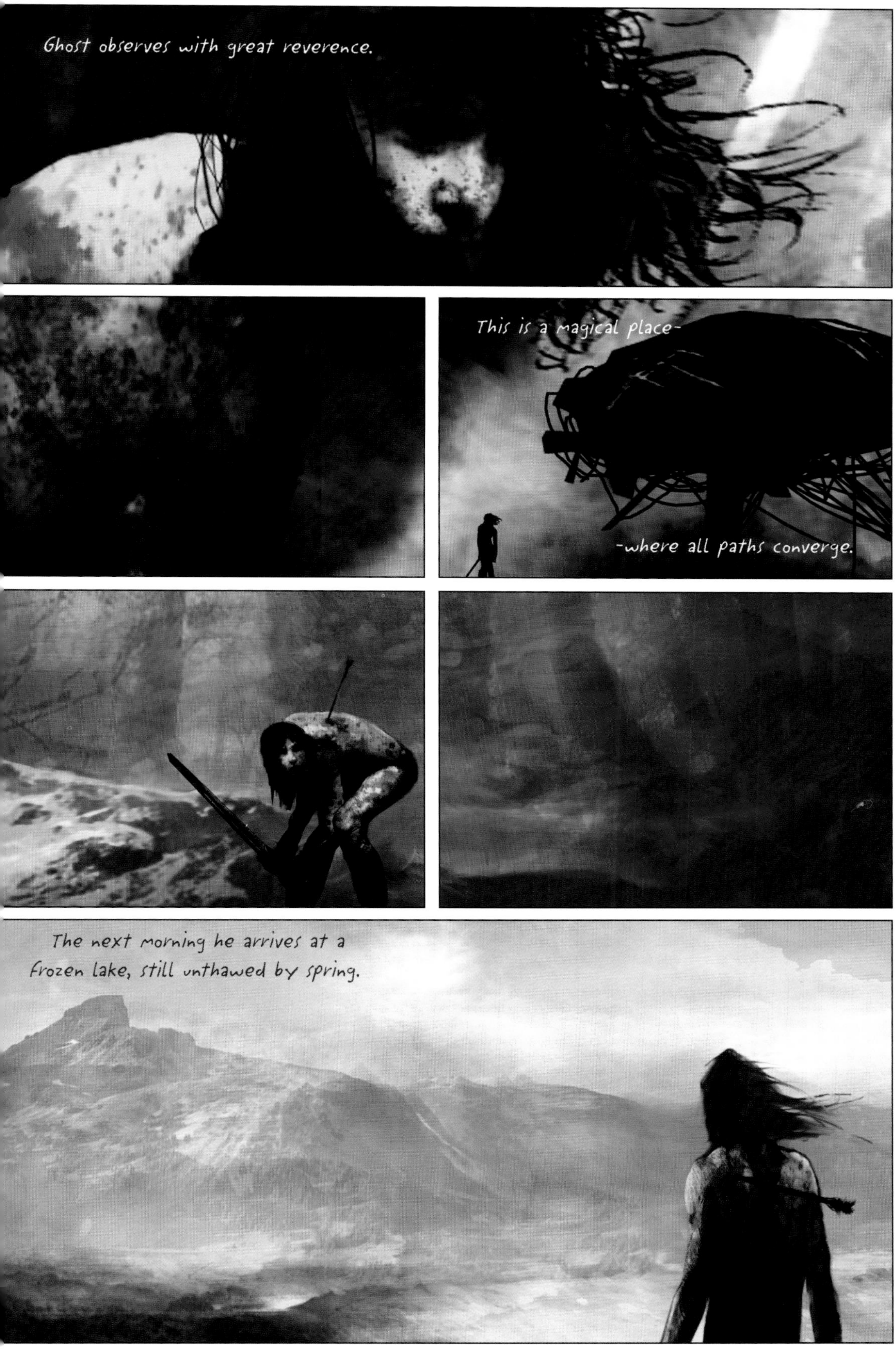
Ghost observes with great reverence.
This is a magical place-
-where all paths converge.
The next morning he arrives at a frozen lake, still unthawed by spring.

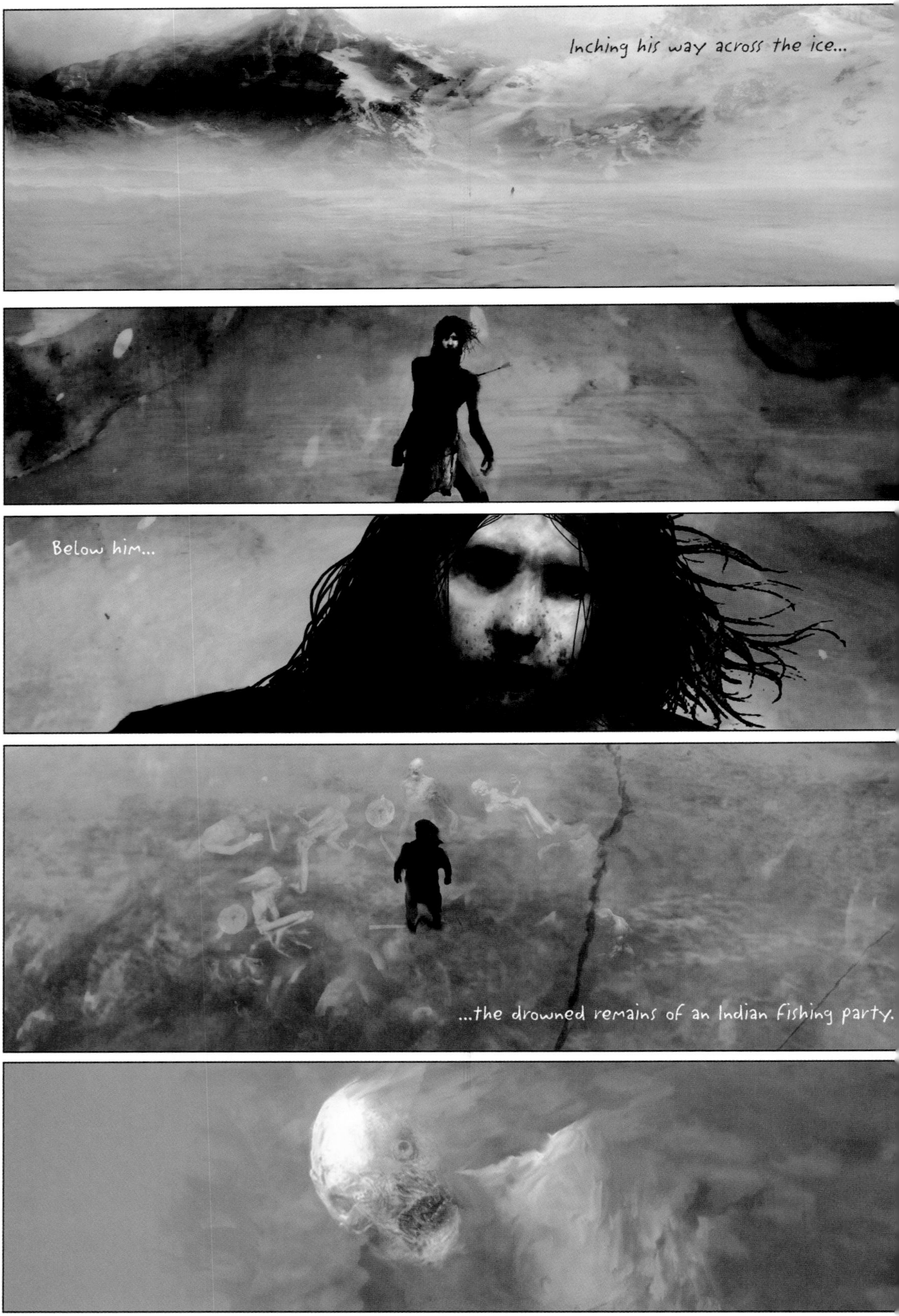
Inching his way across the ice...
Below him...
...the drowned remains of an Indian fishing party.

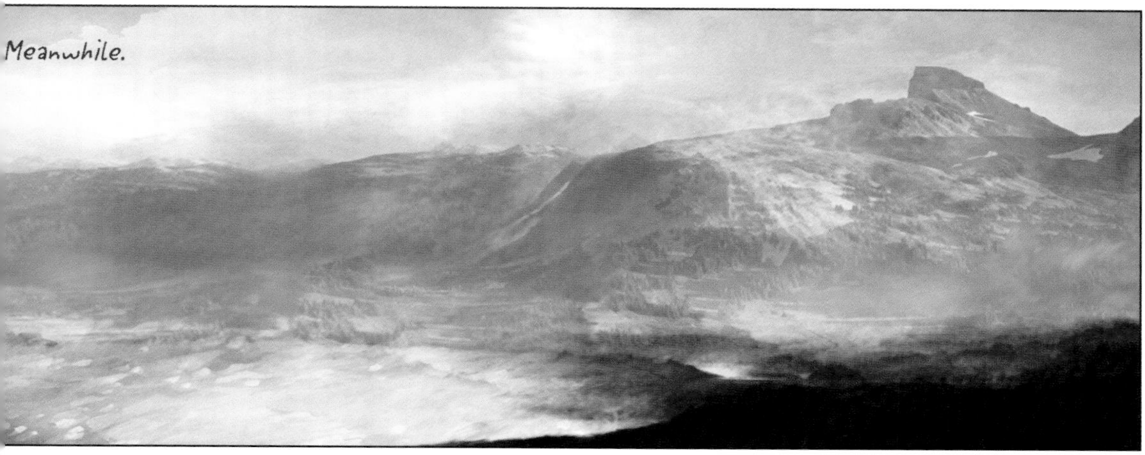
Meanwhile.

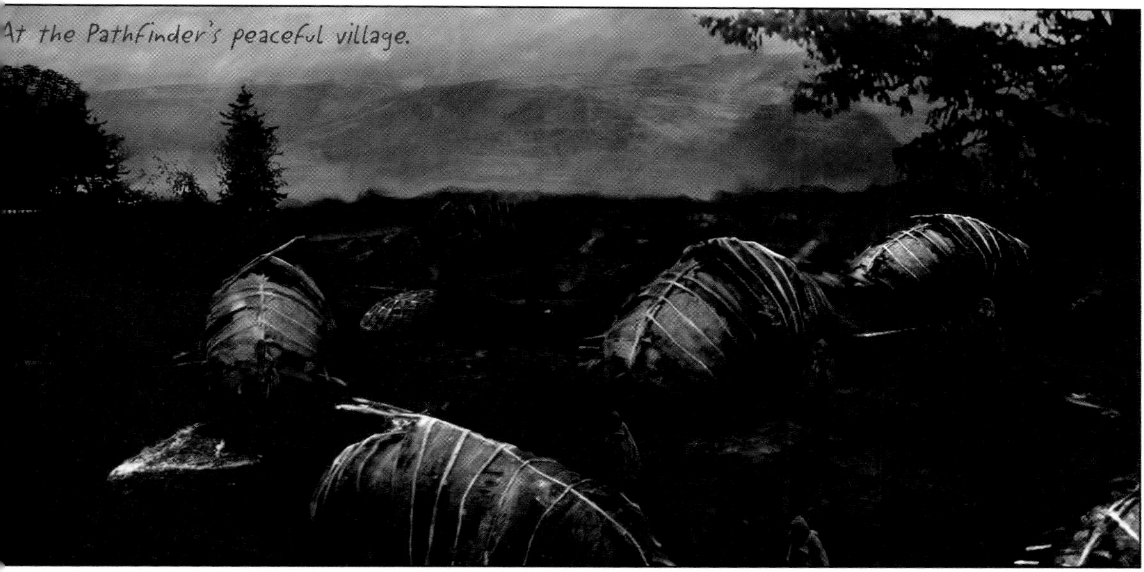
At the Pathfinder's peaceful village.

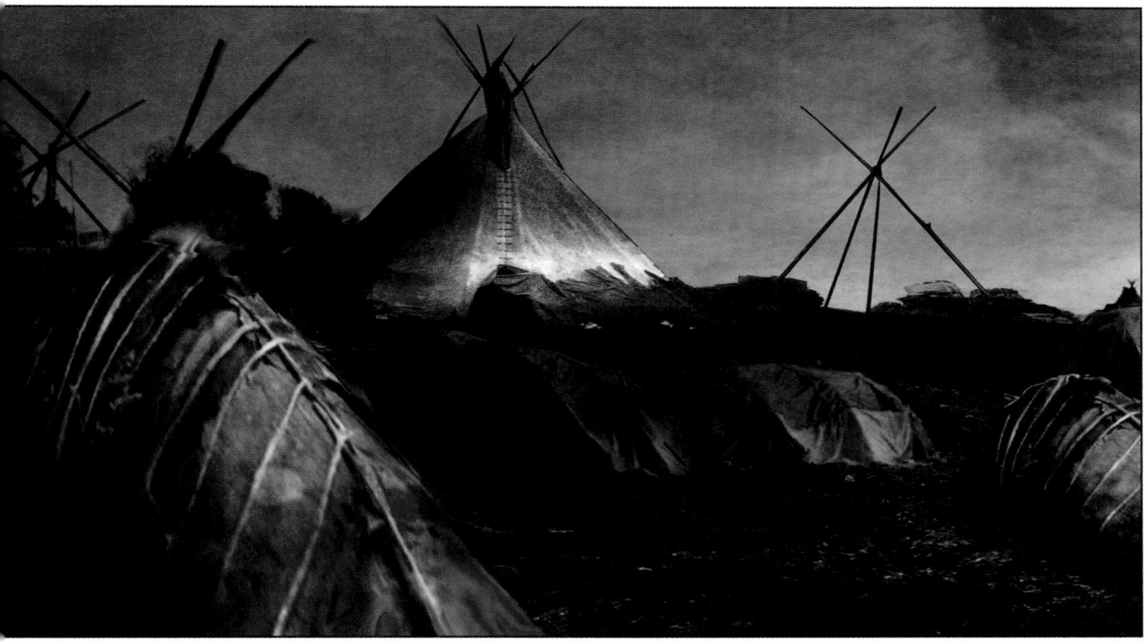

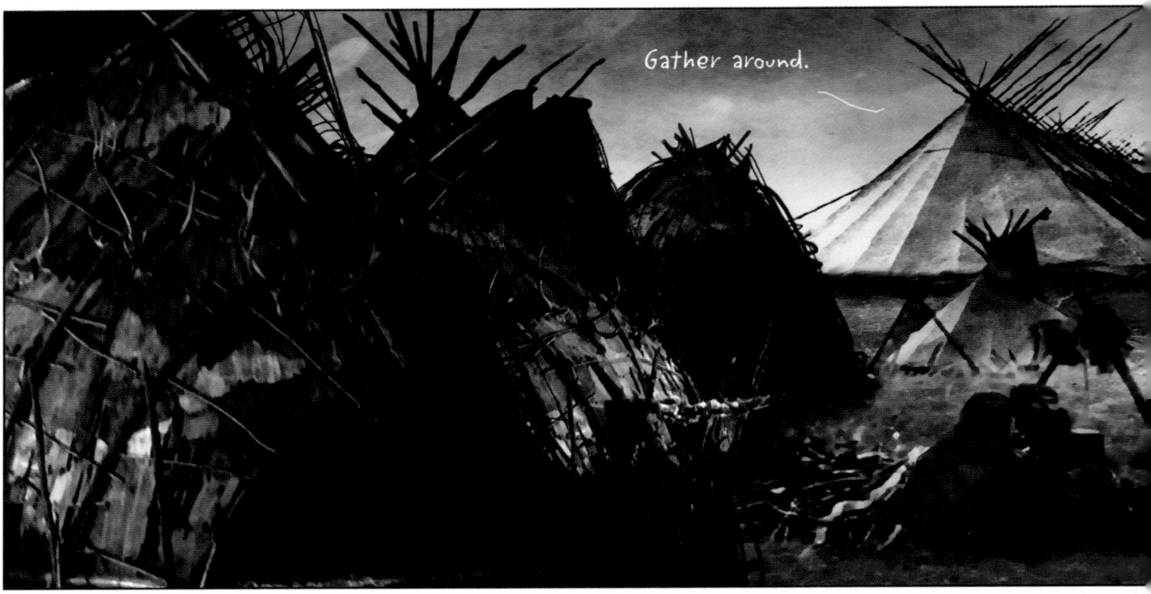
Gather around.

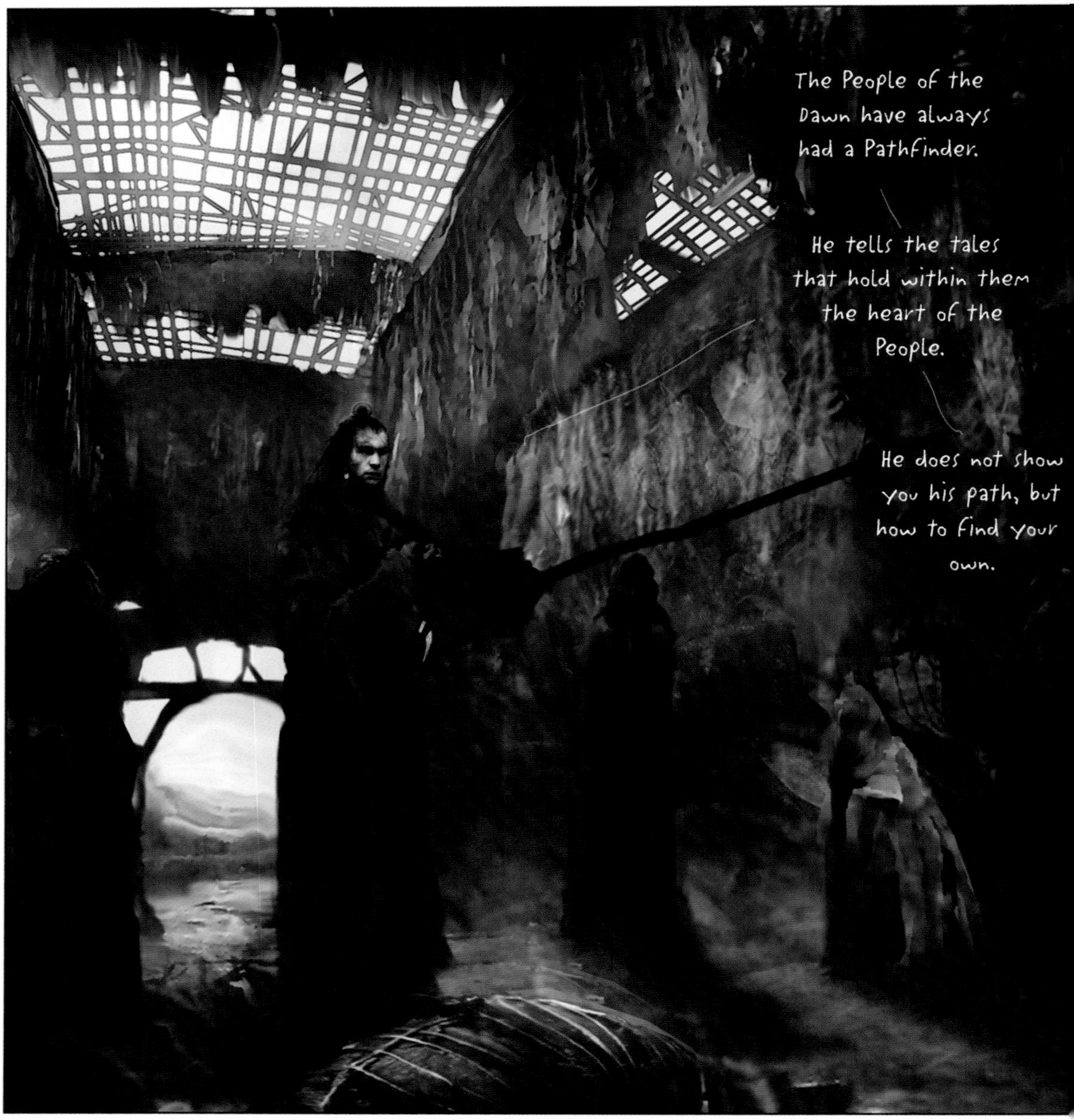
The People of the Dawn have always had a Pathfinder.
He tells the tales that hold within them the heart of the People.
He does not show you his path, but how to find your own.

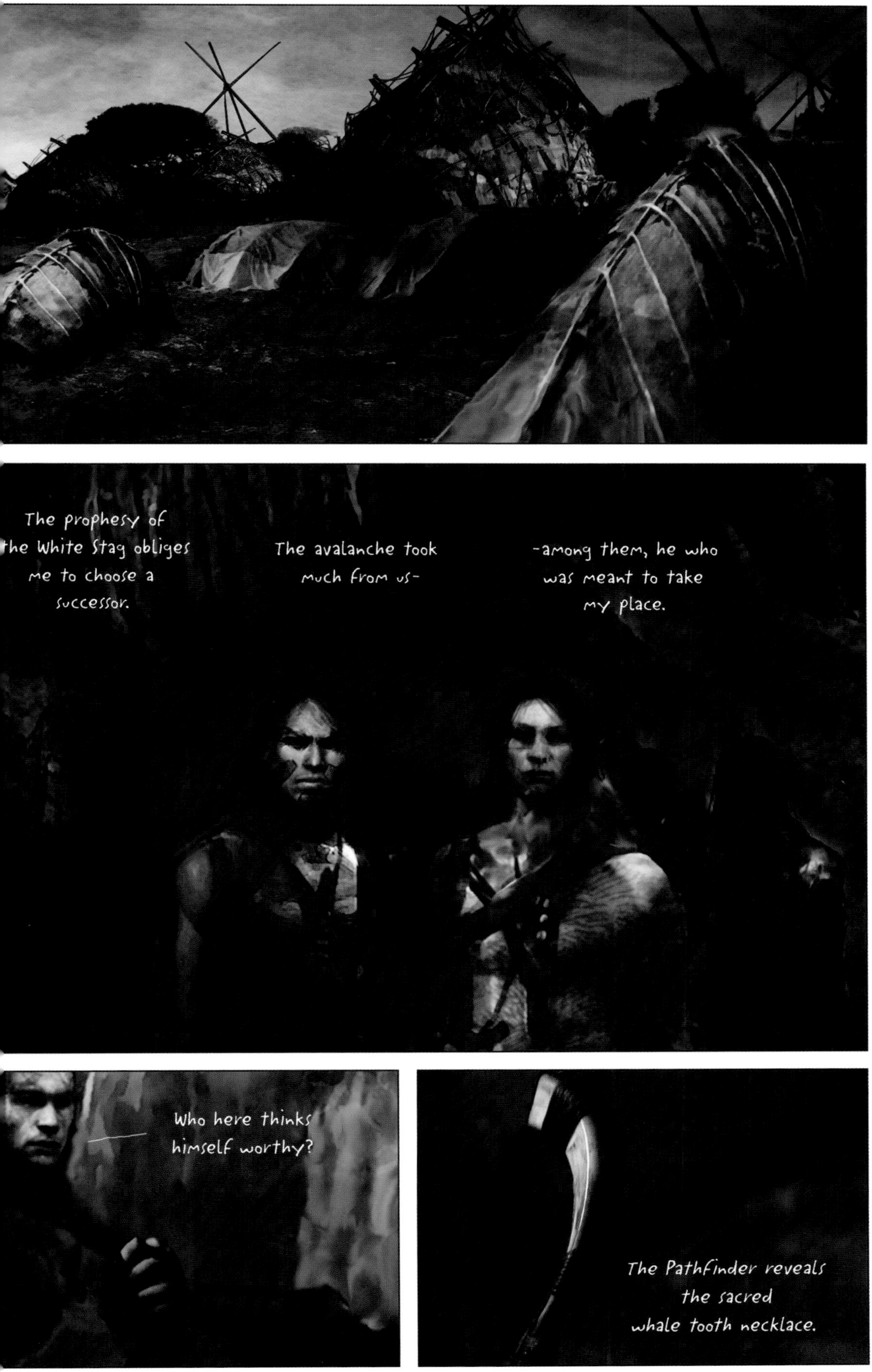
The prophesy of the White Stag obliges me to choose a successor.
The avalanche took much from us-
-among them, he who was meant to take my place.
Who here thinks himself worthy?
The Pathfinder reveals the sacred whale tooth necklace.

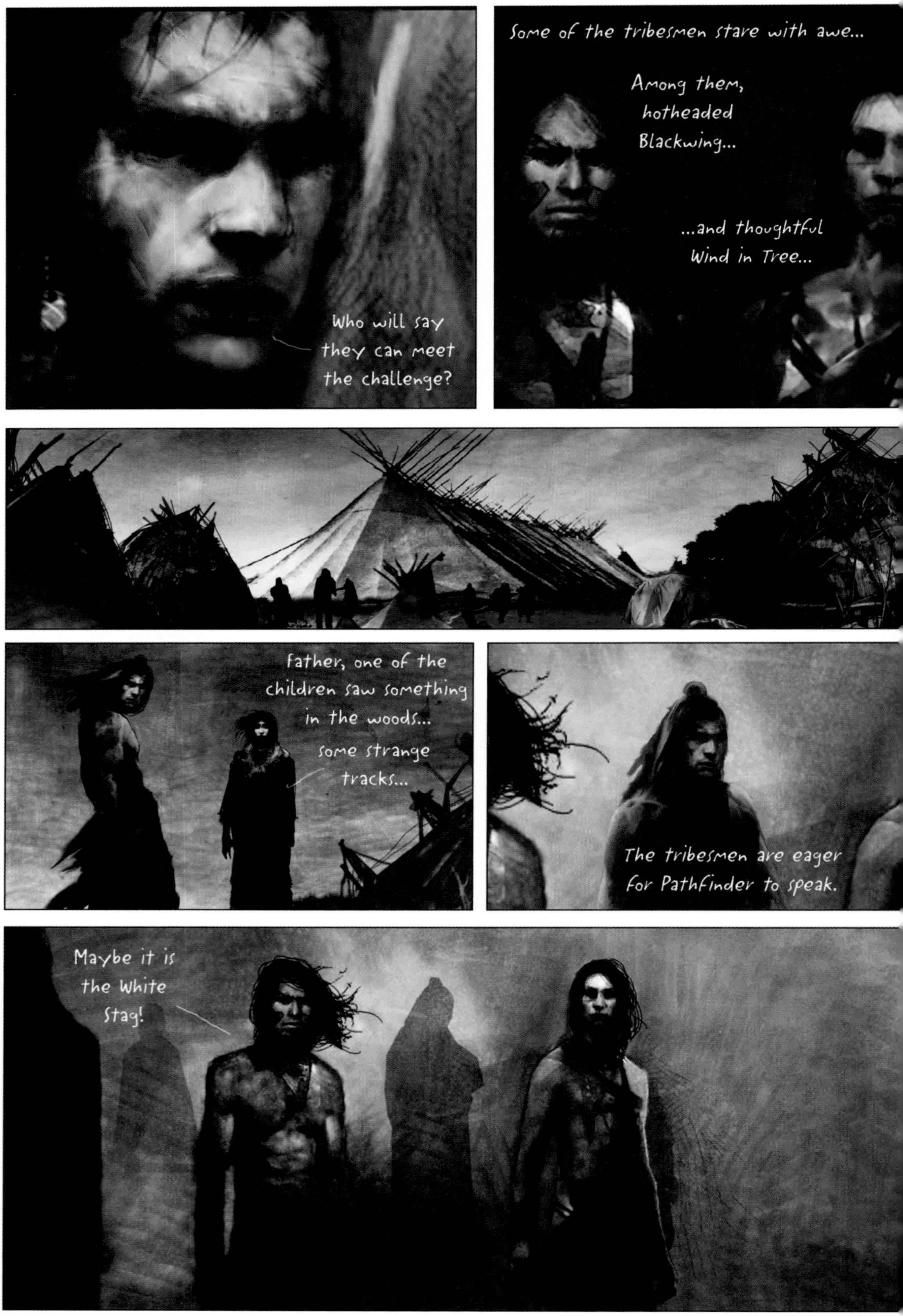
Who will say they can meet the challenge?
Some of the tribesmen stare with awe...
Among them, hotheaded Blackwing...
...and thoughtful Wind in Tree...
Father, one of the children saw something in the woods... some strange tracks...
The tribesmen are eager for Pathfinder to speak.
Maybe it is the White Stag!

It's a challenge.

But father-

I saw the tracks. They were not those of a stag-

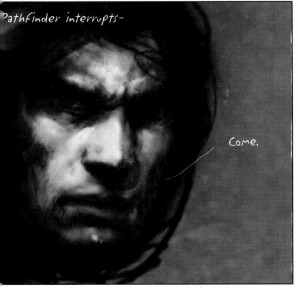

Pathfinder interrupts-

Come.

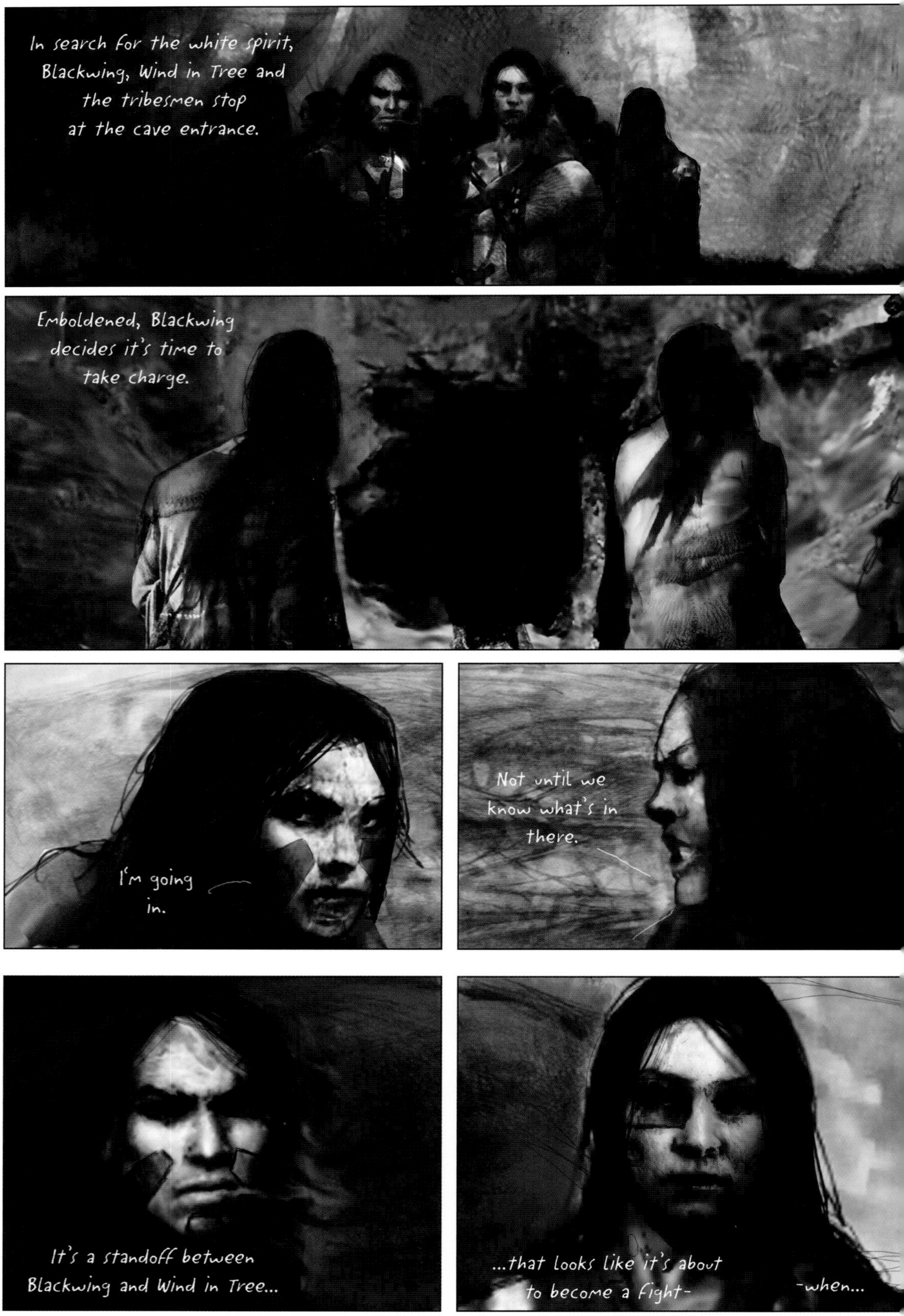
In search for the white spirit, Blackwing, Wind in Tree and the tribesmen stop at the cave entrance.
Emboldened, Blackwing decides it's time to take charge.
I'm going in.
Not until we know what's in there.
It's a standoff between Blackwing and Wind in Tree...
...that looks like it's about to become a fight-
-when...

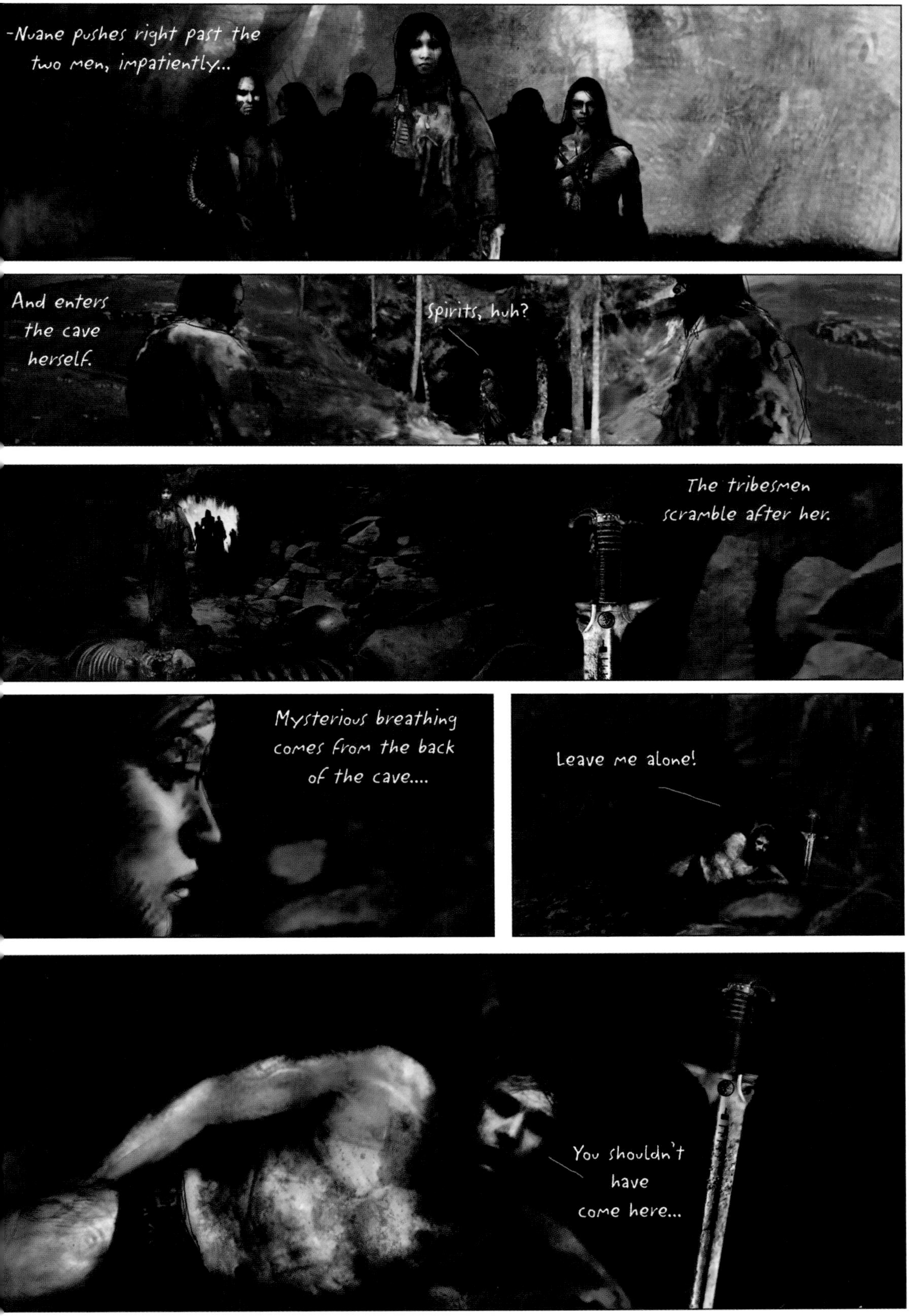
-Nuane pushes right past the two men, impatiently...
And enters the cave herself.
Spirits, huh?
The tribesmen scramble after her.
Mysterious breathing comes from the back of the cave....
Leave me alone!
You shouldn't have come here...

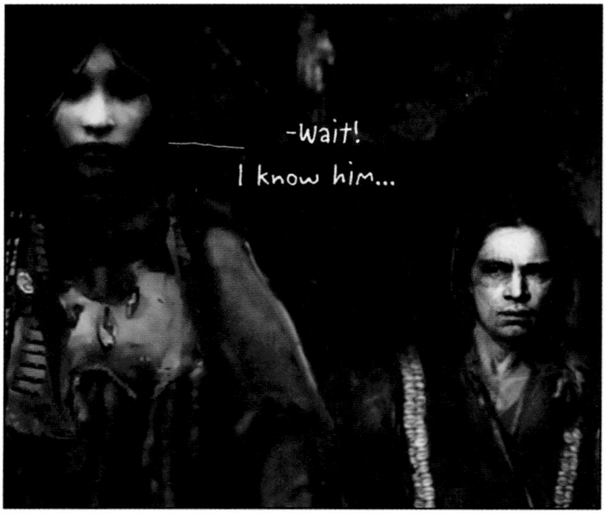
-Wait!
I know him...

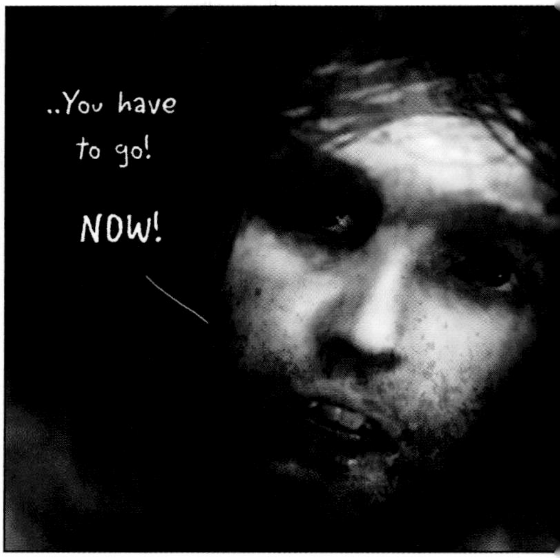
..You have
to go!
NOW!

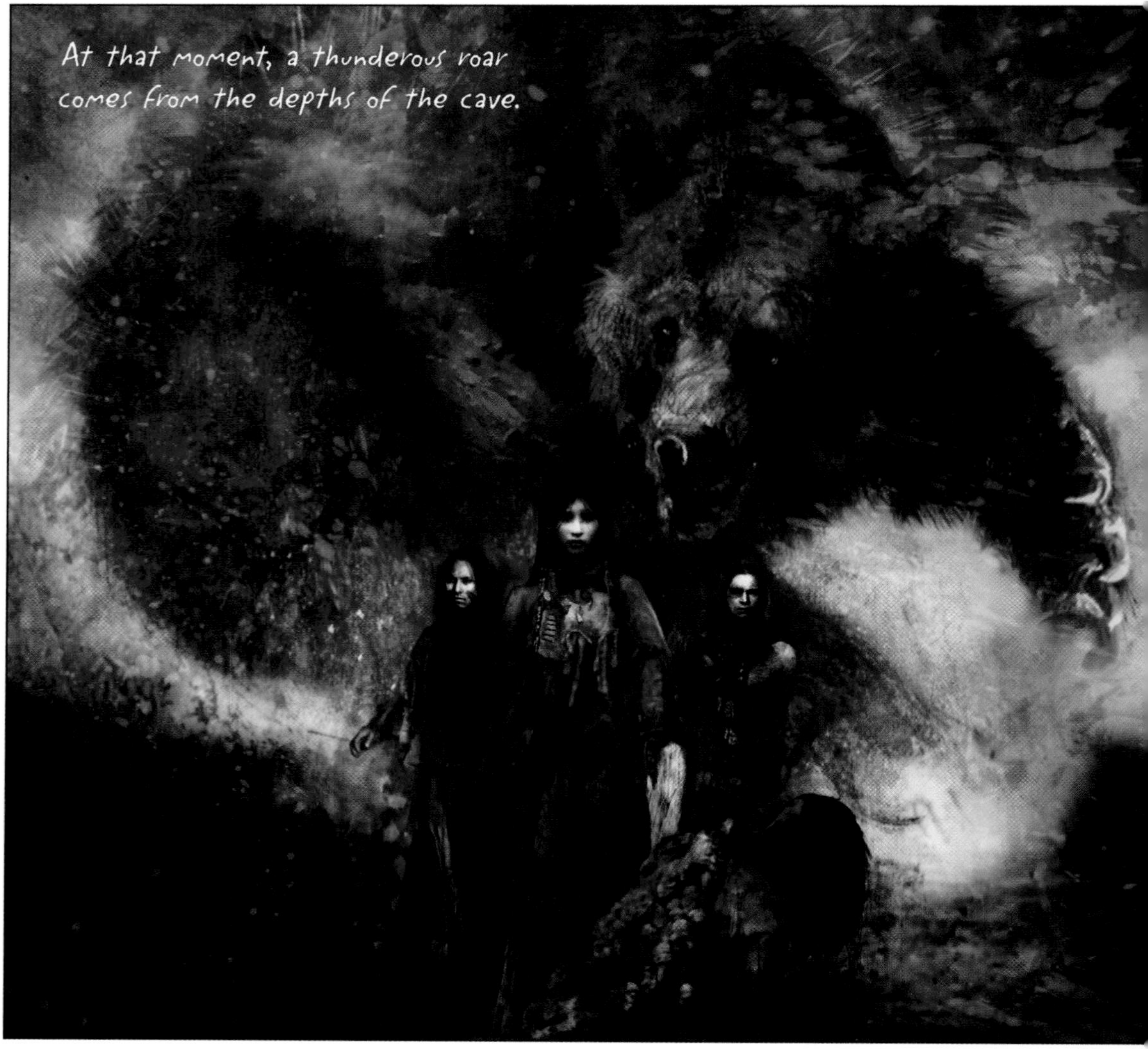
At that moment, a thunderous roar
comes from the depths of the cave.

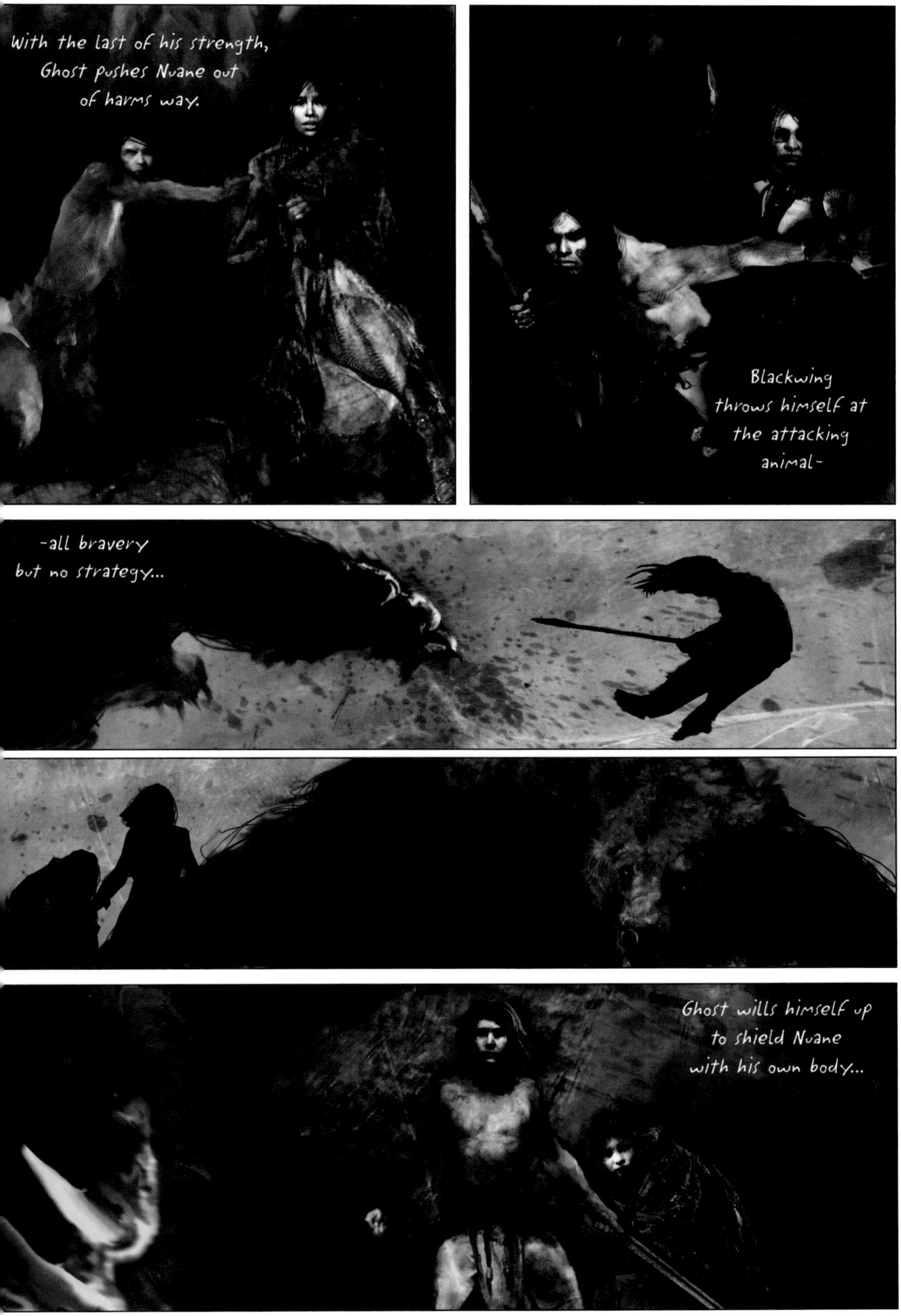
With the last of his strength, Ghost pushes Nuane out of harms way.
Blackwing throws himself at the attacking animal-
-all bravery but no strategy...
Ghost wills himself up to shield Nuane with his own body...

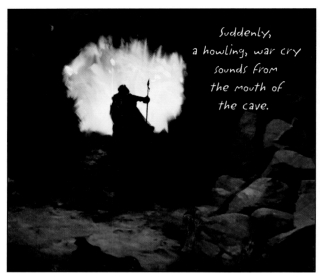

Suddenly,
a howling, war cry
sounds from
the mouth of
the cave.

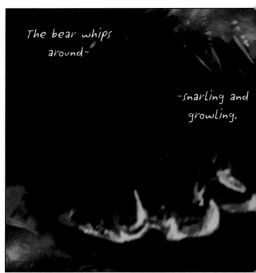

The bear whips
around-

-snarling and
growling.

The Pathfinder's
face is calm-

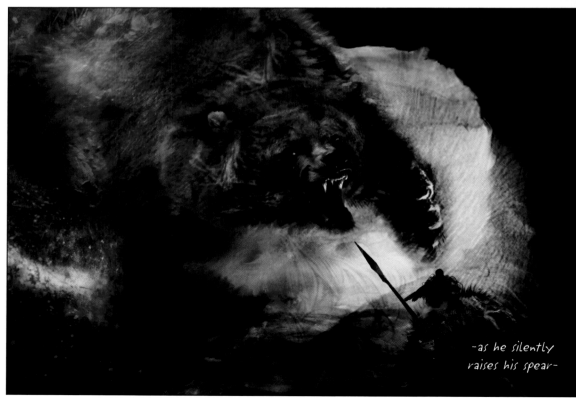

-as he silently
raises his spear-

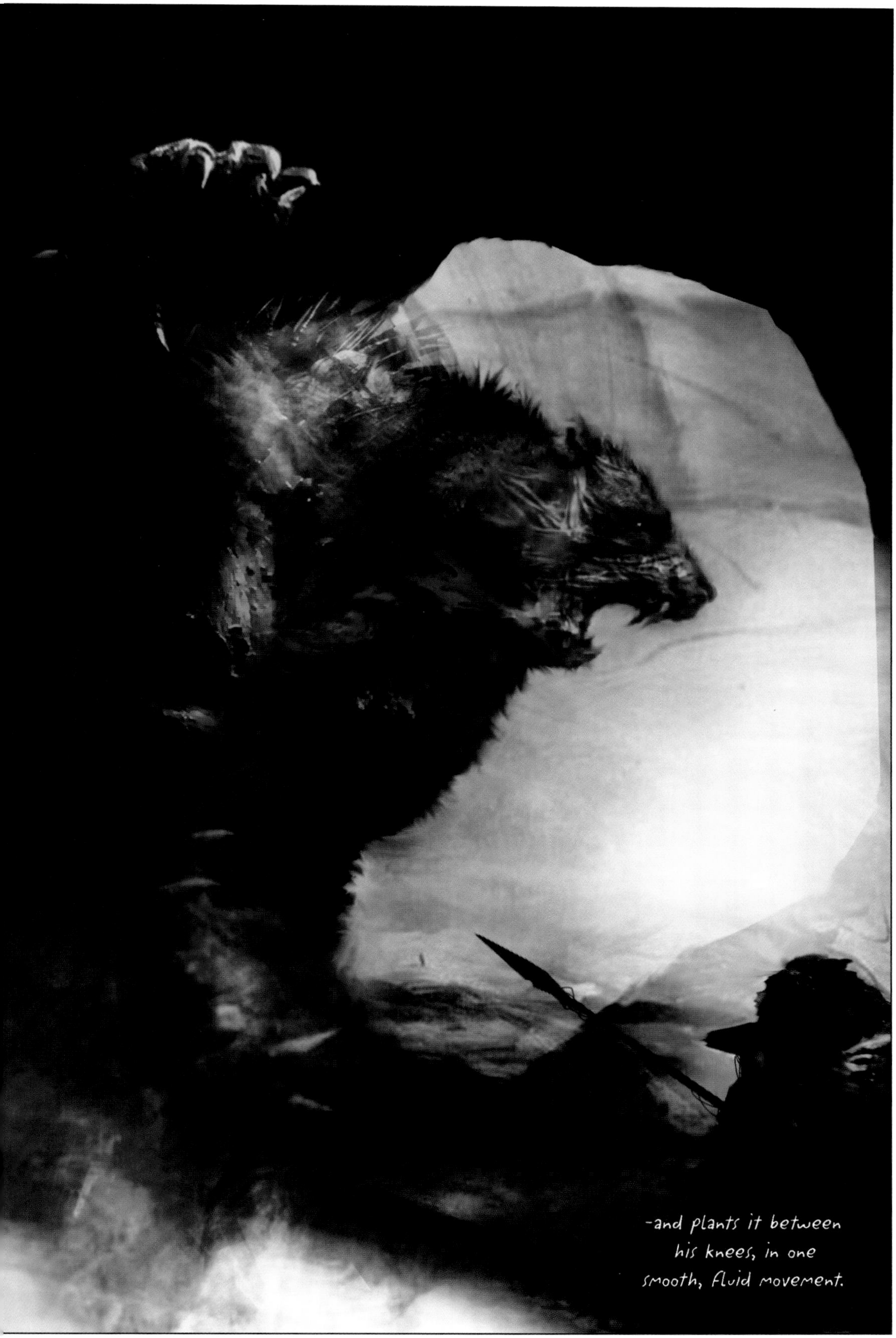
-and plants it between
his knees, in one
smooth, fluid movement.

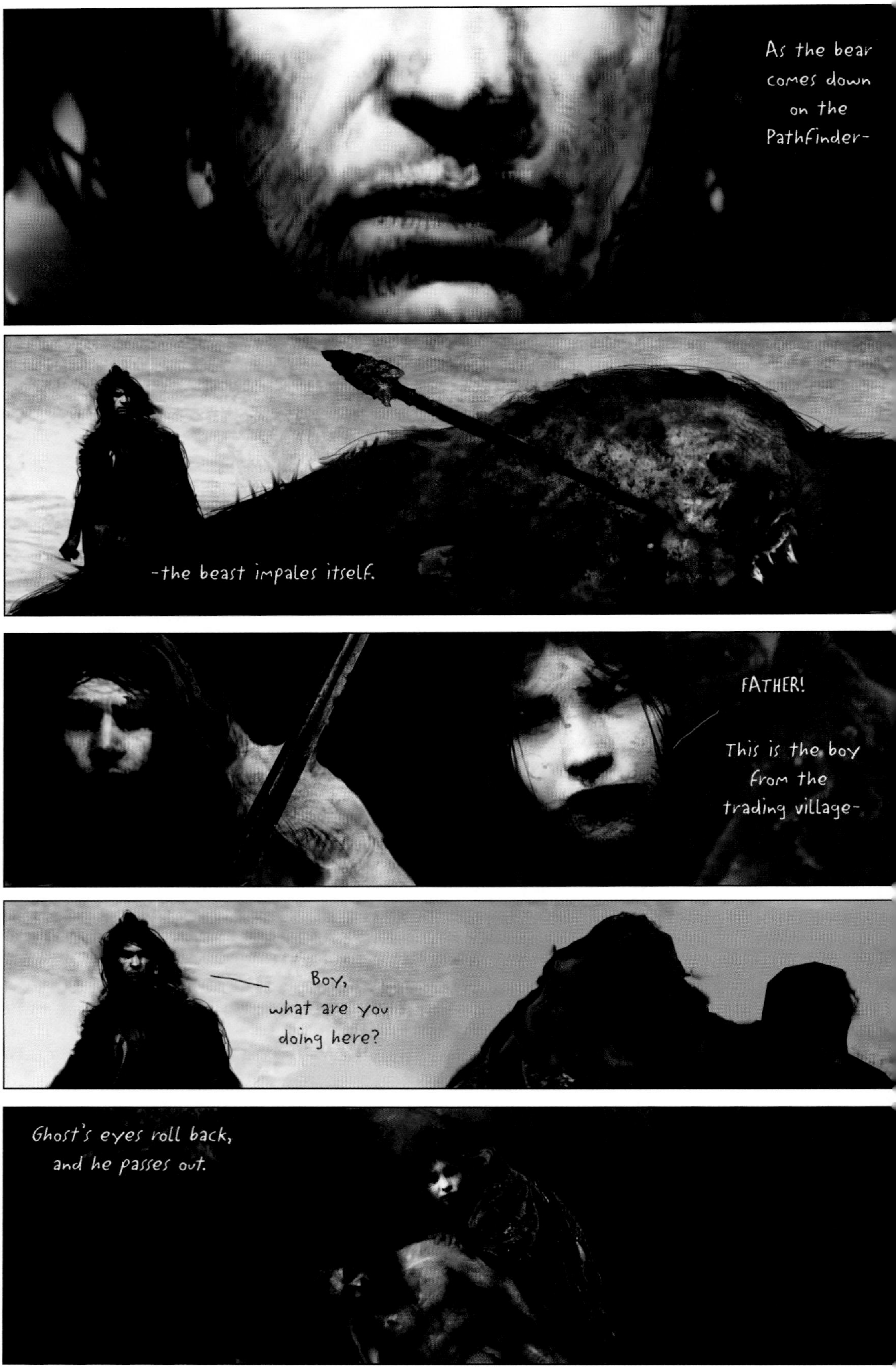
As the bear comes down on the Pathfinder-
-the beast impales itself.
FATHER!
This is the boy from the trading village-
Boy, what are you doing here?
Ghost's eyes roll back, and he passes out.

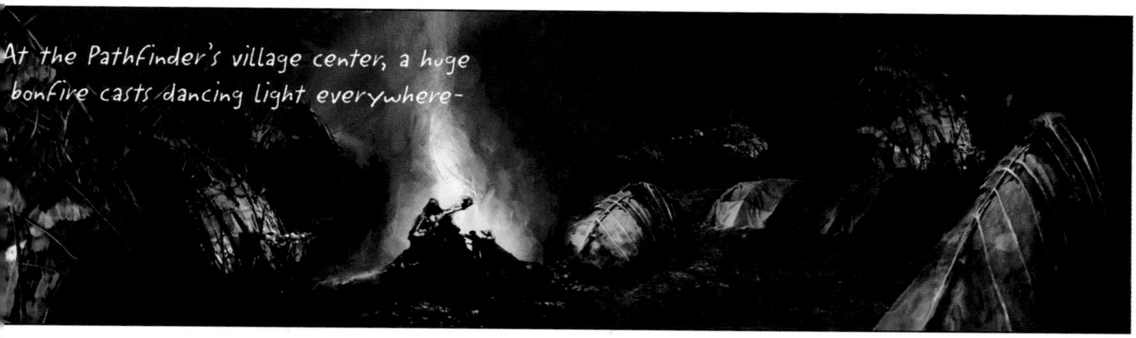
At the Pathfinder's village center, a huge bonfire casts dancing light everywhere-

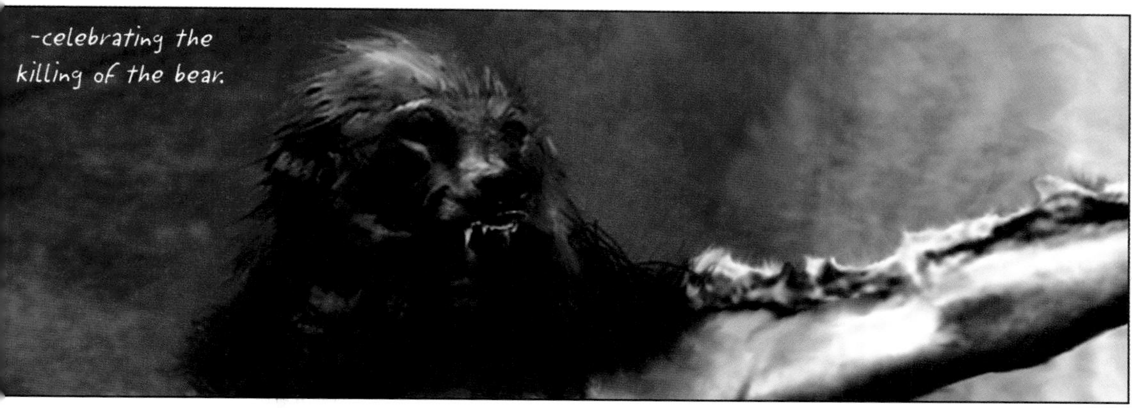
-celebrating the killing of the bear.

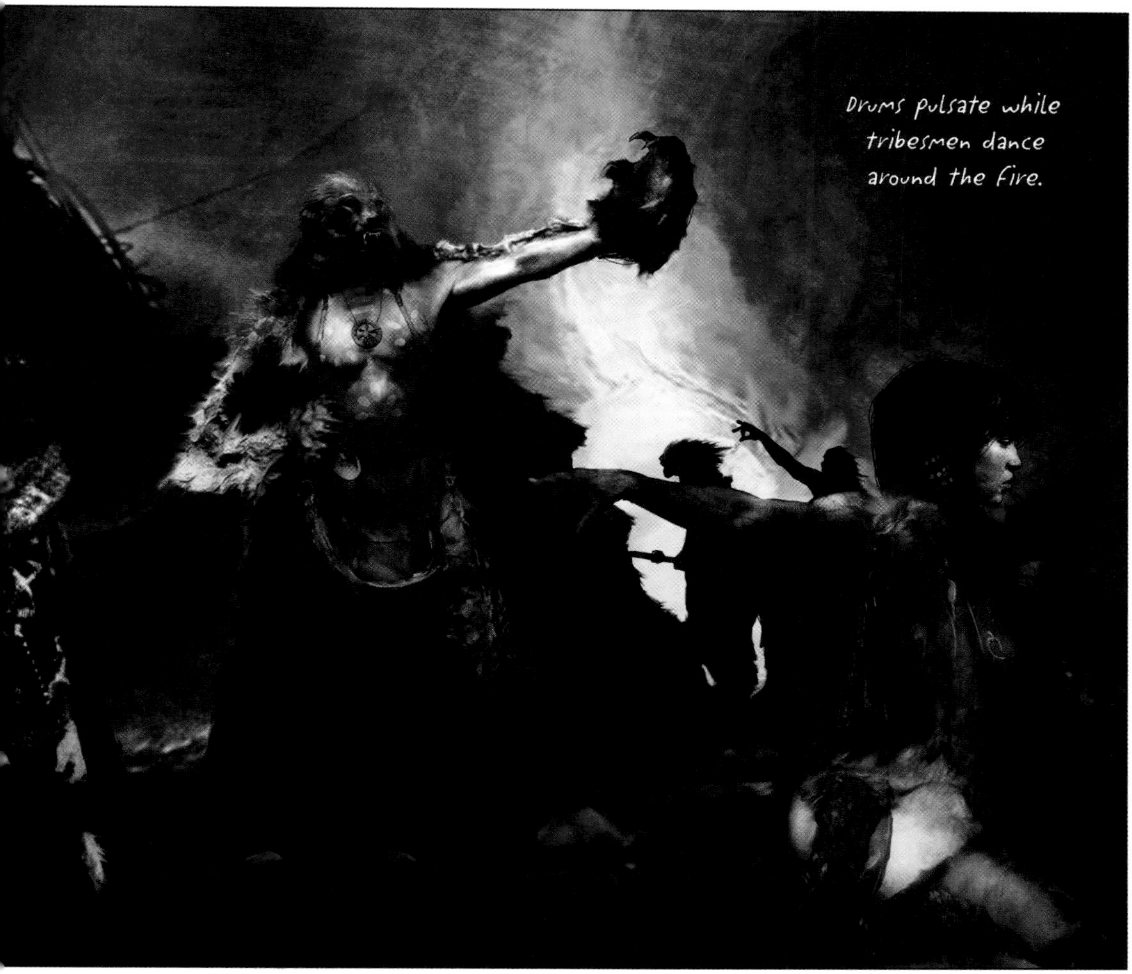
Drums pulsate while tribesmen dance around the fire.

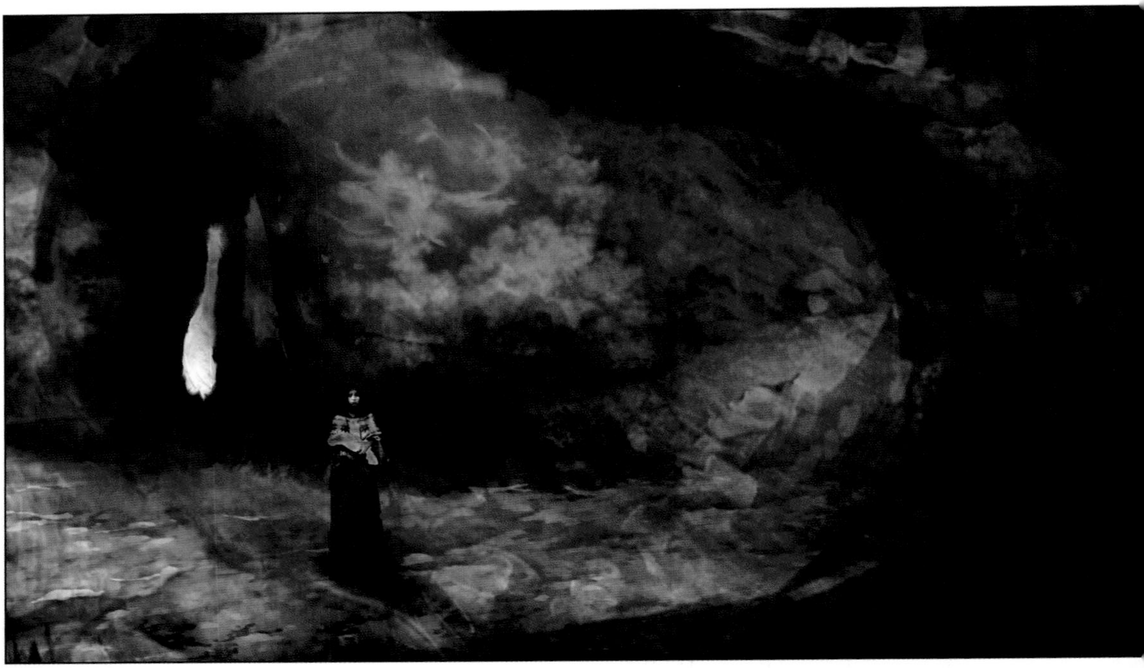

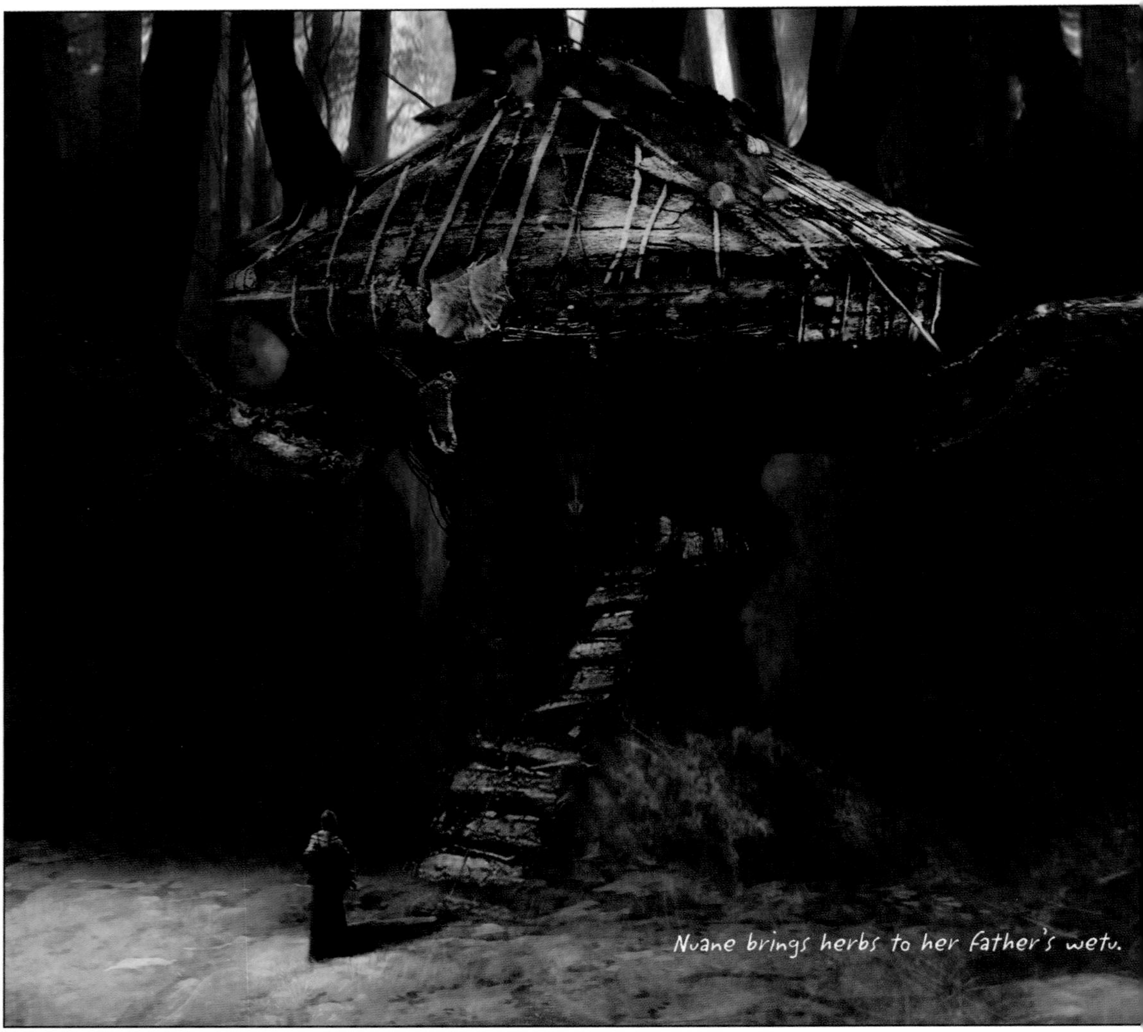
Nuane brings herbs to her father's wetu.

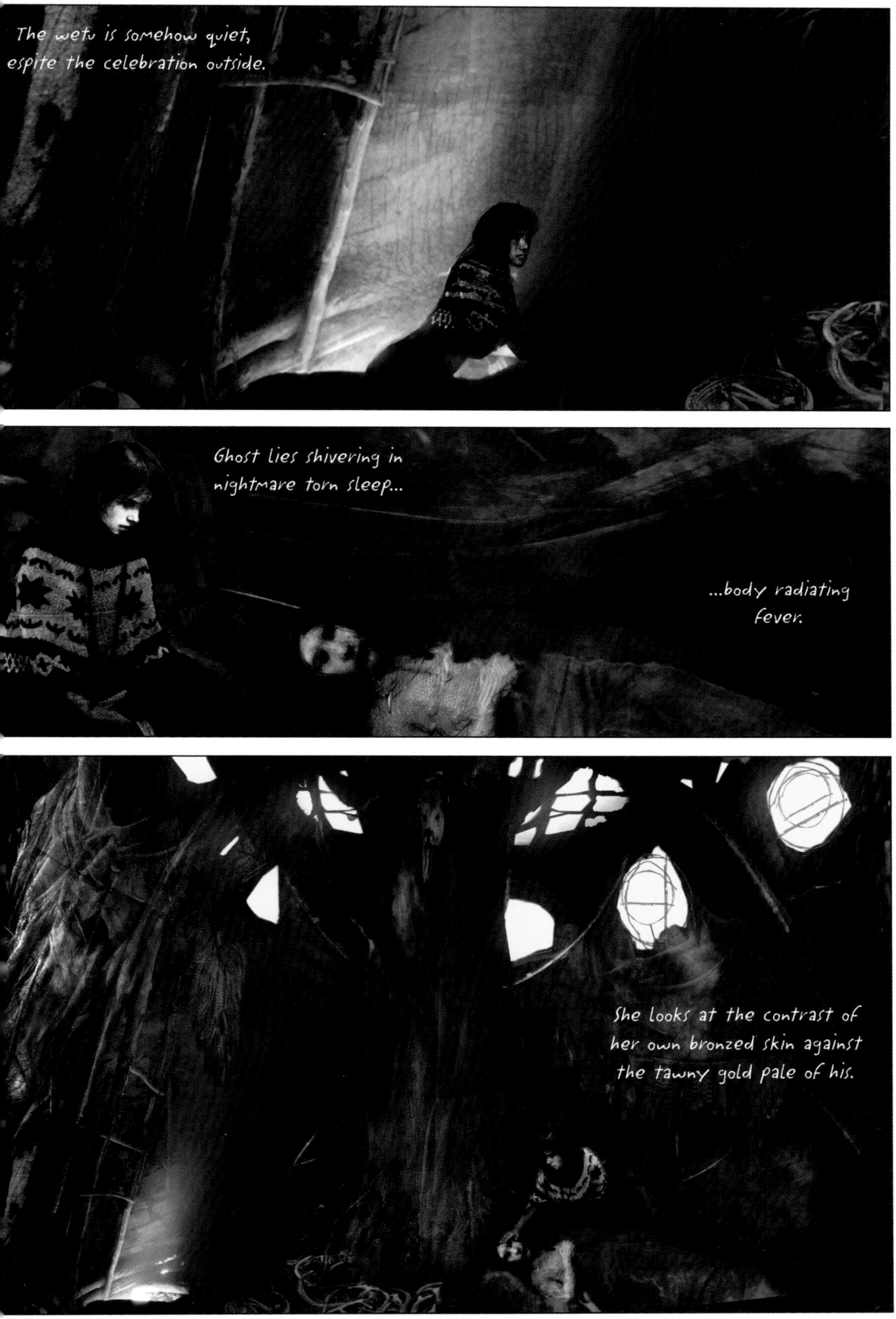
The wetu is somehow quiet,
espite the celebration outside.
Ghost lies shivering in
nightmare torn sleep...
...body radiating
fever.
She looks at the contrast of
her own bronzed skin against
the tawny gold pale of his.

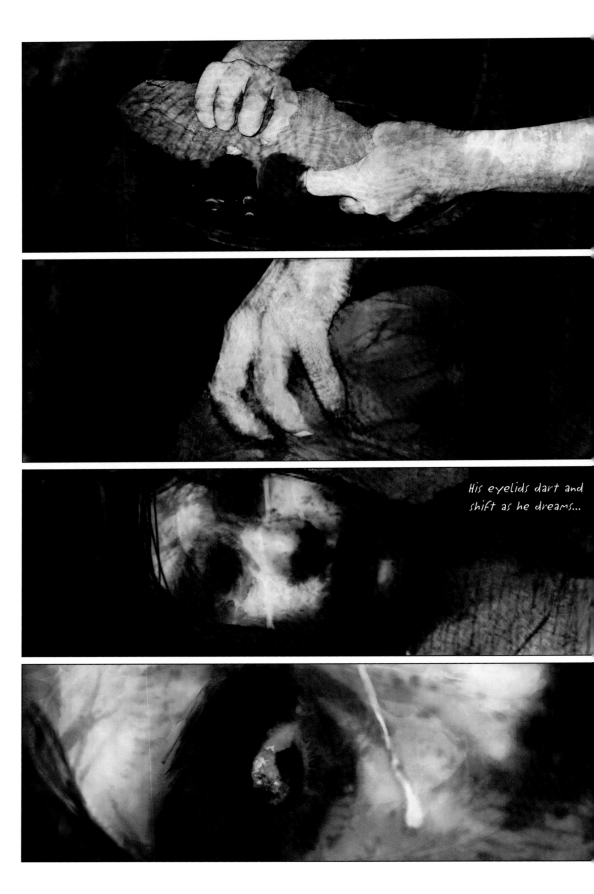

His eyelids dart and shift as he dreams...

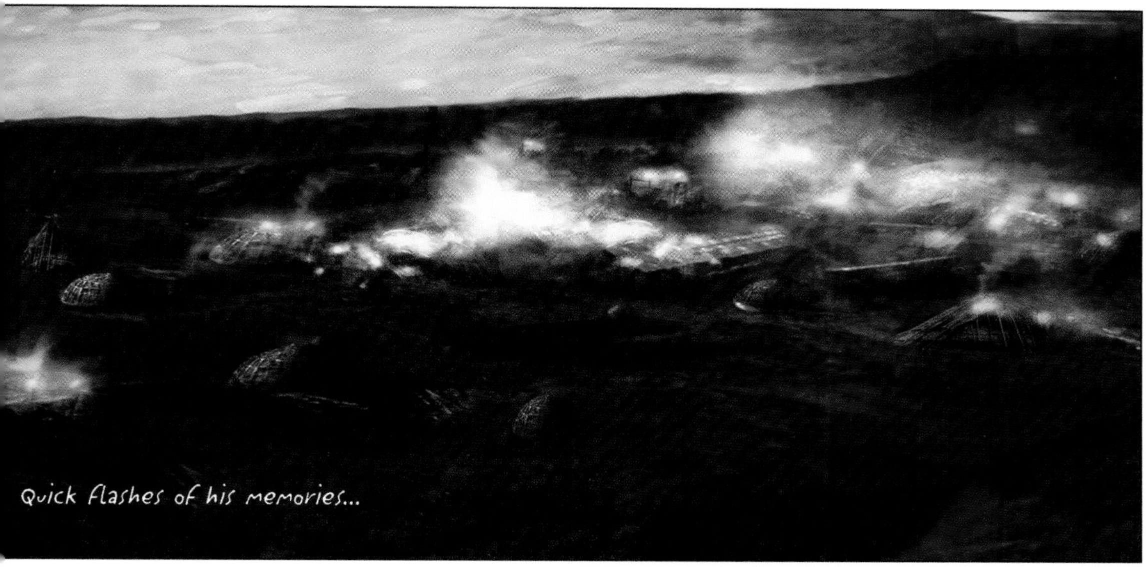
Quick flashes of his memories...

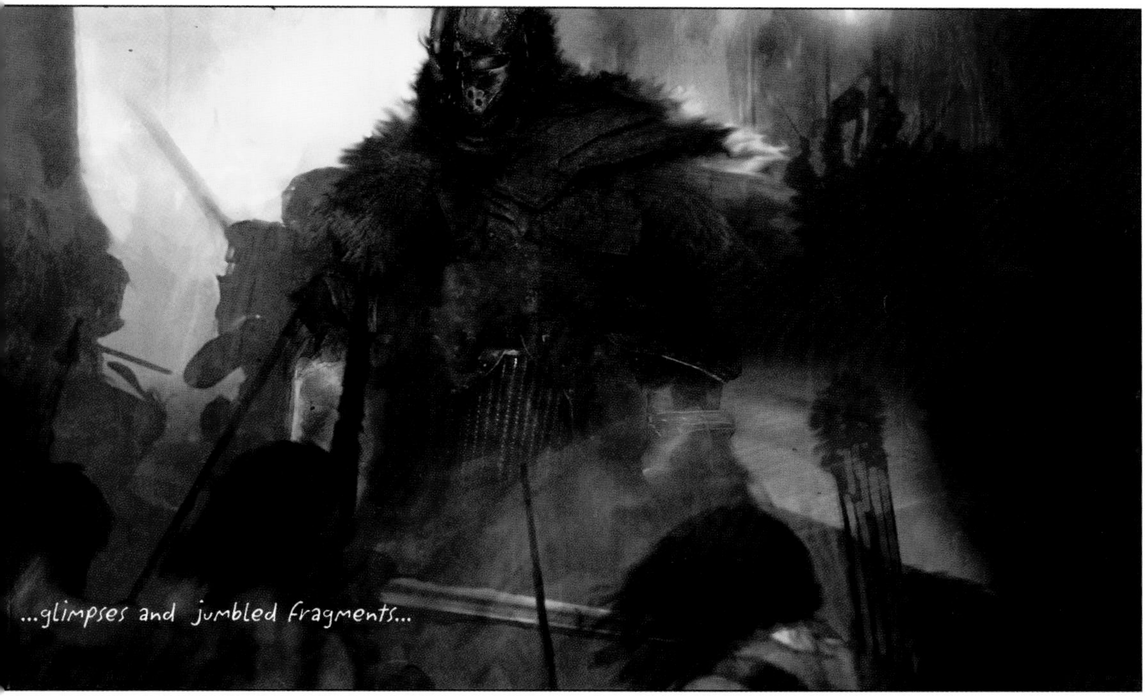
...glimpses and jumbled fragments...

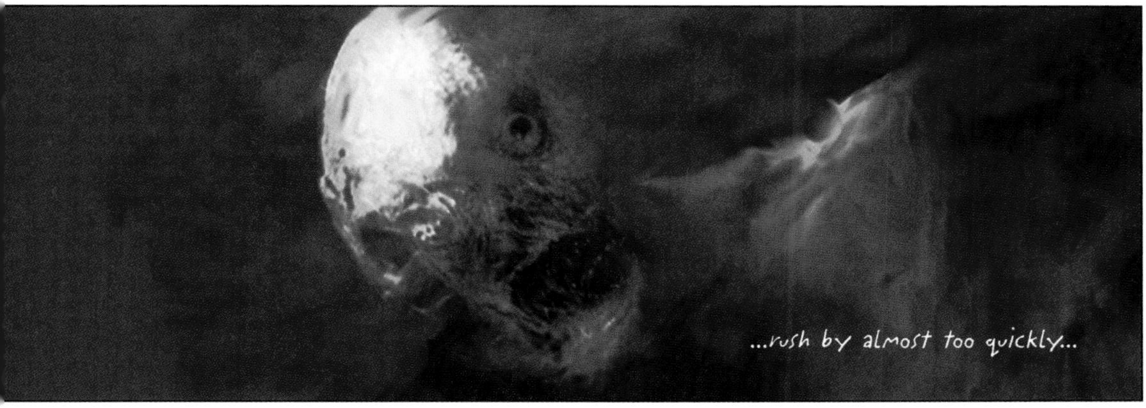
...rush by almost too quickly...

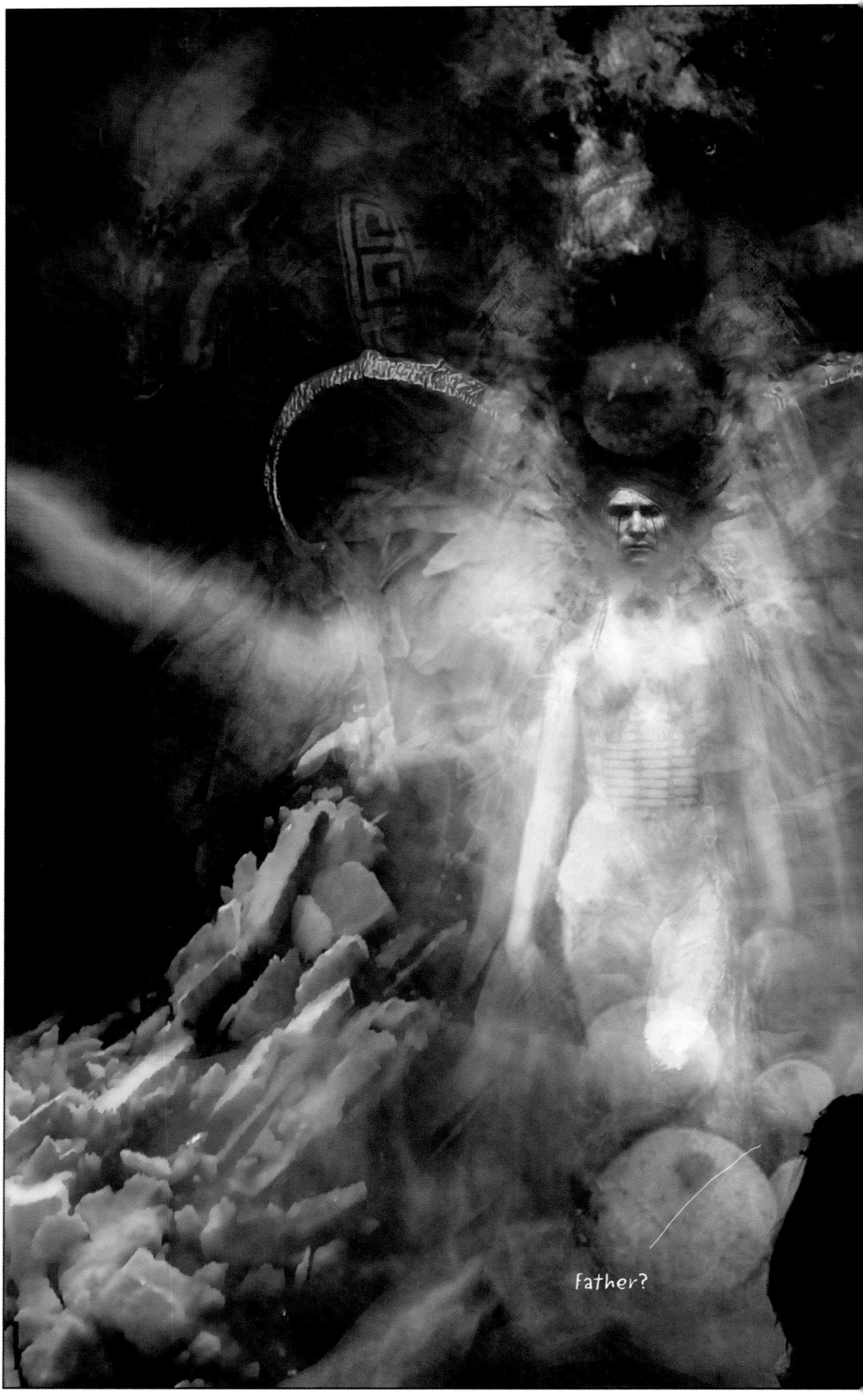
father?

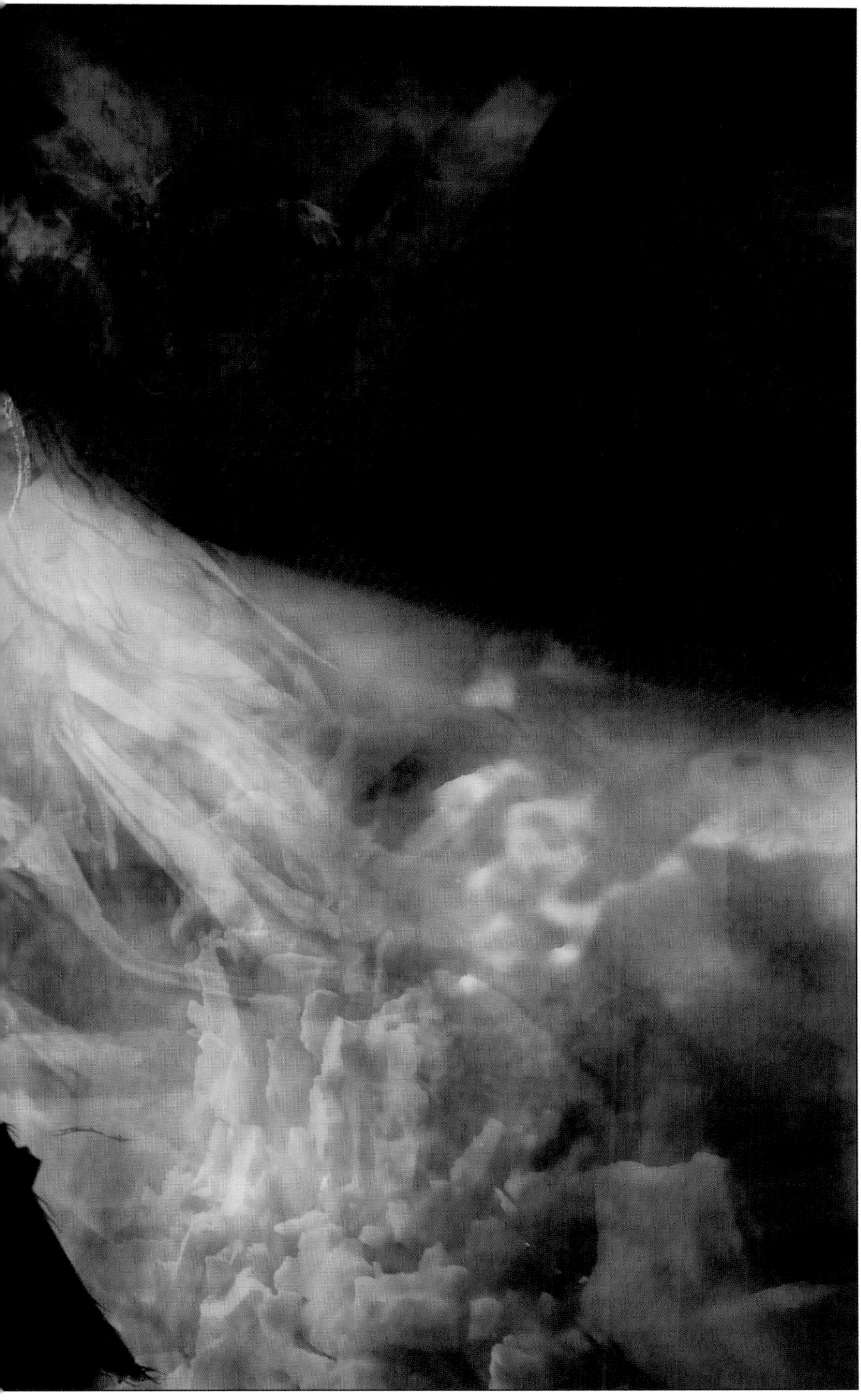

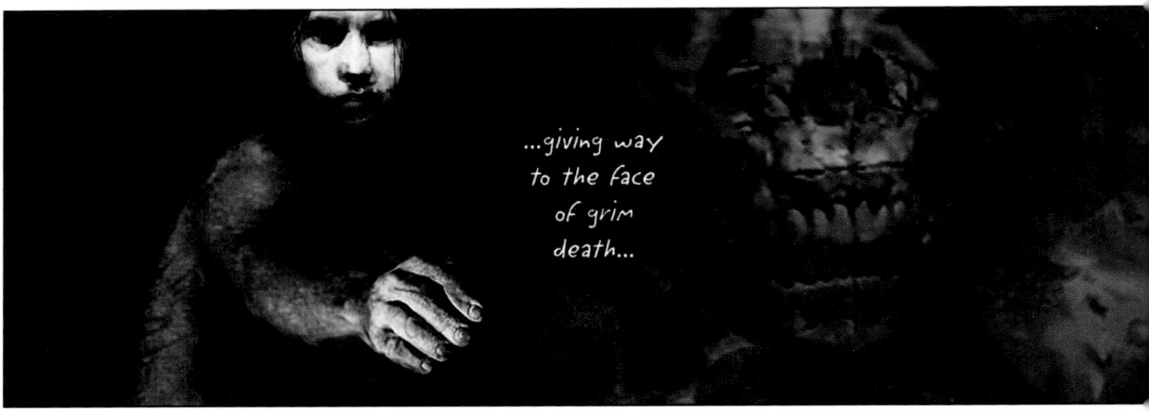
...giving way to the face of grim death...

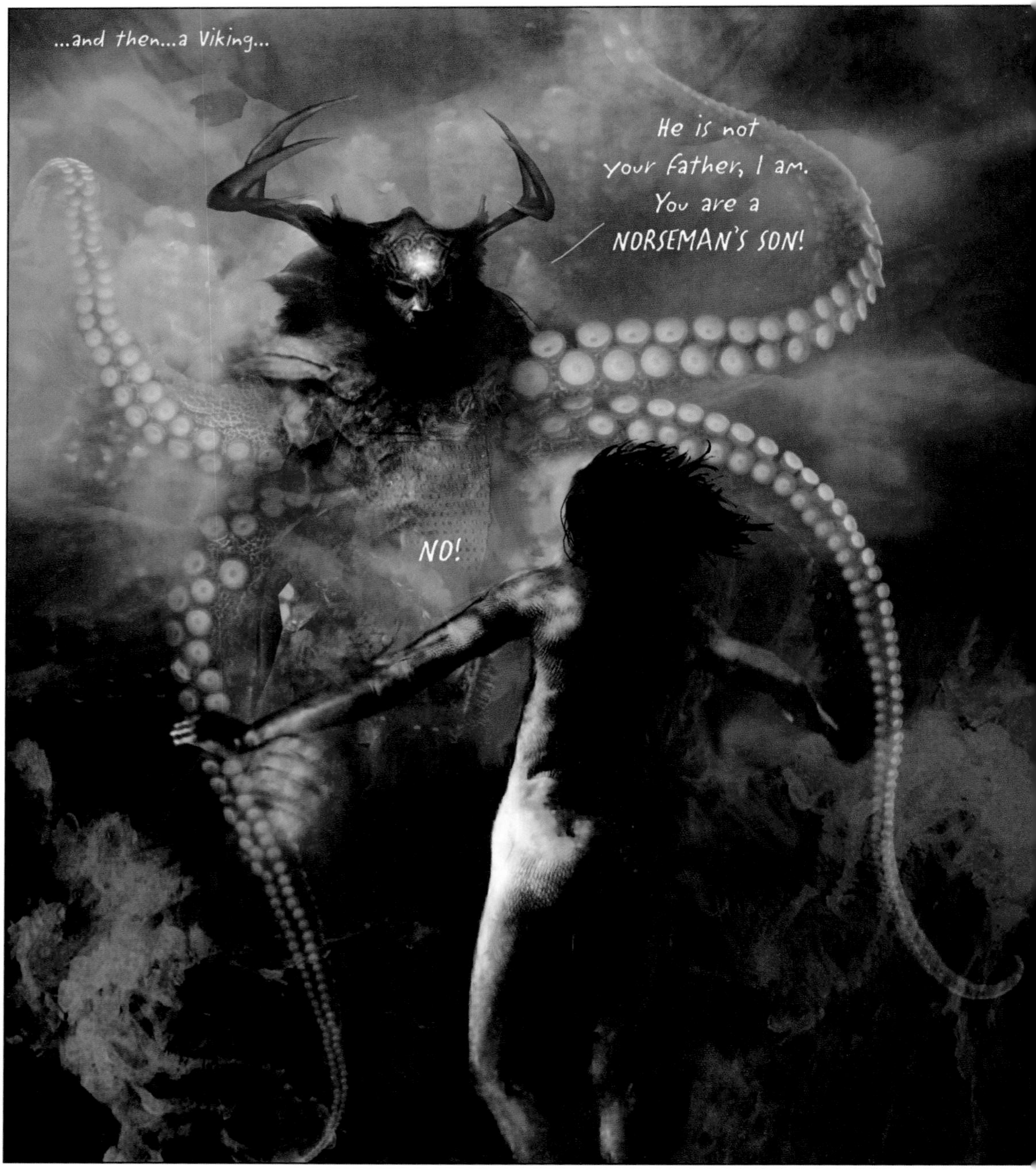
...and then...a Viking...
He is not your father, I am. You are a NORSEMAN'S SON!
NO!

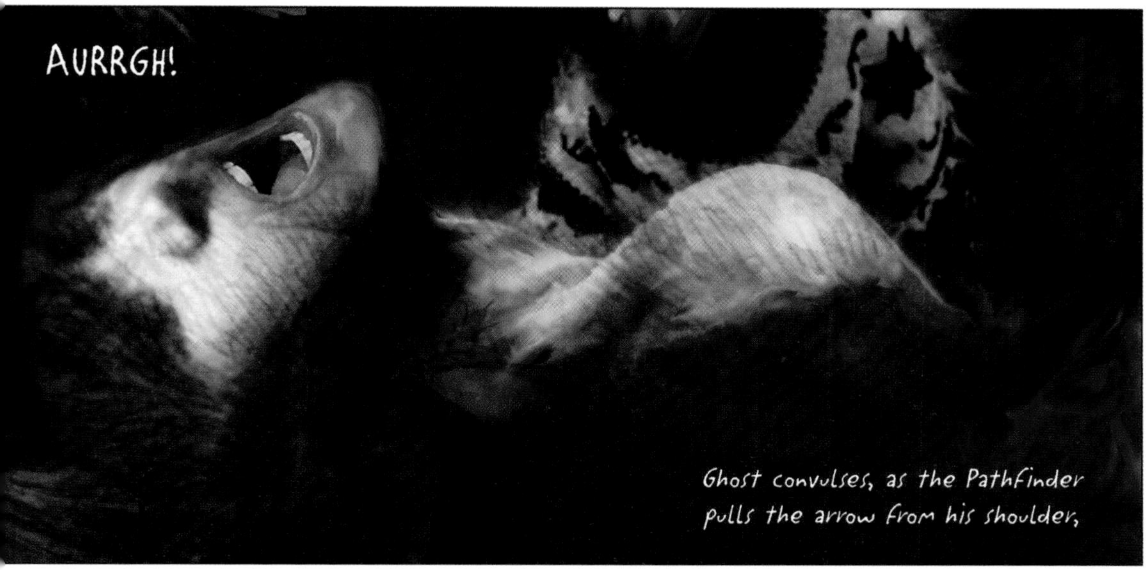
AURRGH!
Ghost convulses, as the Pathfinder pulls the arrow from his shoulder,

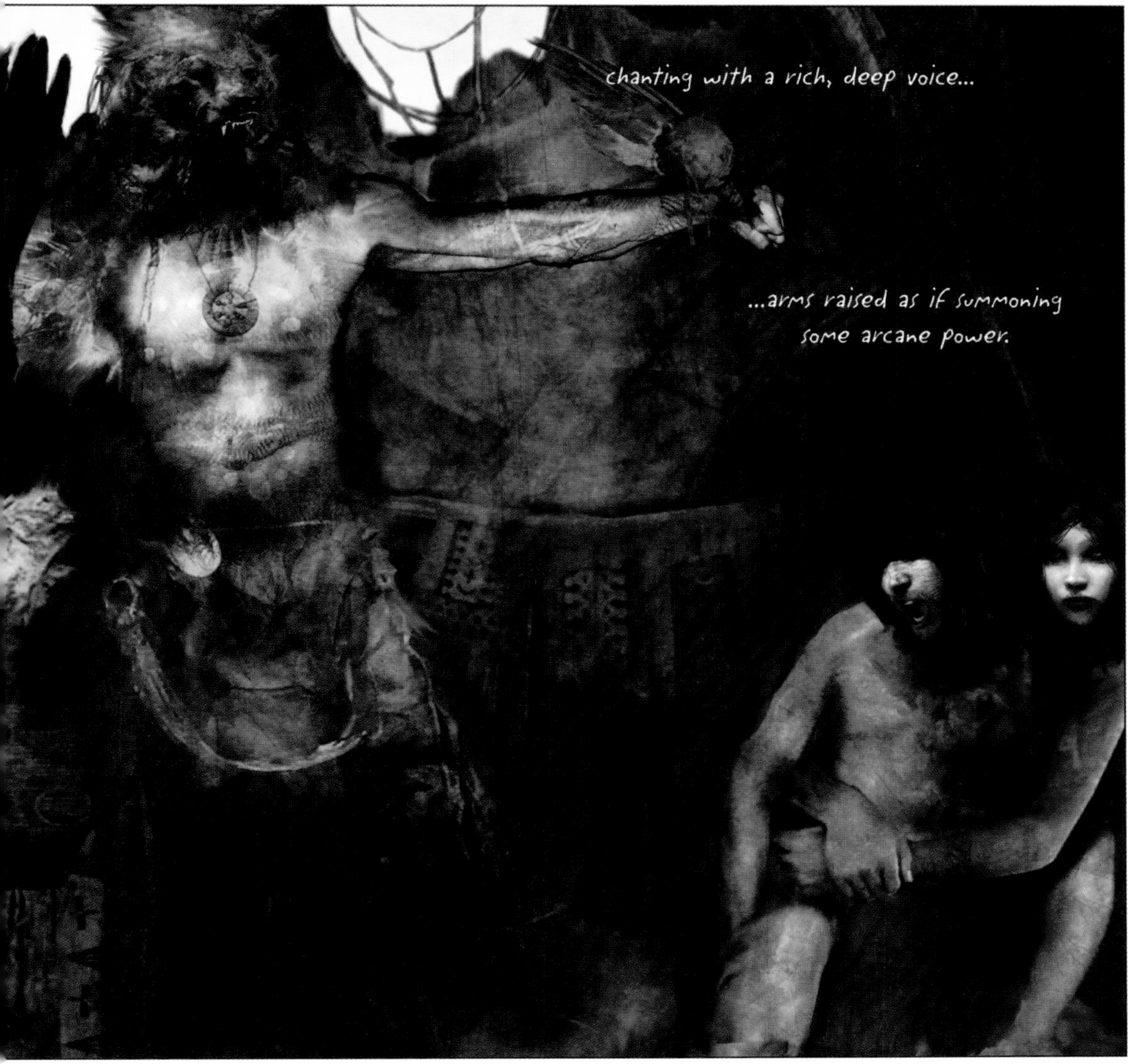
chanting with a rich, deep voice...
...arms raised as if summoning some arcane power.

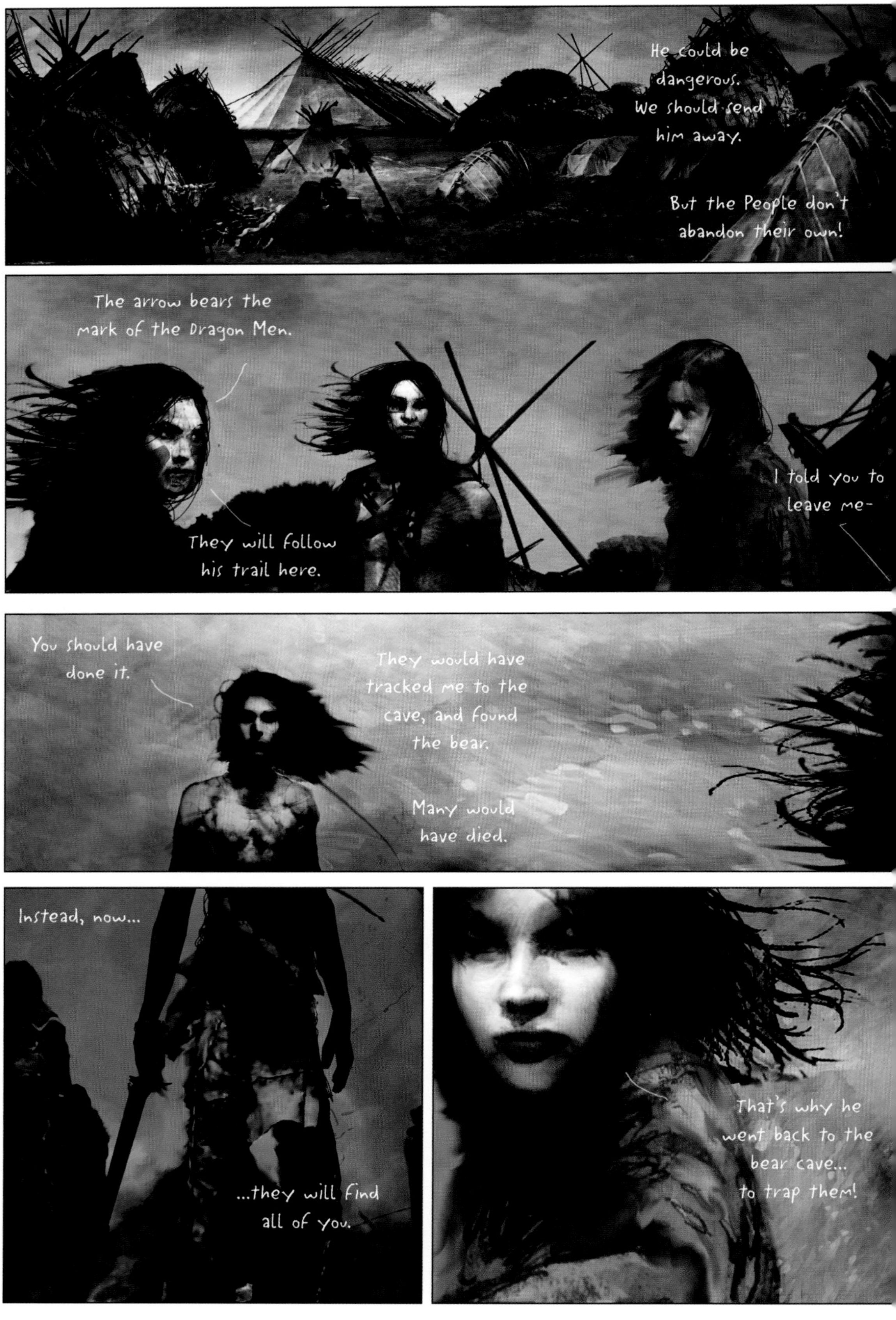
He could be dangerous. We should send him away.
But the People don't abandon their own!
The arrow bears the mark of the Dragon Men.
They will follow his trail here.
I told you to leave me-
You should have done it.
They would have tracked me to the cave, and found the bear.
Many would have died.
Instead, now...
...they will find all of you.
That's why he went back to the bear cave... to trap them!

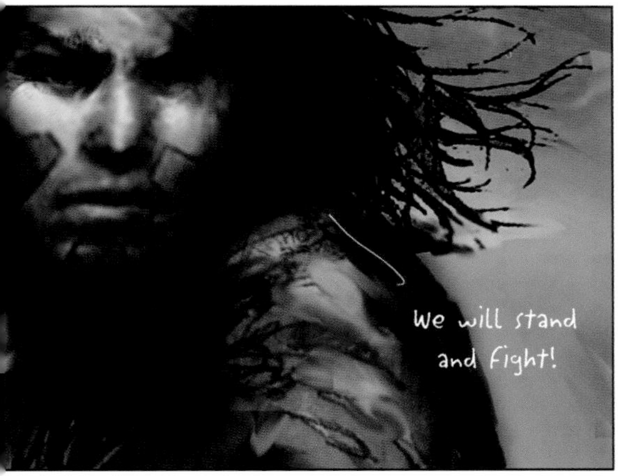
We will stand and fight!

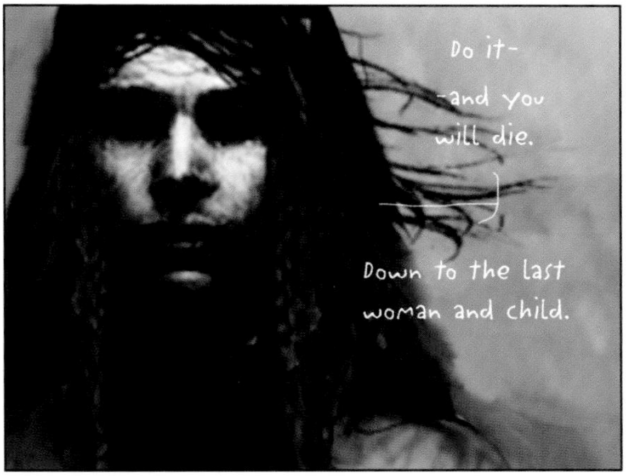
Do it-
-and you will die.
Down to the last woman and child.

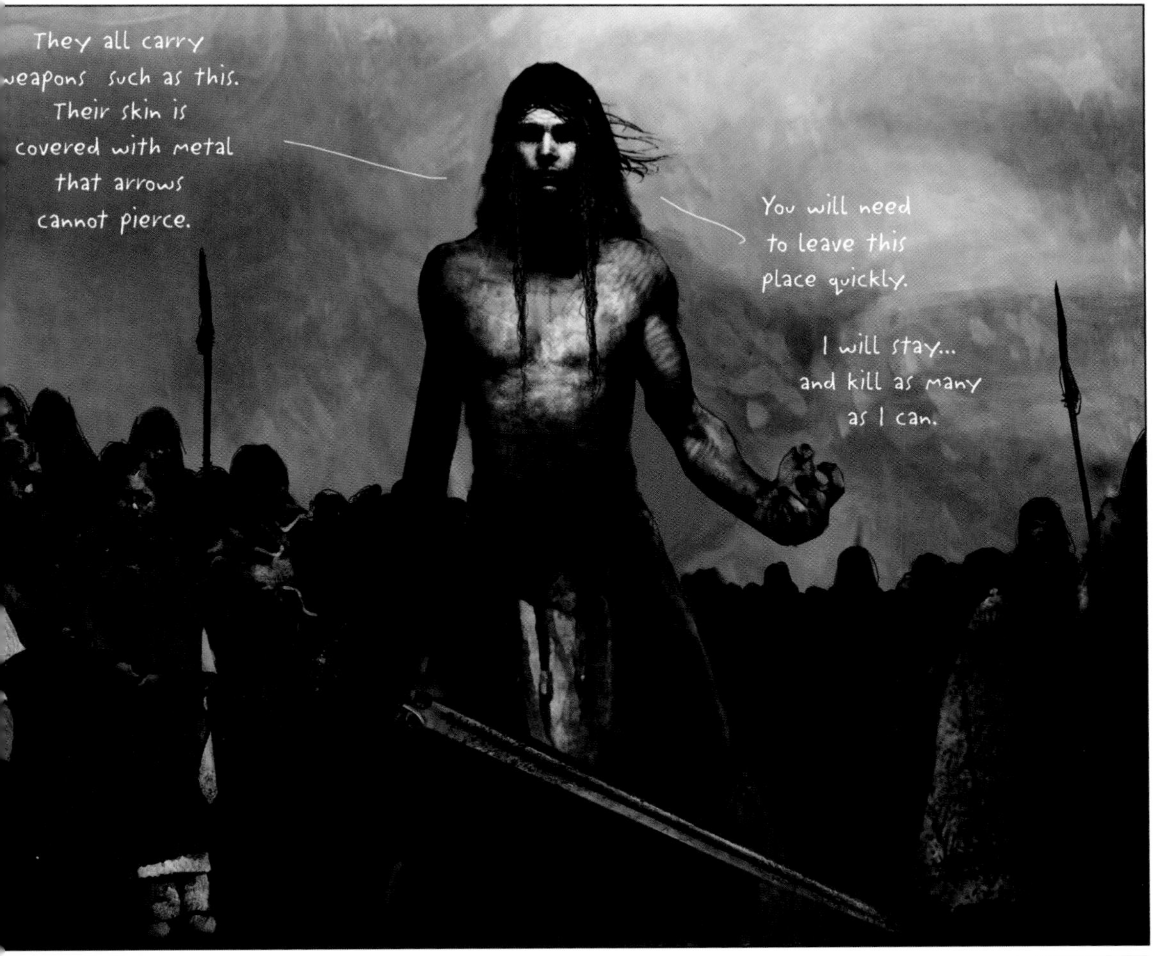
They all carry weapons such as this. Their skin is covered with metal that arrows cannot pierce.
You will need to leave this place quickly.
I will stay... and kill as many as I can.

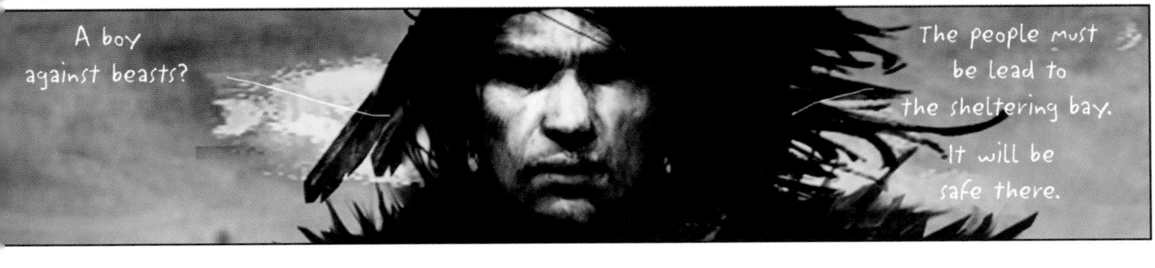
A boy against beasts?
The people must be lead to the sheltering bay.
It will be safe there.

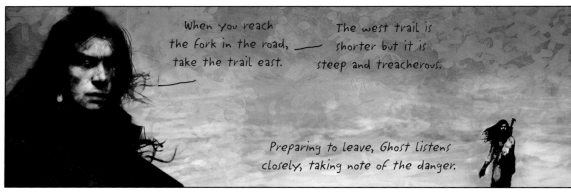

When you reach the fork in the road, take the trail east.

The west trail is shorter but it is steep and treacherous.

Preparing to leave, Ghost listens closely, taking note of the danger.

-Wind In Tree- -you will lead them to the bay.

At the fork in the mountain pass, take the east trail.

Yes Pathfinder-

No- let me lead the way.

The Dragon Men are not the worst of what he must face.

He has vengeance in his heart. His journey will be cursed-

Nuane watches Ghost heading back in the forest.

Father, you cannot abandon him...

...to fight a battle against such monsters.

He must choose his own path.

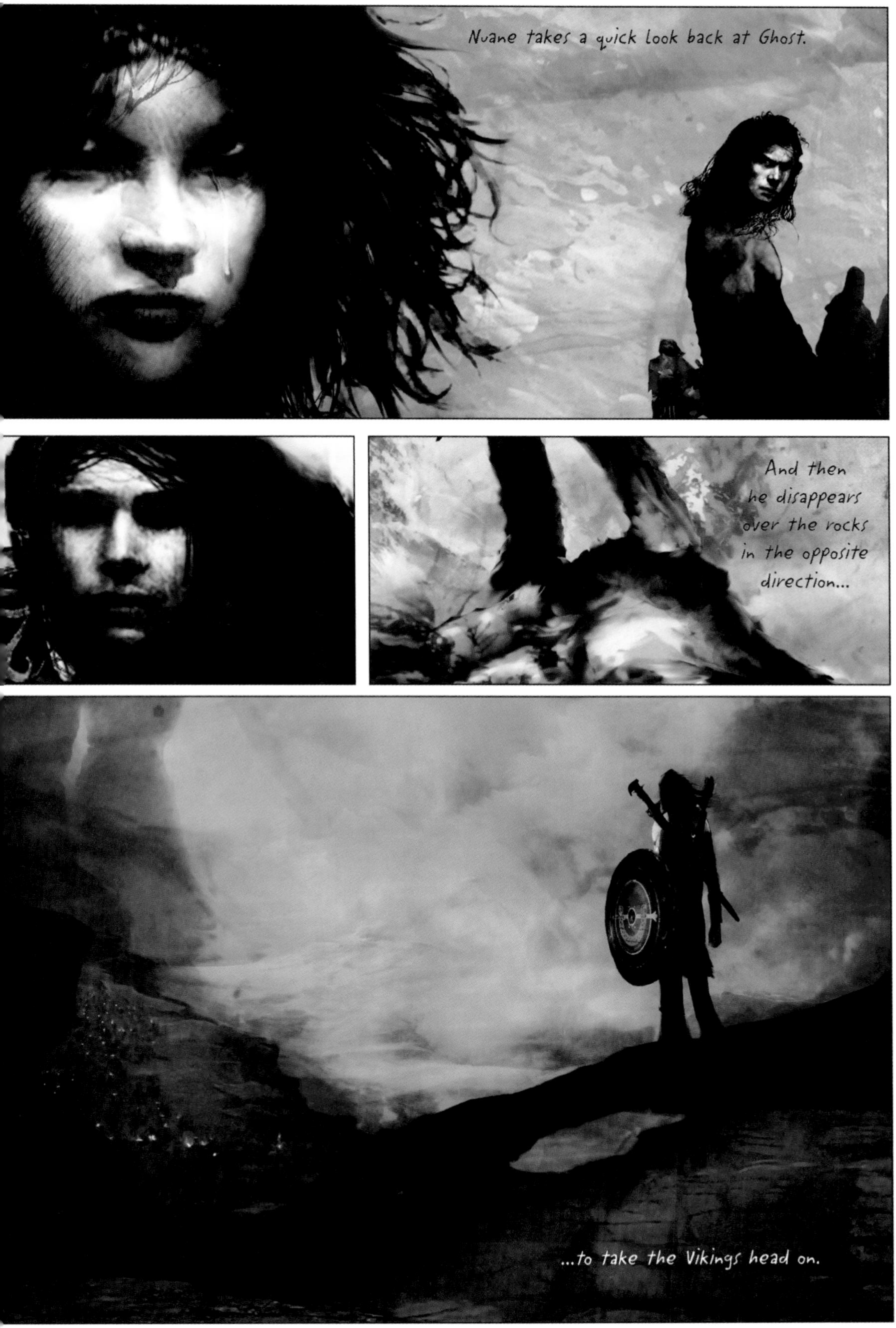
Nuane takes a quick look back at Ghost.
And then he disappears over the rocks in the opposite direction...
...to take the Vikings head on.

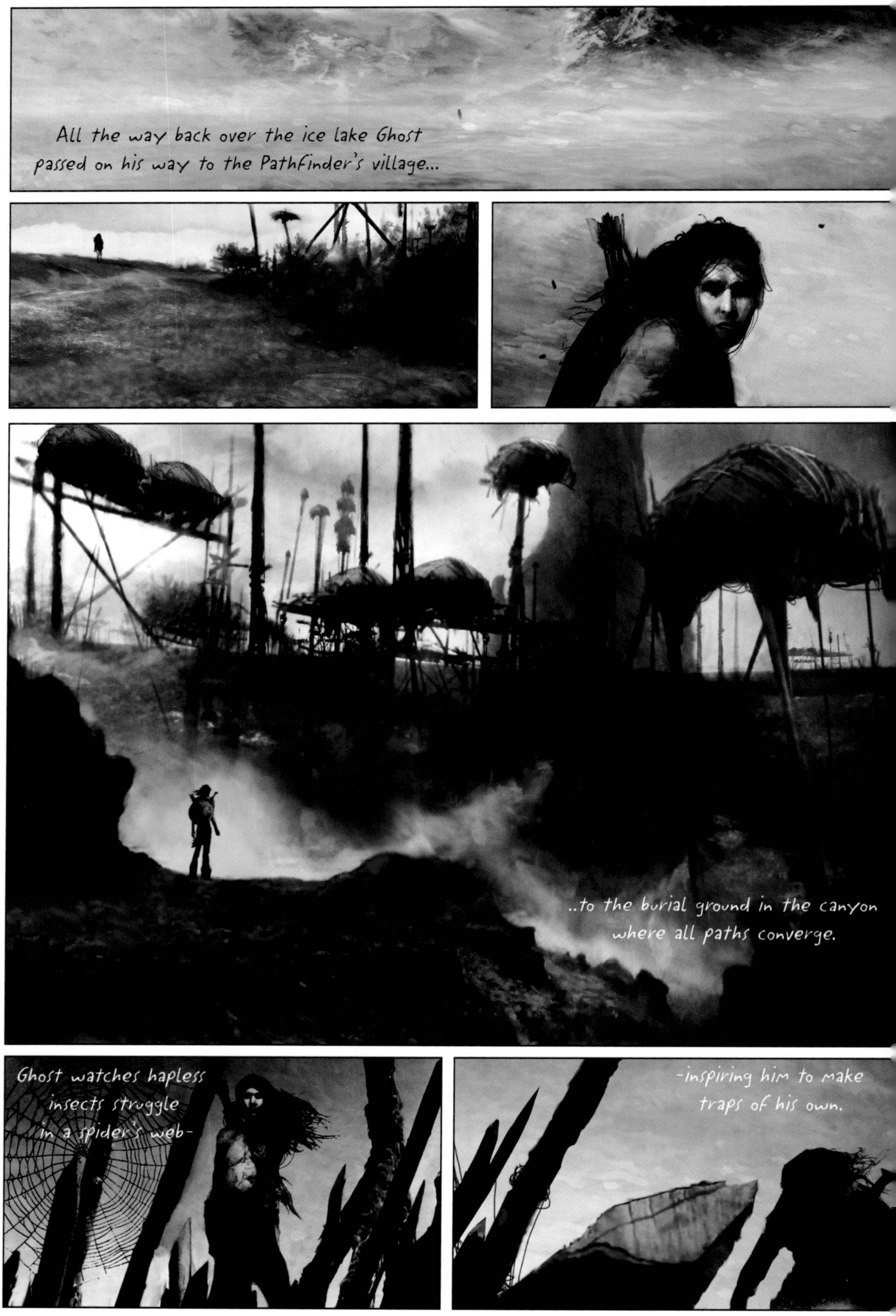
All the way back over the ice lake Ghost passed on his way to the Pathfinder's village...
..to the burial ground in the canyon where all paths converge.
Ghost watches hapless insects struggle in a spider's web-
-inspiring him to make traps of his own.

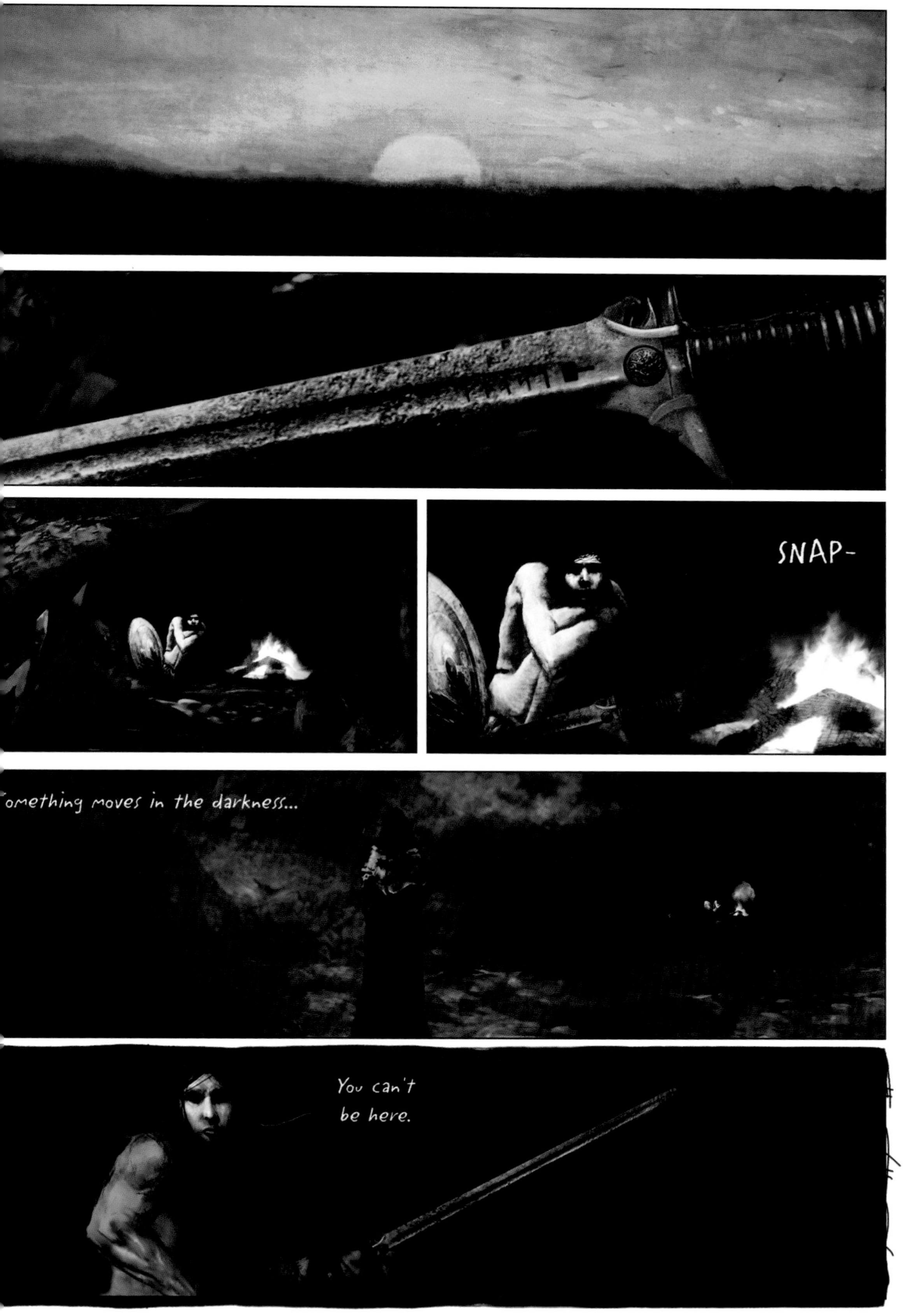
SNAP-
omething moves in the darkness...
You can't be here.

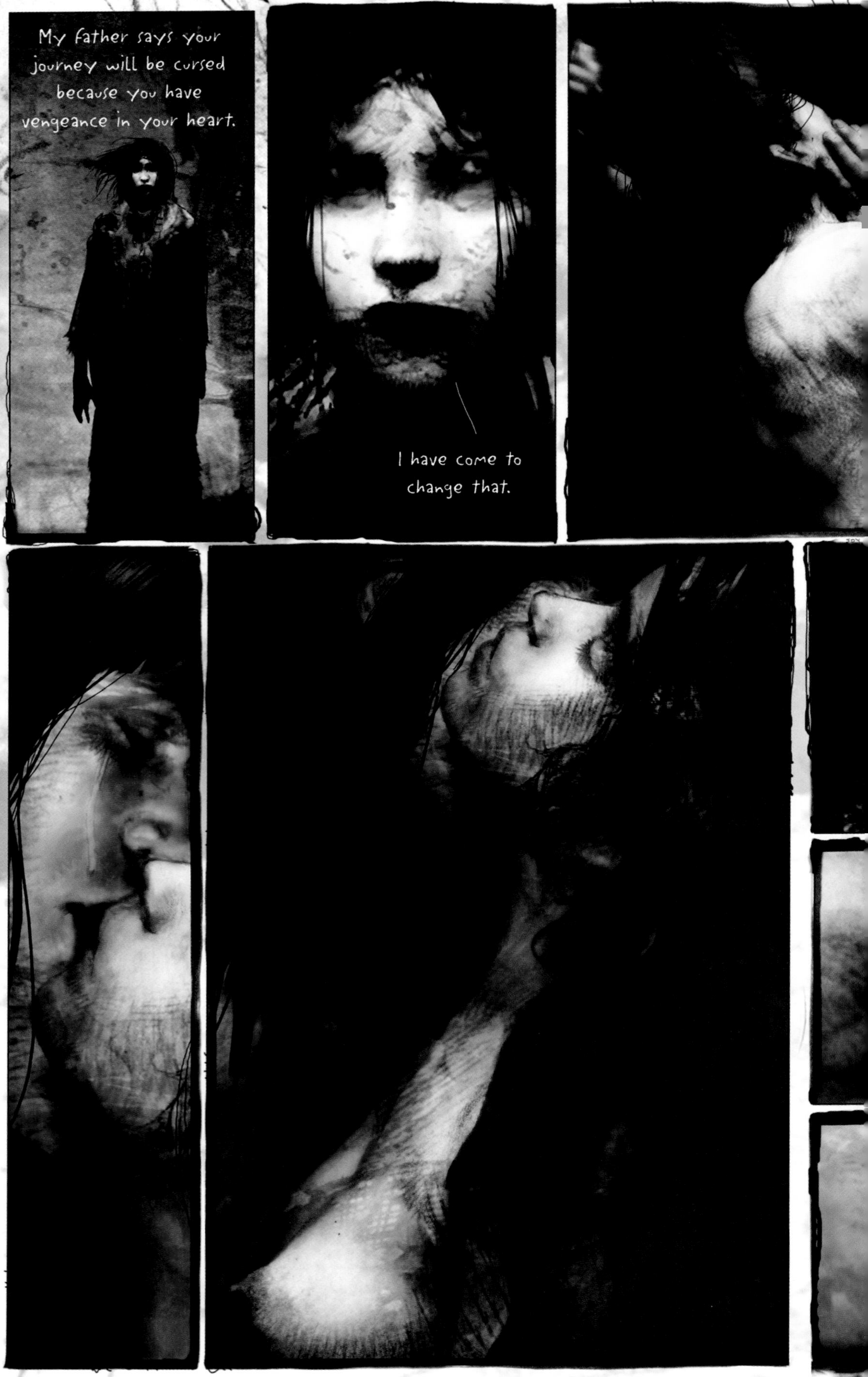
My father says your journey will be cursed because you have vengeance in your heart.
I have come to change that.

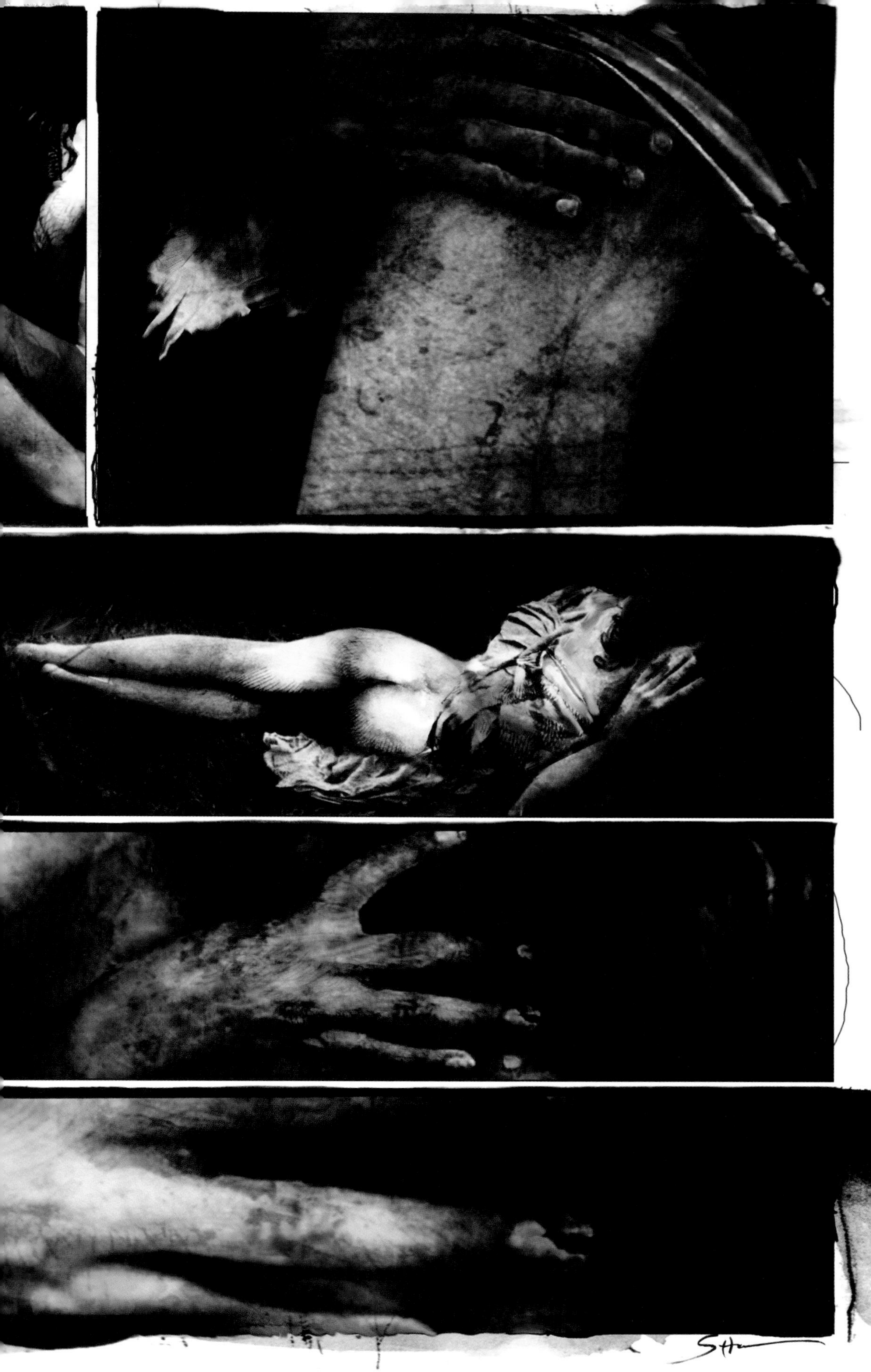

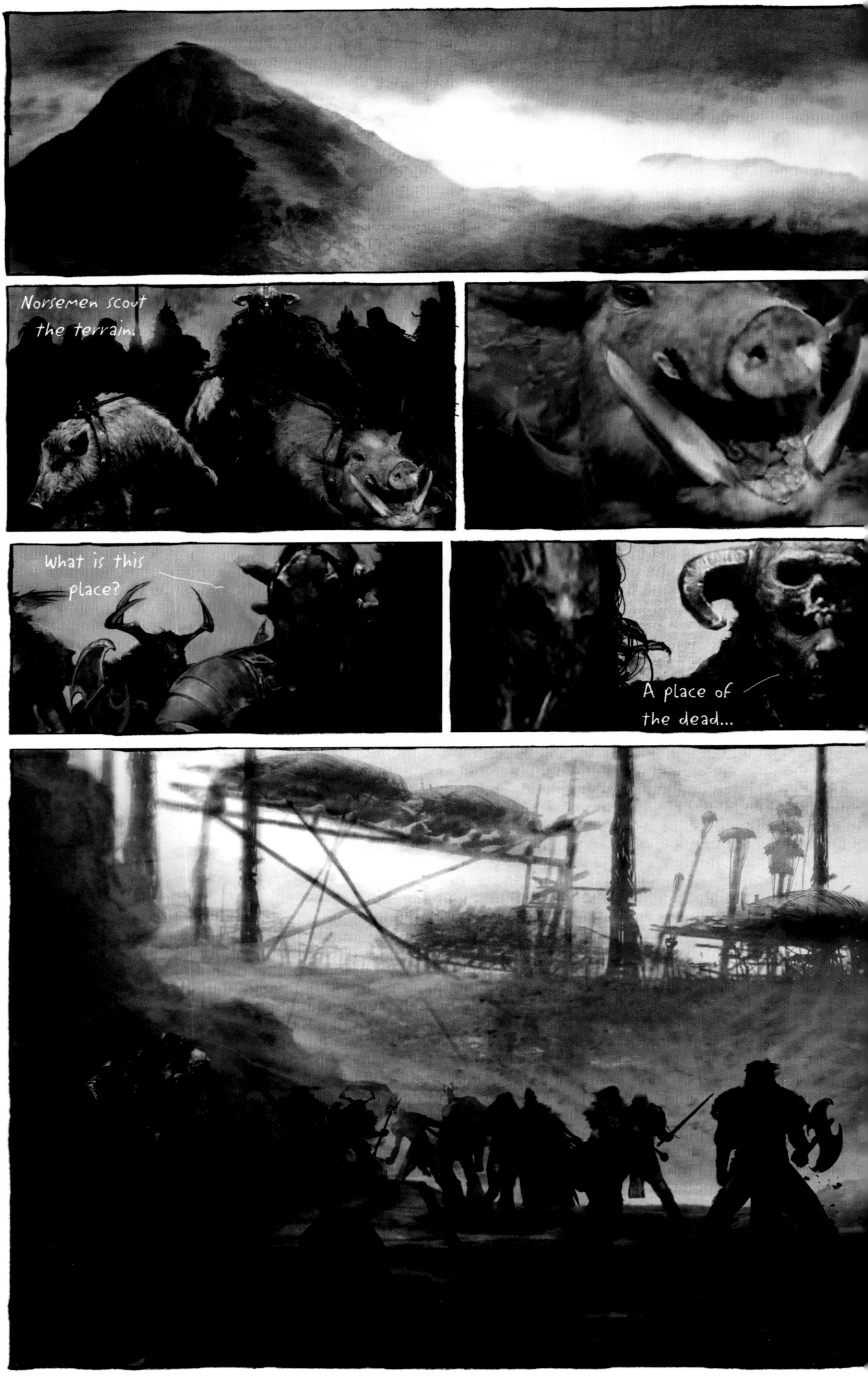
Norsemen scout the terrain.
What is this place?
A place of the dead...

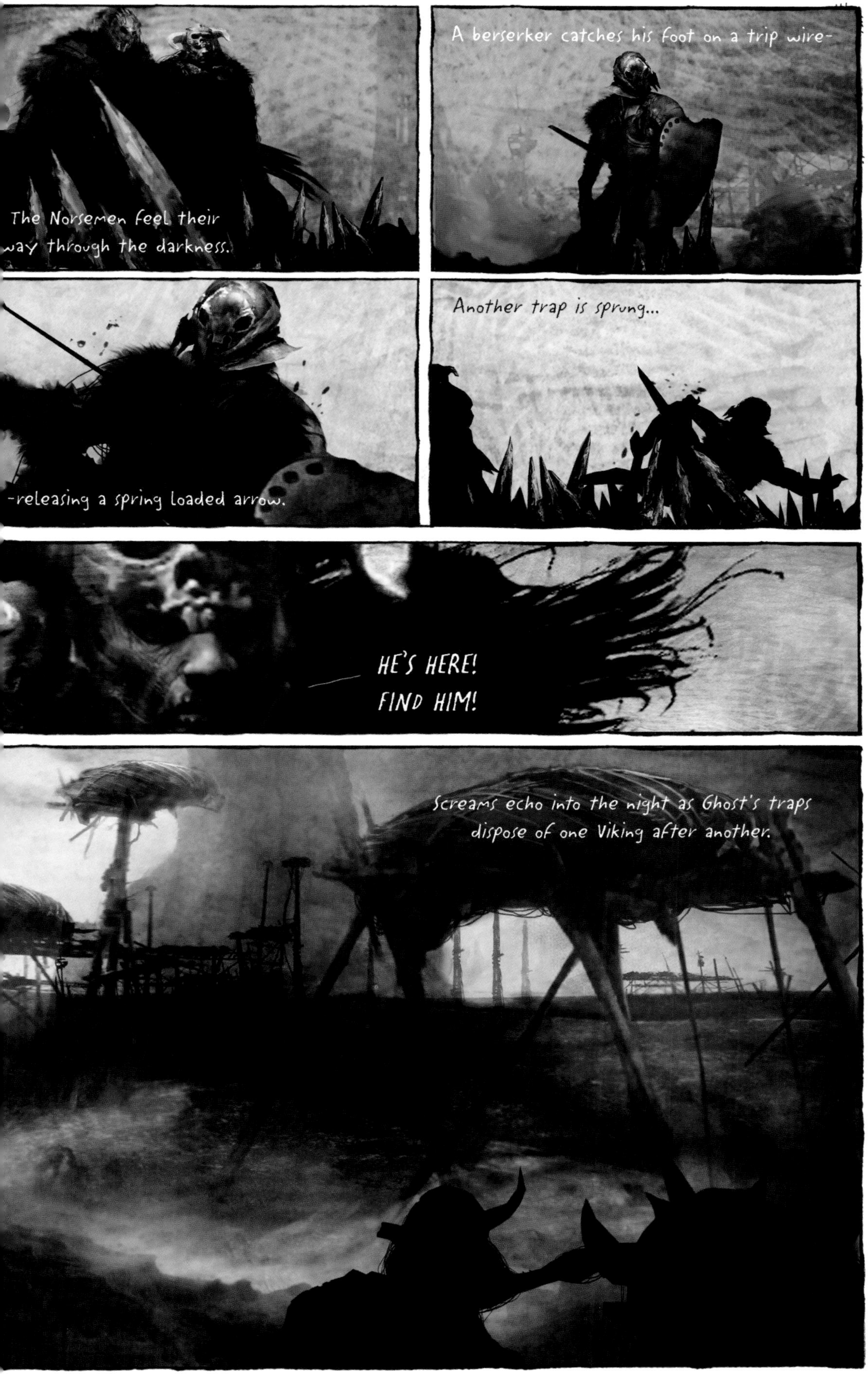
The Norsemen feel their way through the darkness.
A berserker catches his foot on a trip wire-
-releasing a spring loaded arrow.
Another trap is sprung...
HE'S HERE!
FIND HIM!
Screams echo into the night as Ghost's traps dispose of one Viking after another.

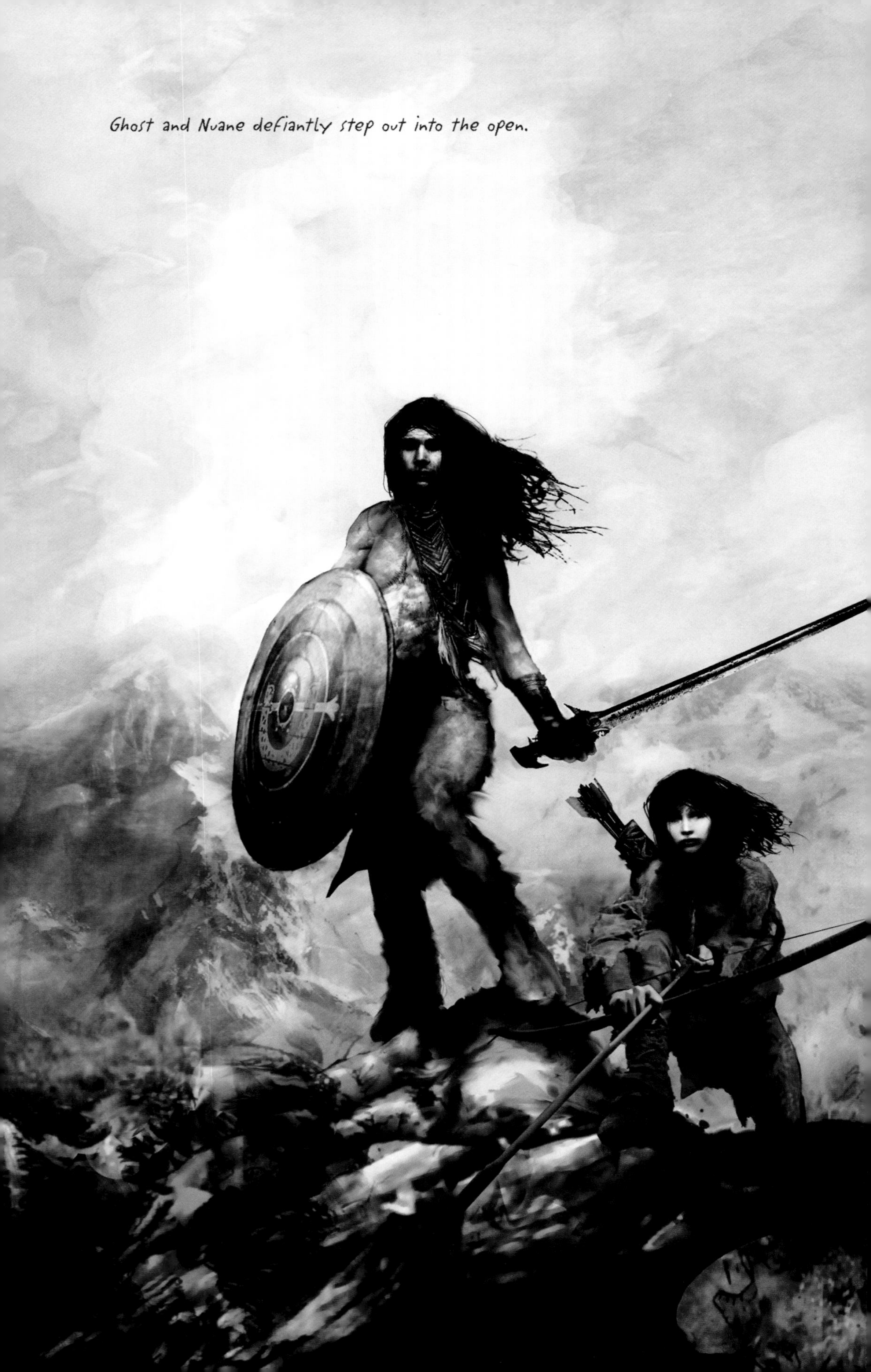
Ghost and Nuane defiantly step out into the open.

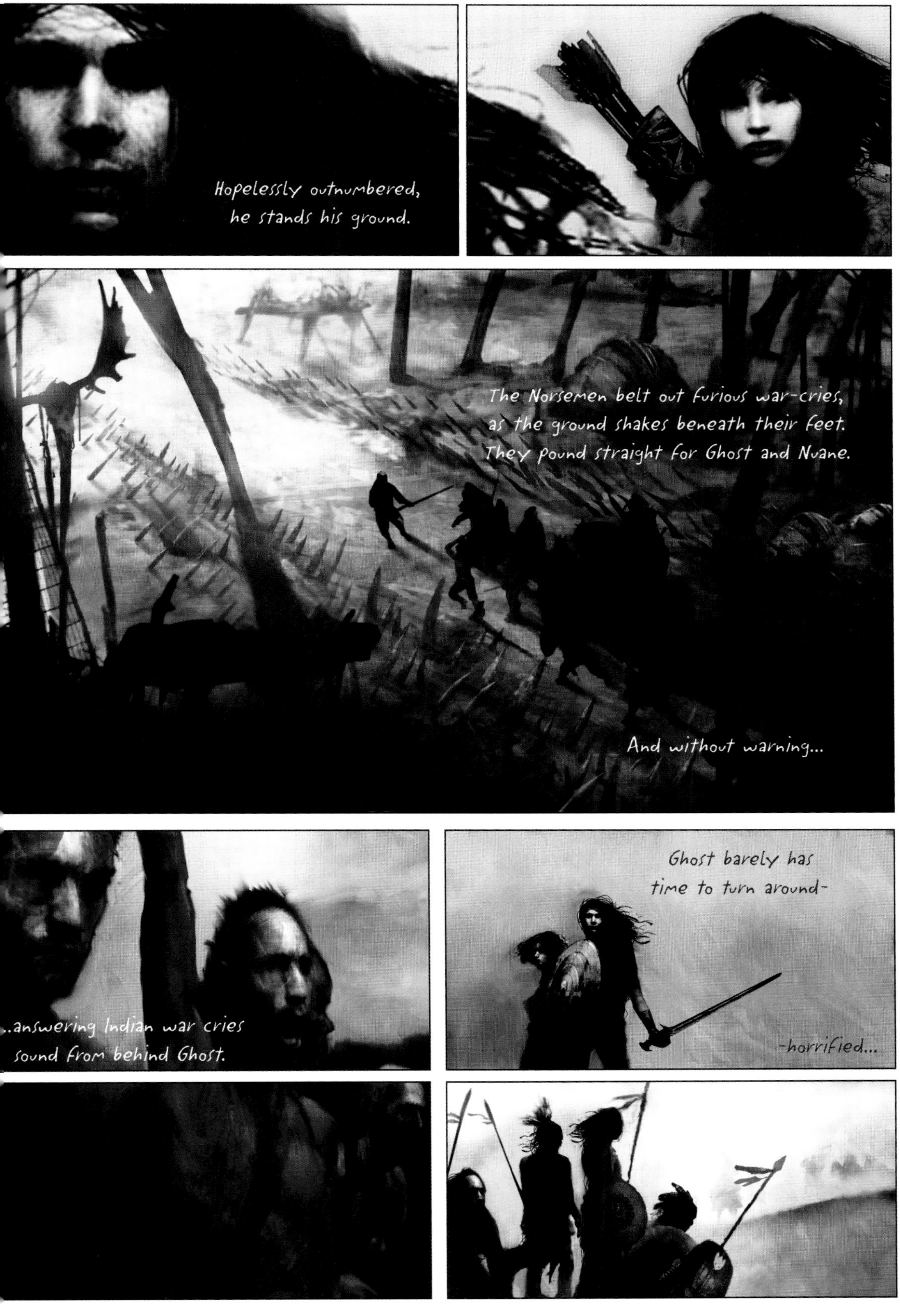
Hopelessly outnumbered, he stands his ground.
The Norsemen belt out furious war-cries, as the ground shakes beneath their feet. They pound straight for Ghost and Nuane.
And without warning...
..answering Indian war cries sound from behind Ghost.
Ghost barely has time to turn around-
-horrified...

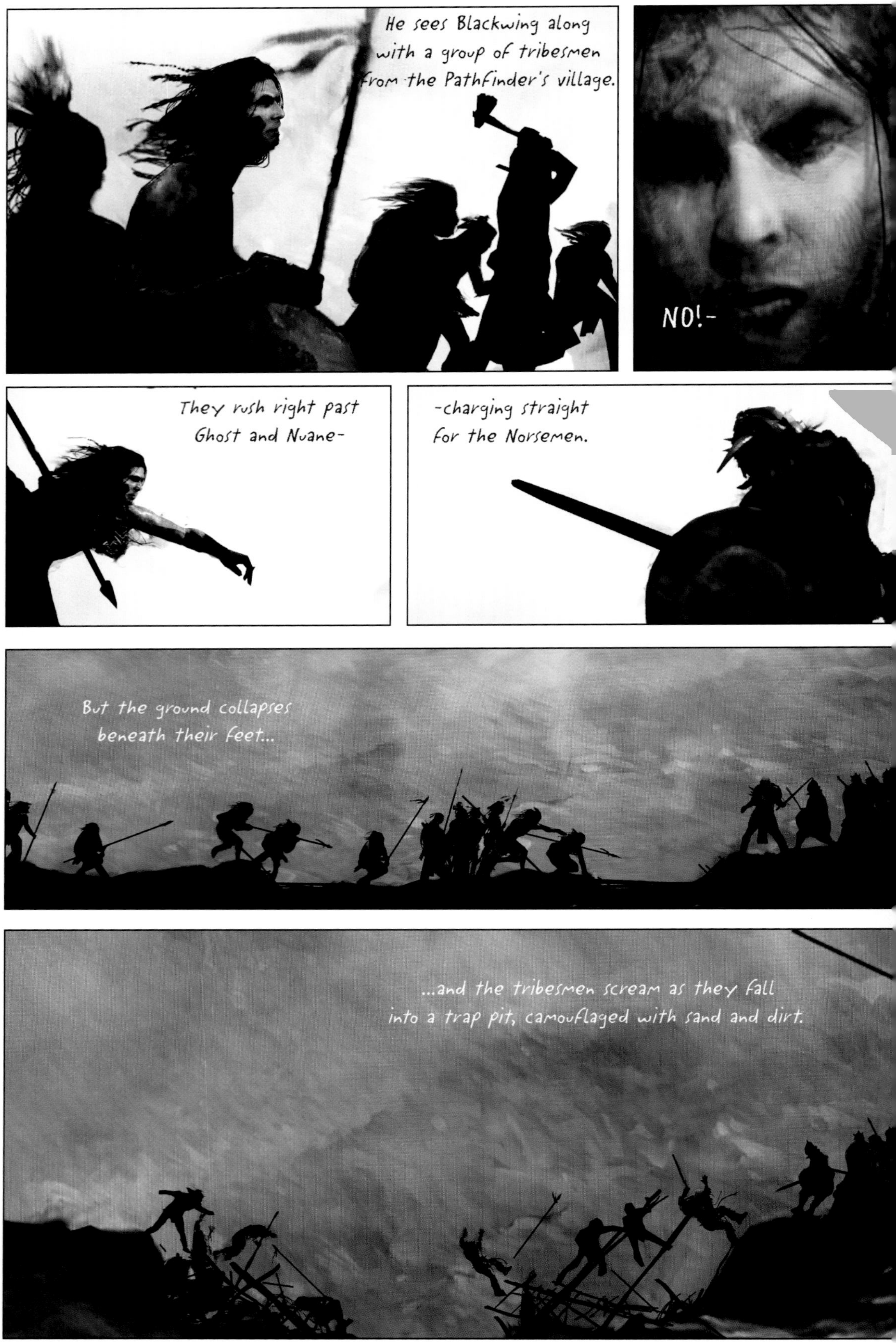
He sees Blackwing along with a group of tribesmen from the Pathfinder's village.
NO!-
They rush right past Ghost and Nuane-
-charging straight for the Norsemen.
But the ground collapses beneath their feet...
...and the tribesmen scream as they fall into a trap pit, camouflaged with sand and dirt.

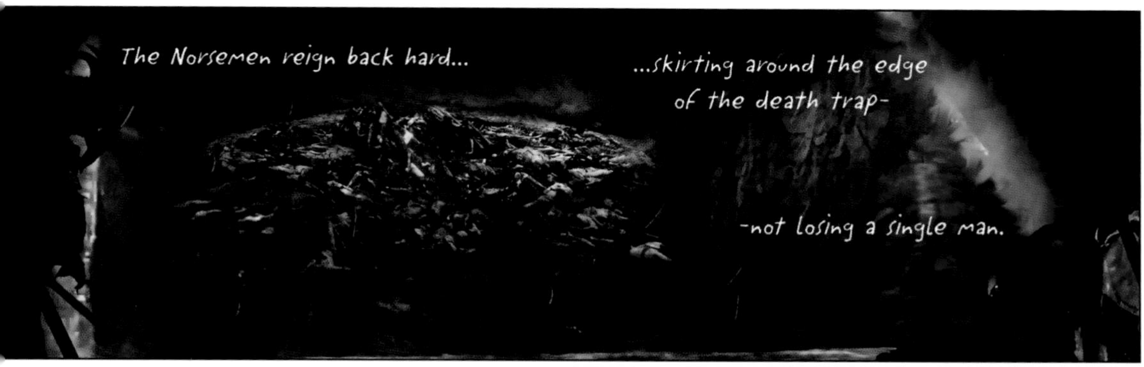
The Norsemen reign back hard...
...skirting around the edge of the death trap-
-not losing a single man.

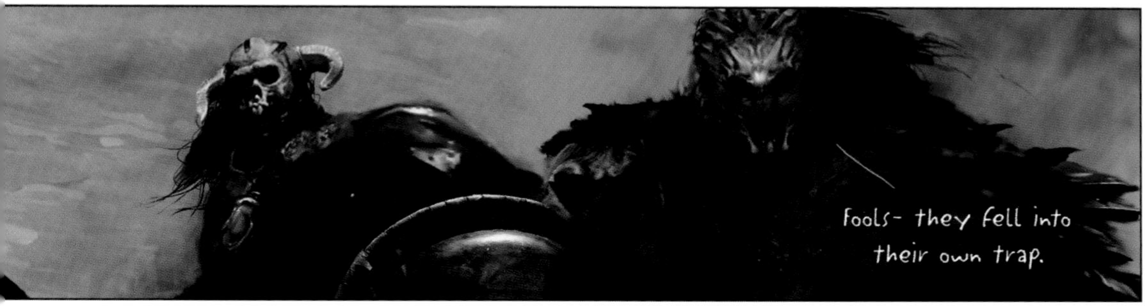
Fools- they fell into their own trap.

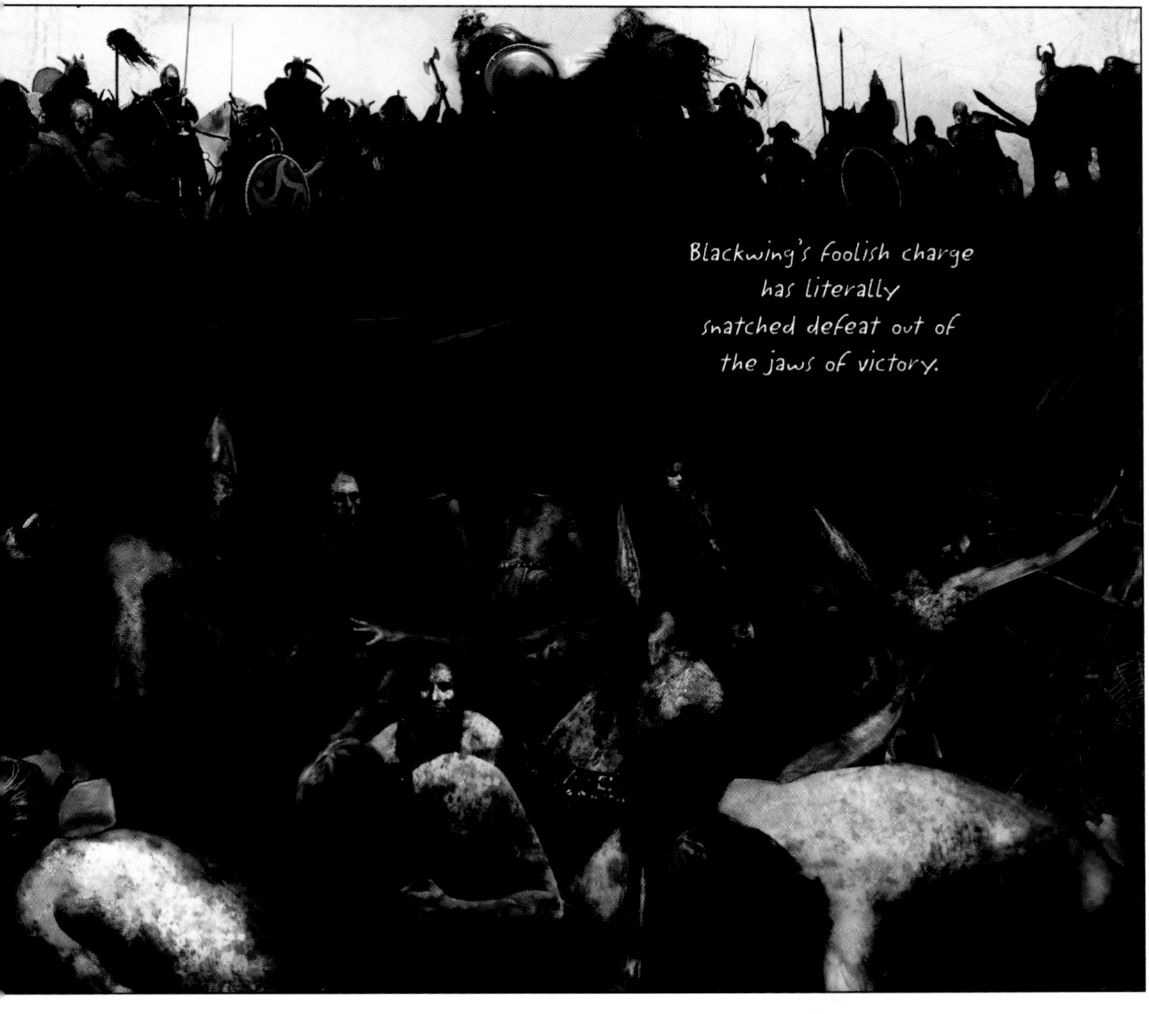
Blackwing's foolish charge has literally snatched defeat out of the jaws of victory.

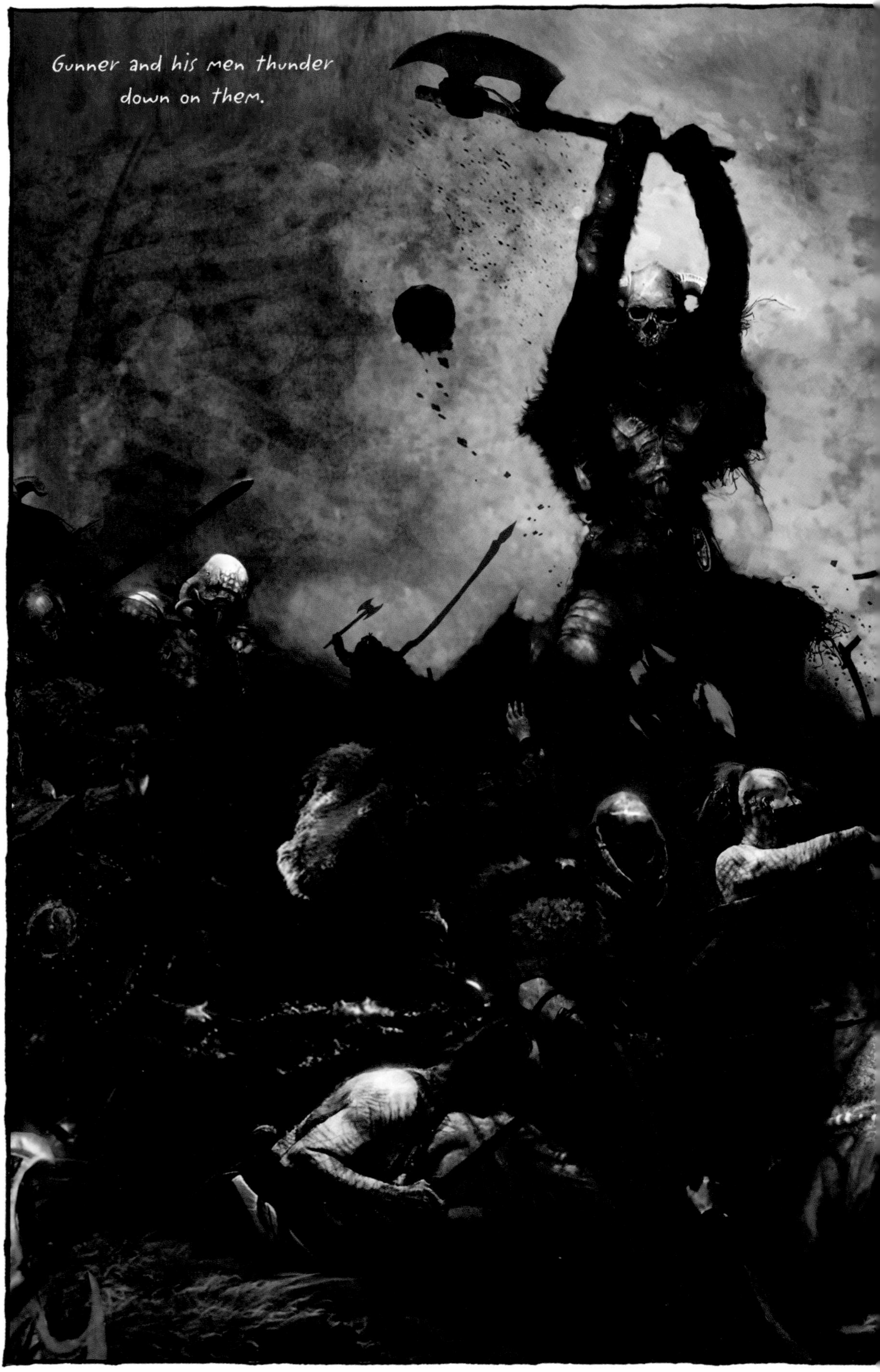
Gunner and his men thunder down on them.

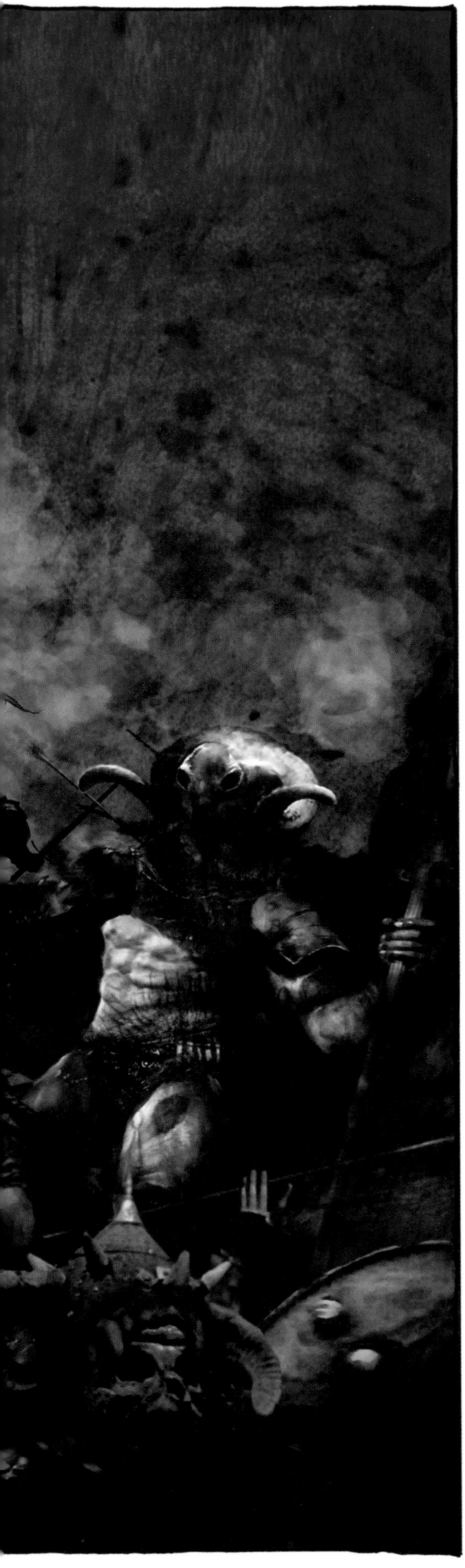

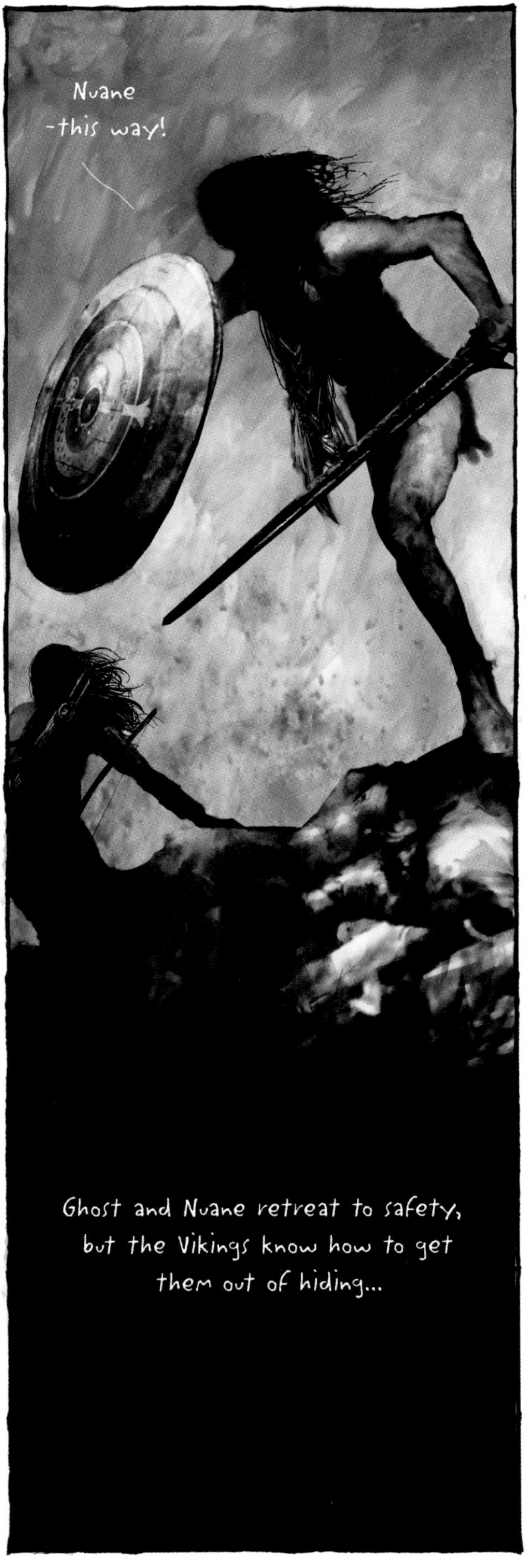
Nuane
-this way!
Ghost and Nuane retreat to safety, but the Vikings know how to get them out of hiding...

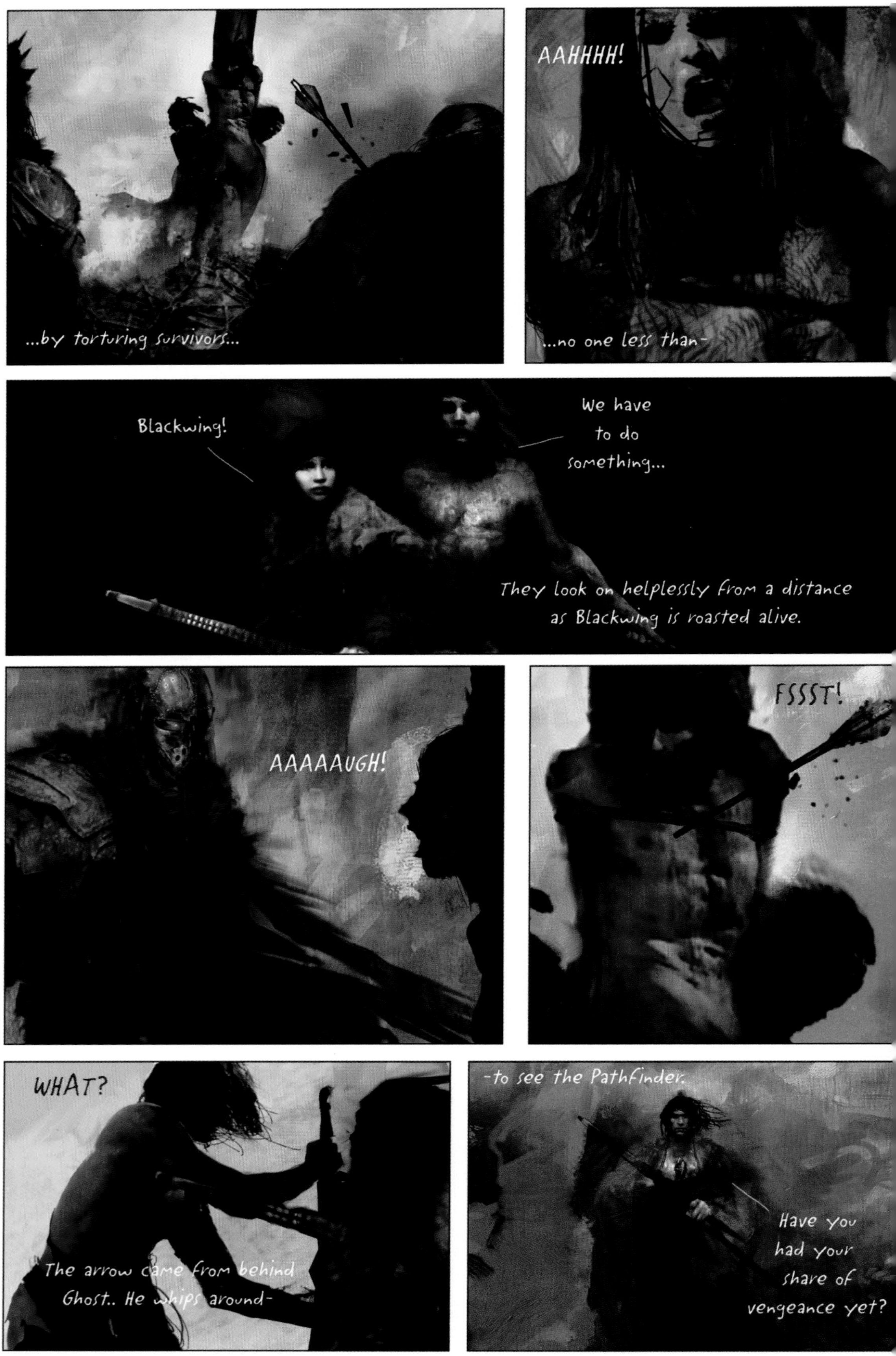
...by torturing survivors...
AAHHHH!
...no one less than-
Blackwing!
We have to do something...
They look on helplessly from a distance as Blackwing is roasted alive.
AAAAAUGH!
FSSST!
WHAT?
The arrow came from behind Ghost.. He whips around-
-to see the Pathfinder.
Have you had your share of vengeance yet?

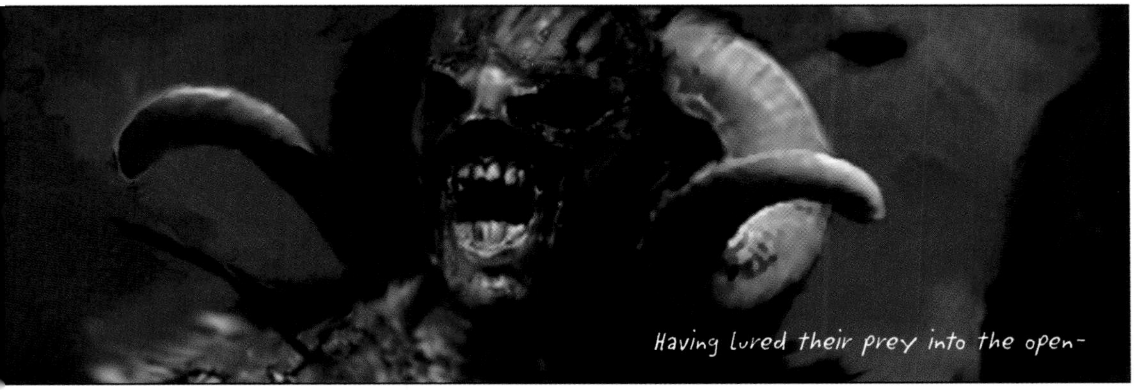
Having lured their prey into the open-

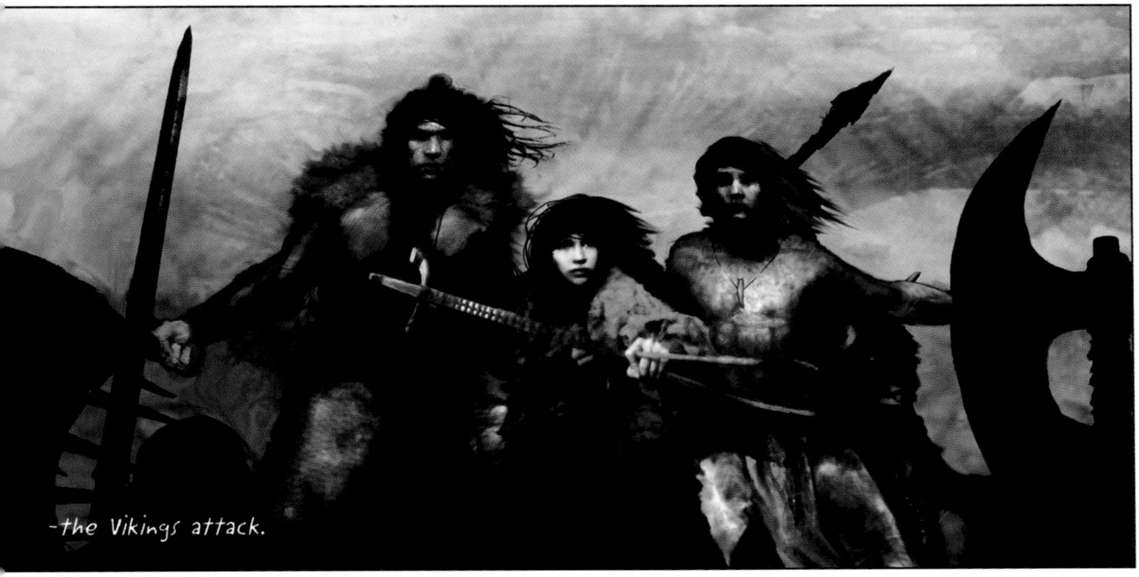
-the Vikings attack.

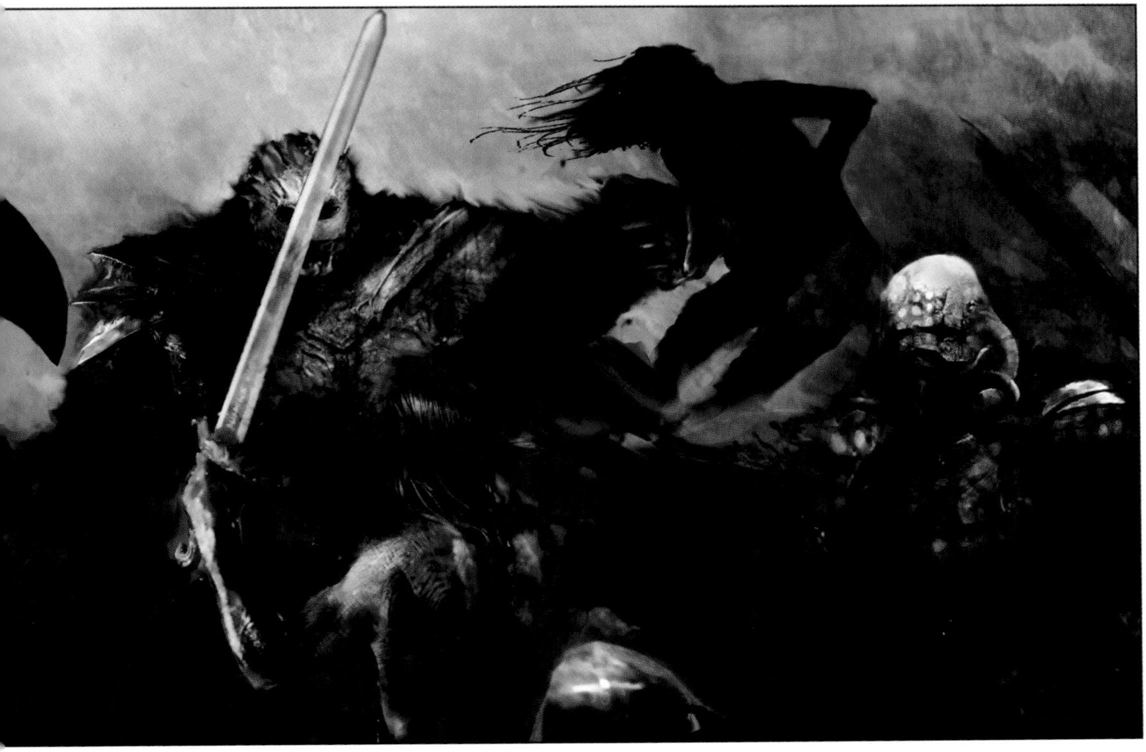

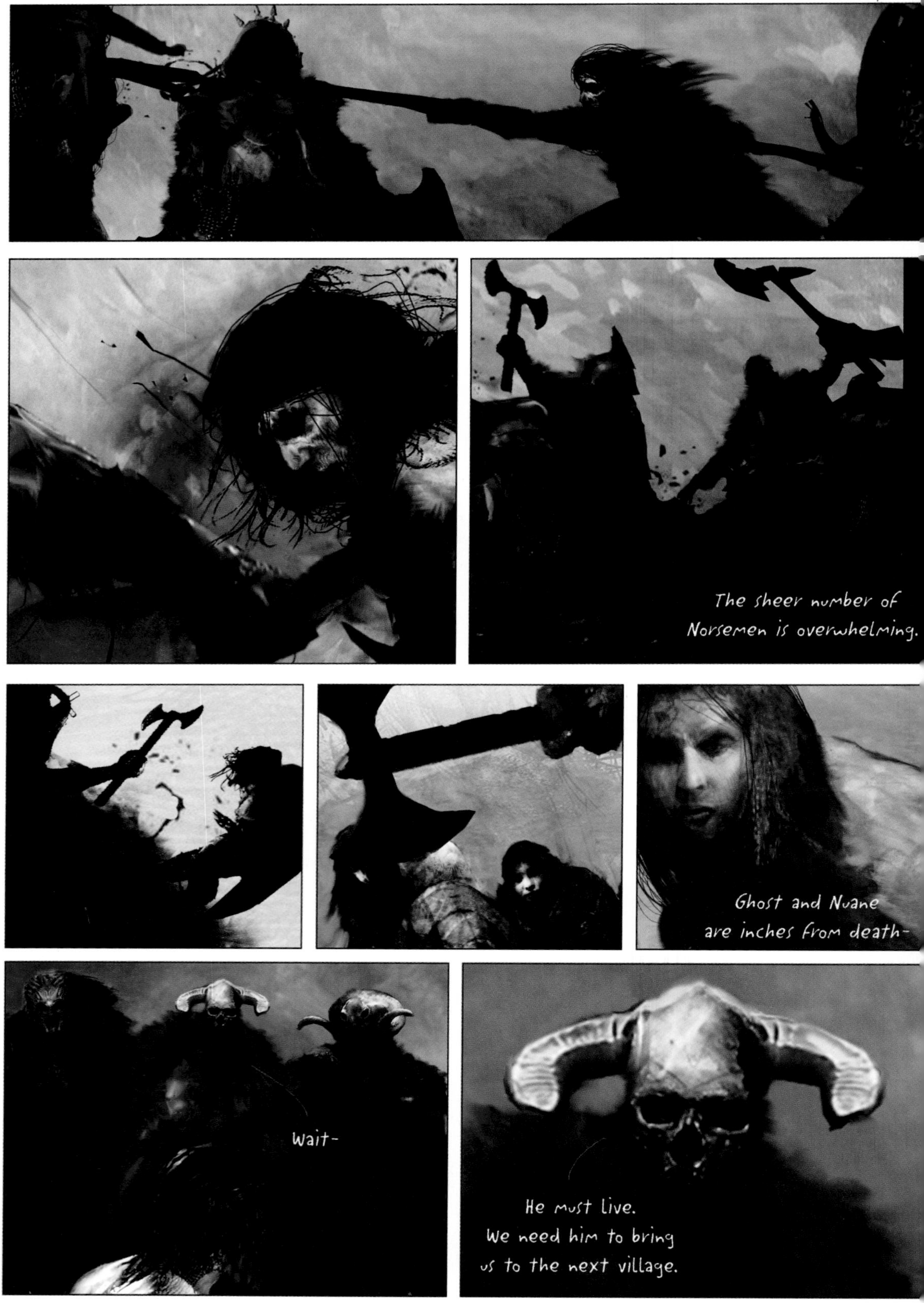
The sheer number of
Norsemen is overwhelming.
Ghost and Nuane
are inches from death-
wait-
He must live.
We need him to bring
us to the next village.

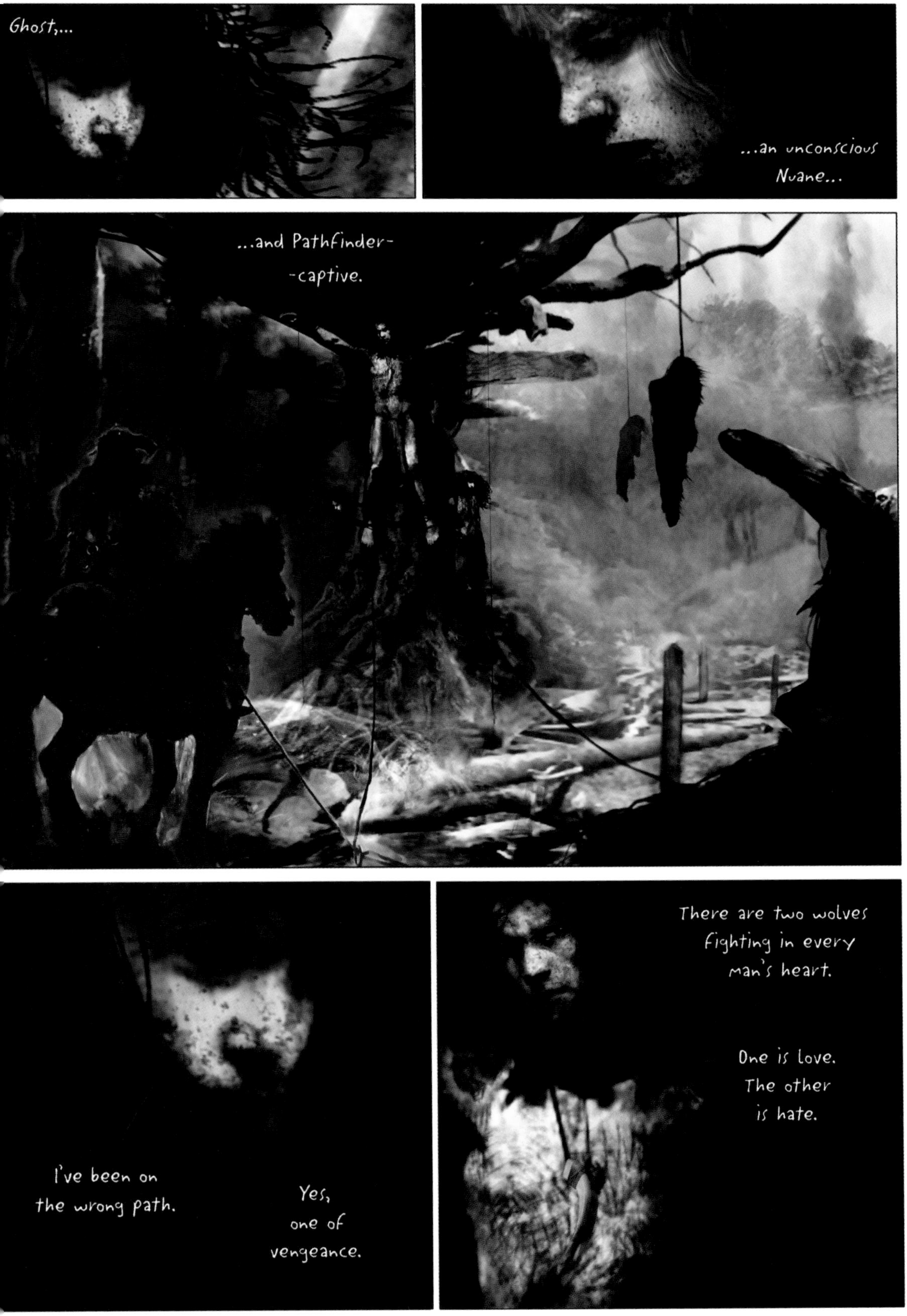

Ghost,...
...an unconscious Nuane...
...and Pathfinder-
-captive.
I've been on the wrong path.
Yes, one of vengeance.
There are two wolves fighting in every man's heart.
One is love. The other is hate.

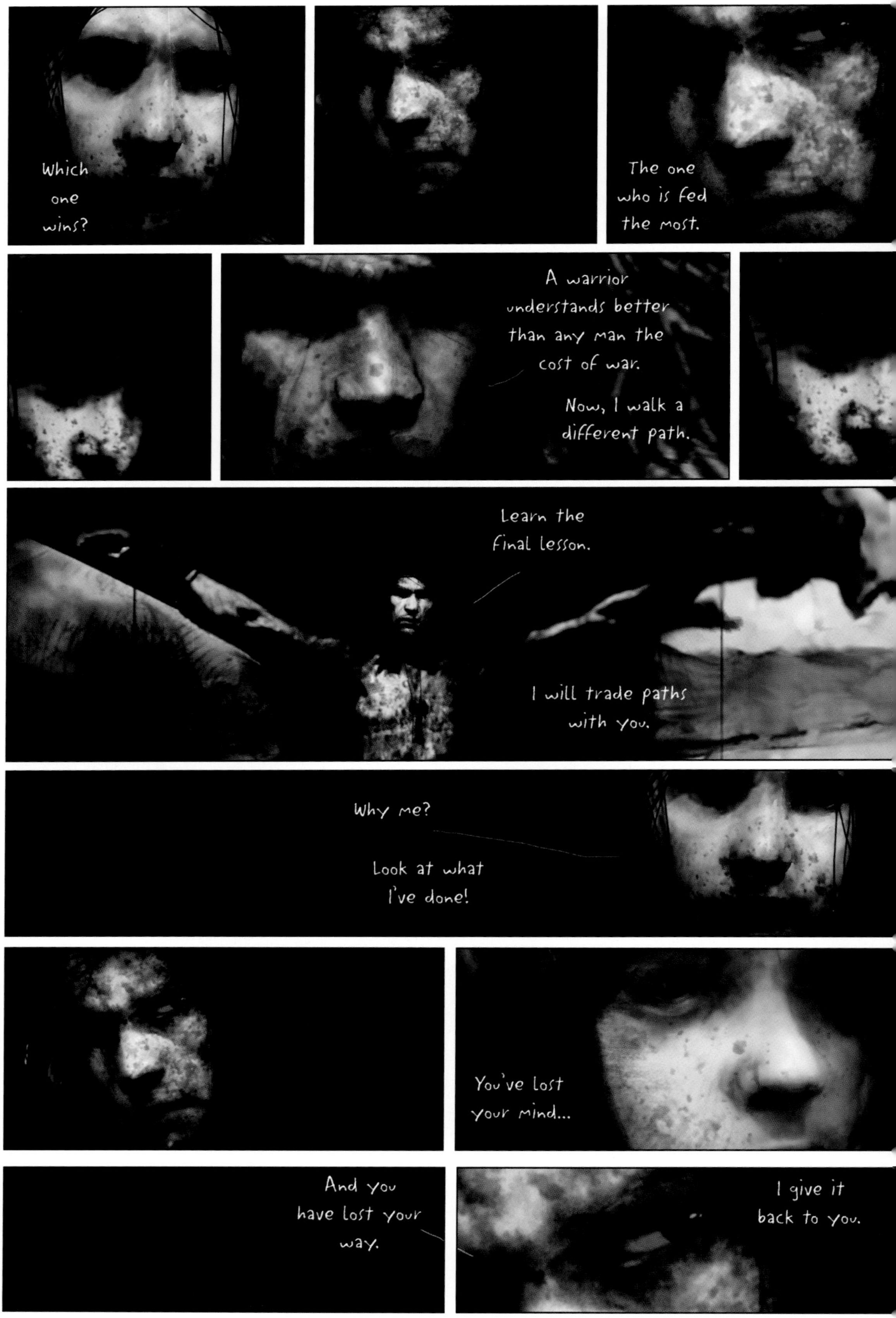
Which one wins?
The one who is fed the most.
A warrior understands better than any man the cost of war.
Now, I walk a different path.
Learn the final lesson.
I will trade paths with you.
Why me?
Look at what I've done!
You've lost your mind...
And you have lost your way.
I give it back to you.

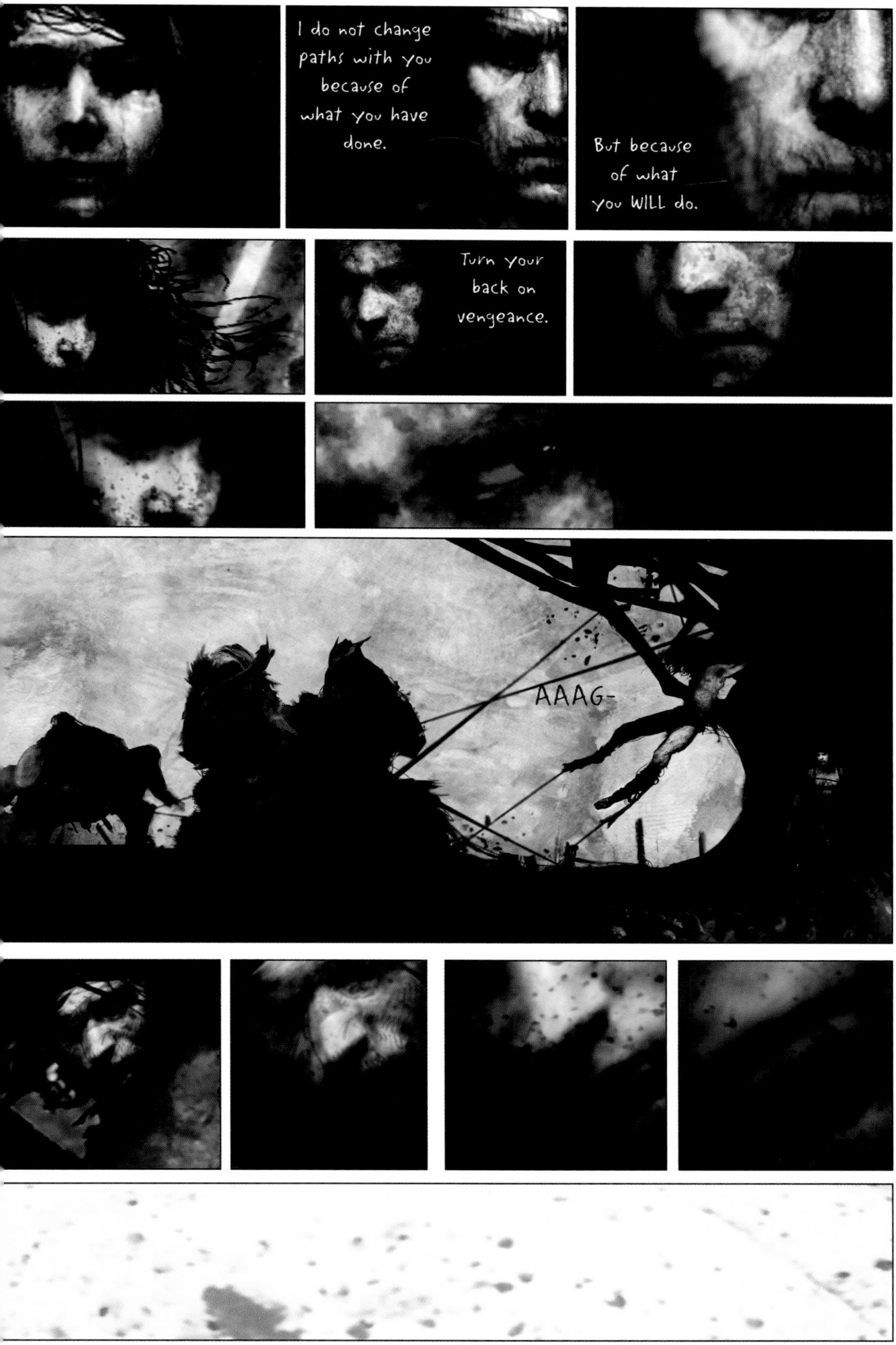
I do not change paths with you because of what you have done.
But because of what you WILL do.
Turn your back on vengeance.
AAAG-

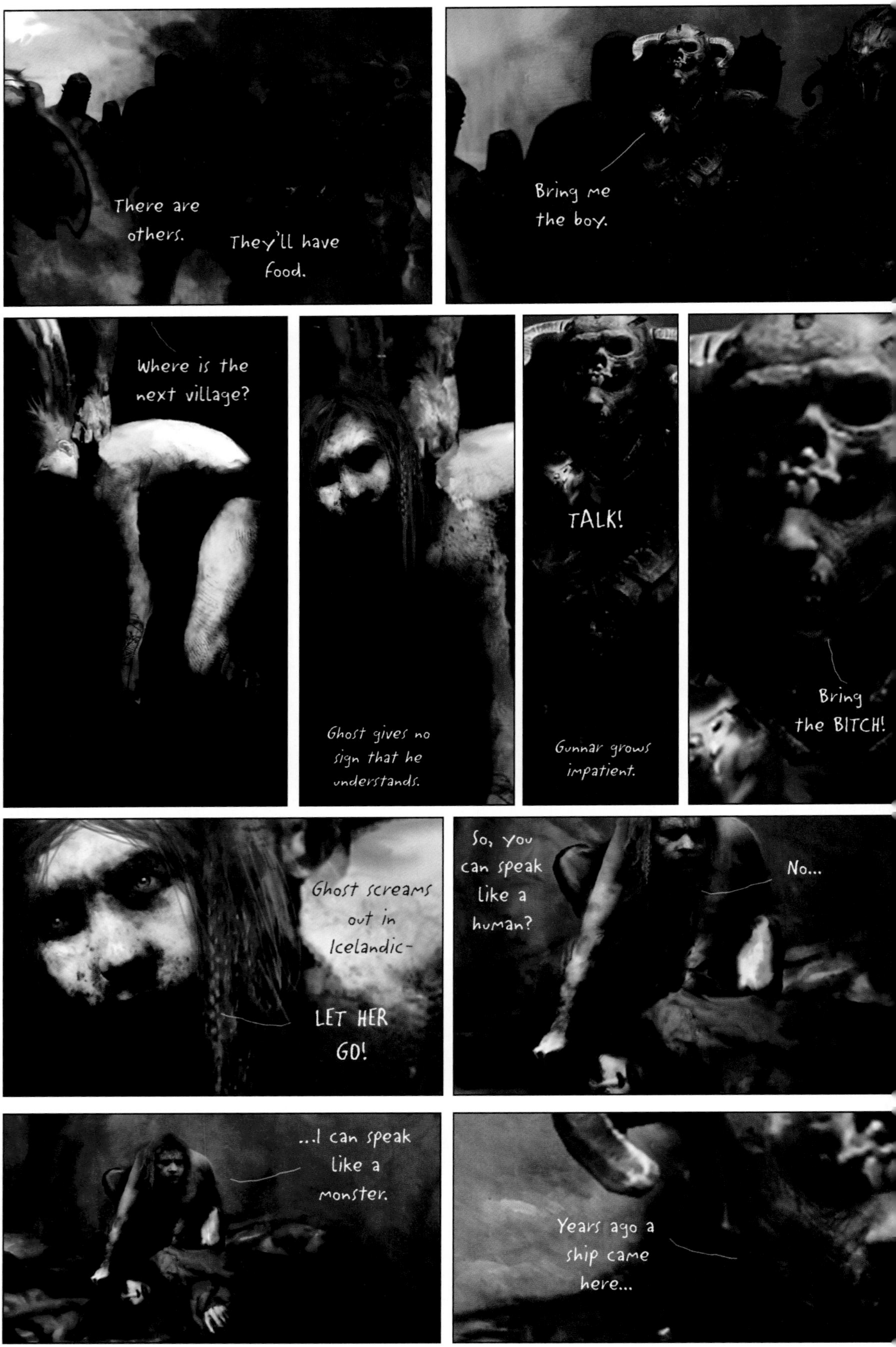

There are others.
They'll have food.
Bring me the boy.
Where is the next village?
Ghost gives no sign that he understands.
TALK!
Gunnar grows impatient.
Bring the BITCH!
Ghost screams out in Icelandic-
LET HER GO!
So, you can speak like a human?
No...
...I can speak like a monster.
Years ago a ship came here...

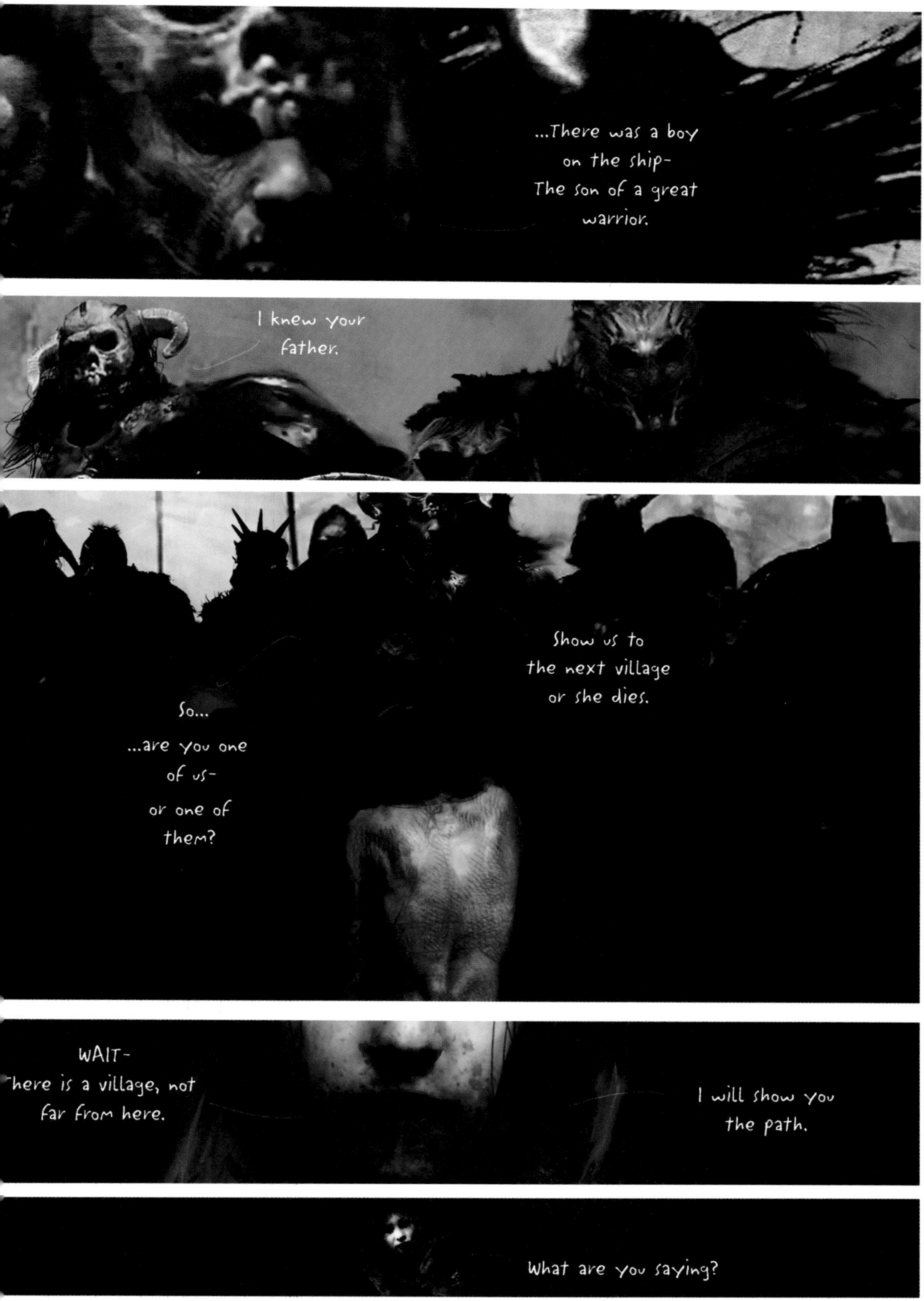
...There was a boy on the ship- The son of a great warrior.
I knew your father.
So... ...are you one of us- or one of them?
Show us to the next village or she dies.
WAIT- here is a village, not far from here.
I will show you the path.
What are you saying?

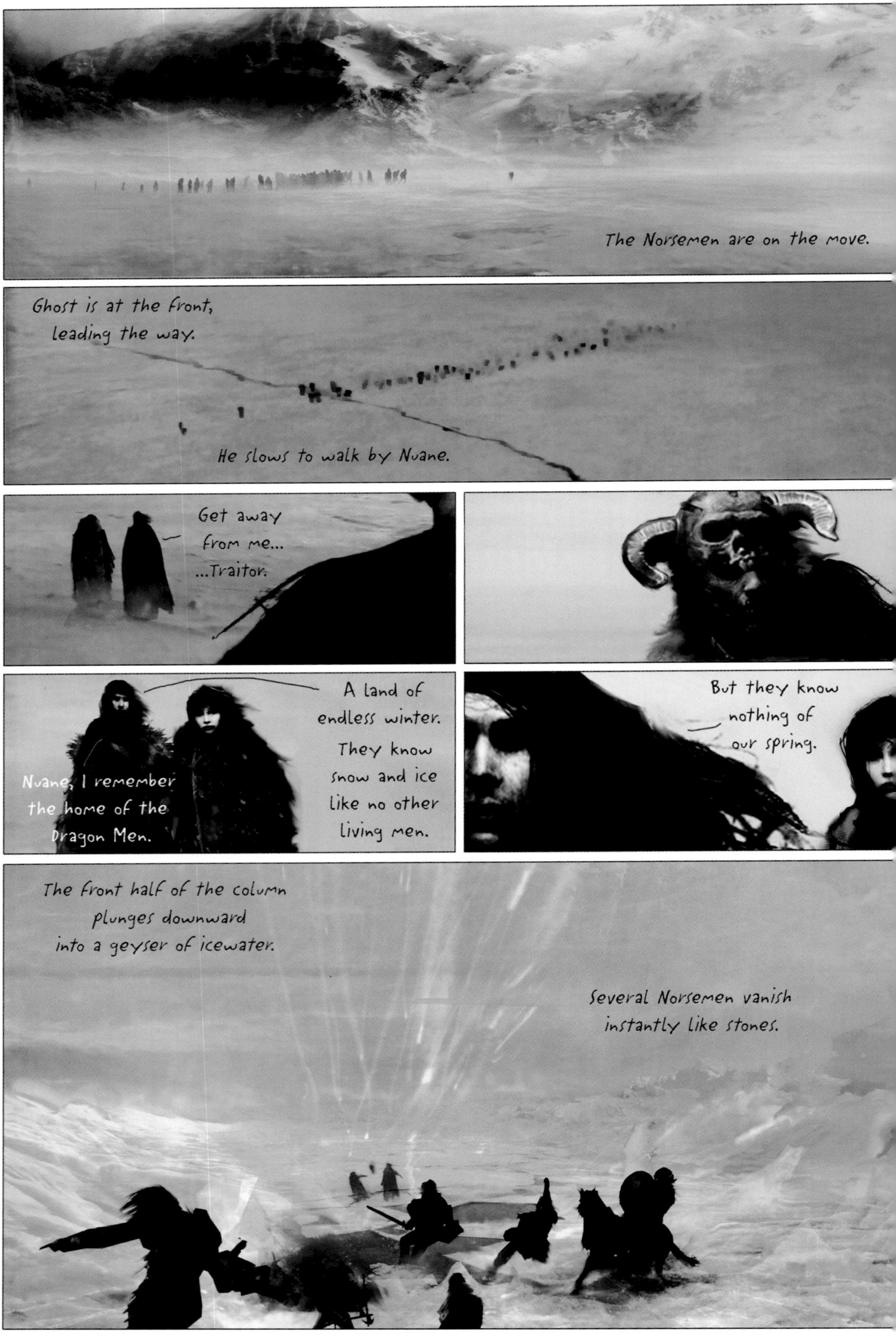
The Norsemen are on the move.
Ghost is at the front, leading the way.
He slows to walk by Nuane.
Get away from me... ...Traitor.
Nuane, I remember the home of the Dragon Men.
A land of endless winter.
They know snow and ice like no other living men.
But they know nothing of our spring.
The front half of the column plunges downward into a geyser of icewater.
Several Norsemen vanish instantly like stones.

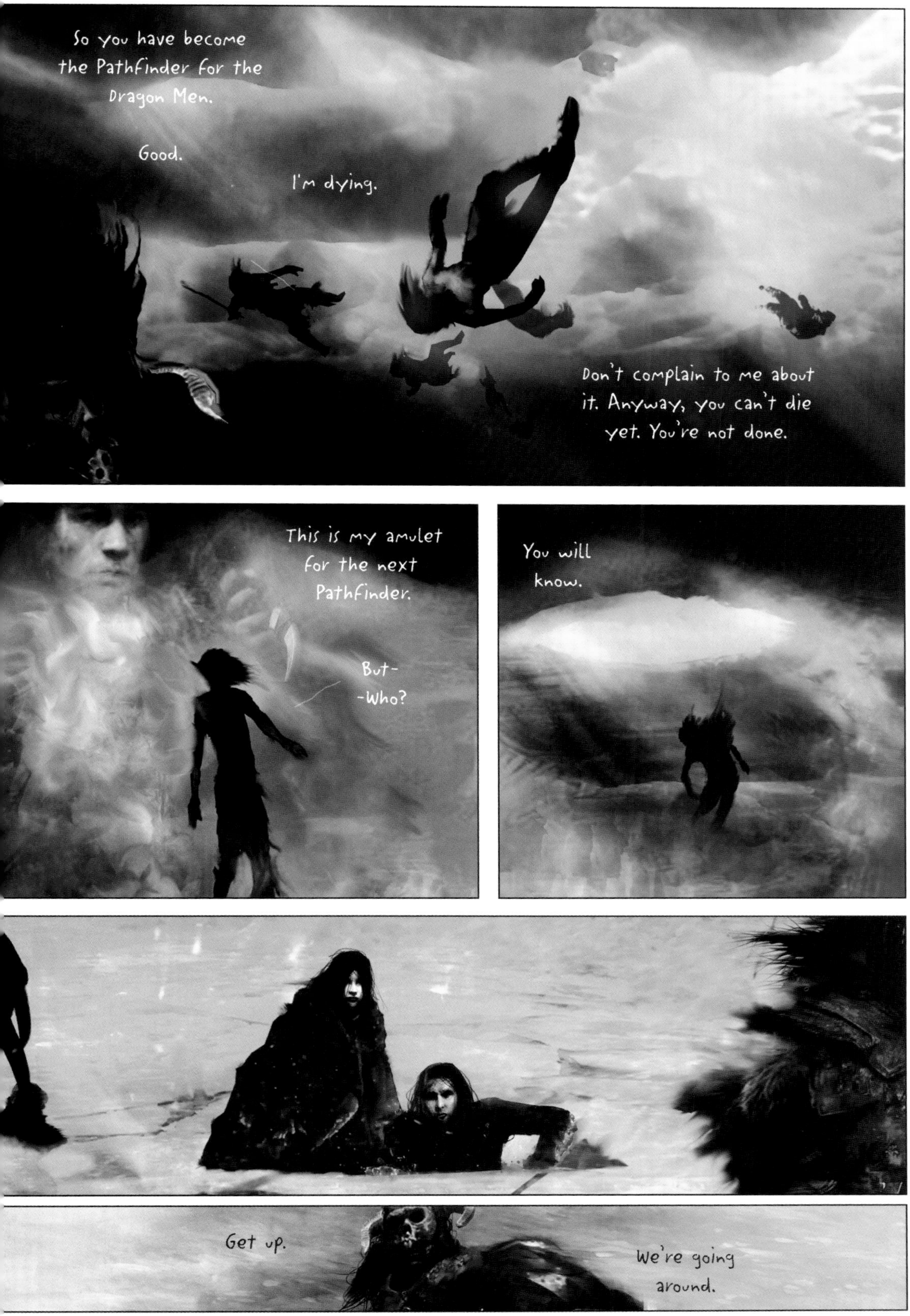

So you have become the Pathfinder for the Dragon Men.
Good.
I'm dying.
Don't complain to me about it. Anyway, you can't die yet. You're not done.
This is my amulet for the next Pathfinder.
But-
-Who?
You will know.
Get up.
We're going around.

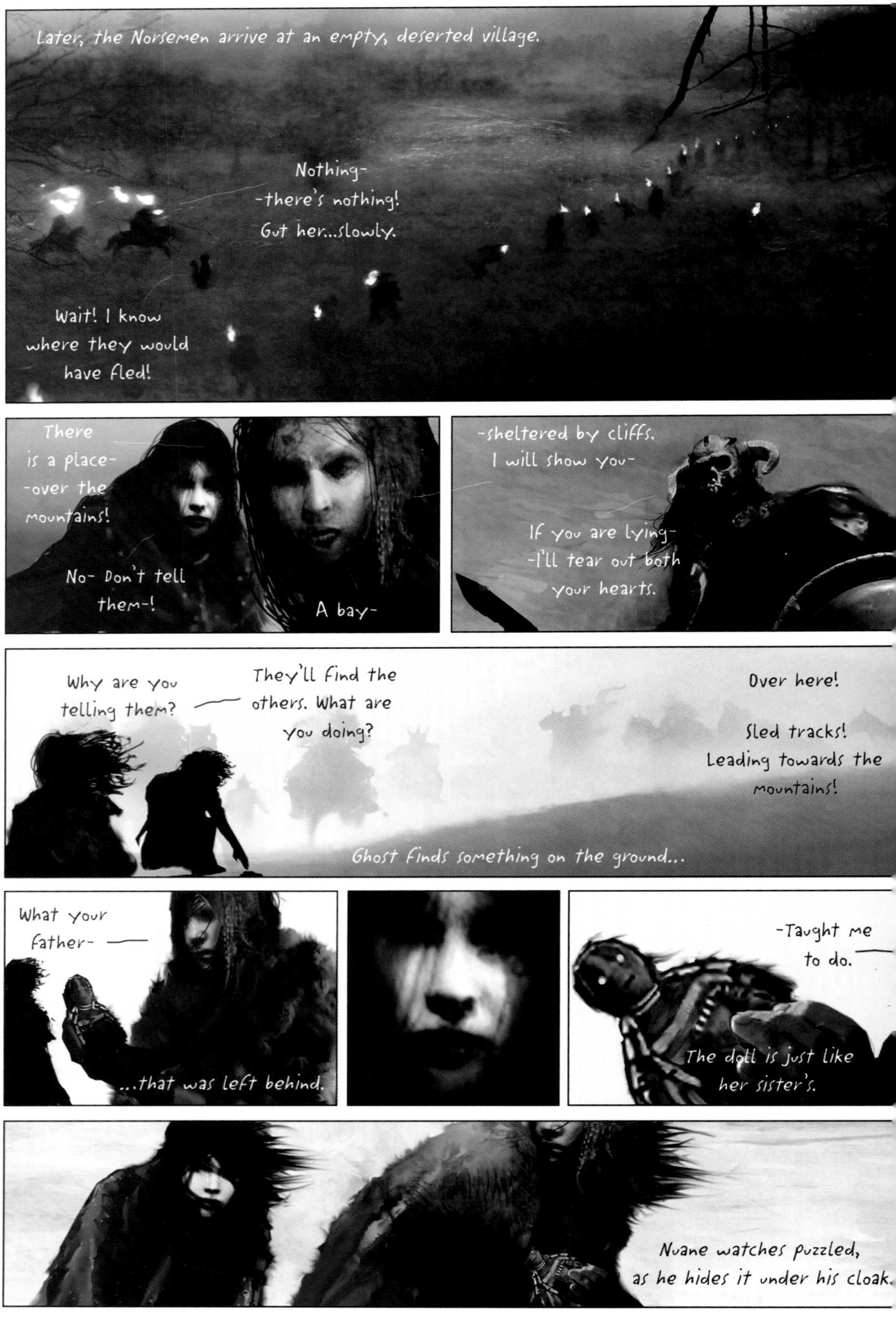
Later, the Norsemen arrive at an empty, deserted village.
Nothing-
-there's nothing!
Gut her...slowly.
Wait! I know where they would have fled!
There is a place-
-over the mountains!
No- Don't tell them-!
A bay-
-sheltered by cliffs.
I will show you-
If you are lying-
-I'll tear out both your hearts.
Why are you telling them?
They'll find the others. What are you doing?
Over here!
Sled tracks!
Leading towards the mountains!
Ghost finds something on the ground...
What your father-
...that was left behind.
-Taught me to do.
The doll is just like her sister's.
Nuane watches puzzled, as he hides it under his cloak.

There are two trails here.

Which one is it?

Get up, you clumsy bitch!

Ghost uses the diversion to plant the doll on the treacherous west path.

A short while later—

Tracker, what did you find?

One of the creatures dropped its doll.

I told you that this is the way.

It was on the west path!

Nuane doesn't understand what Ghost is up to.

Go.

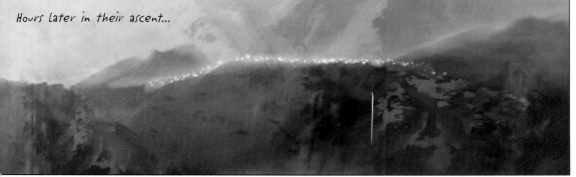

Hours later in their ascent...

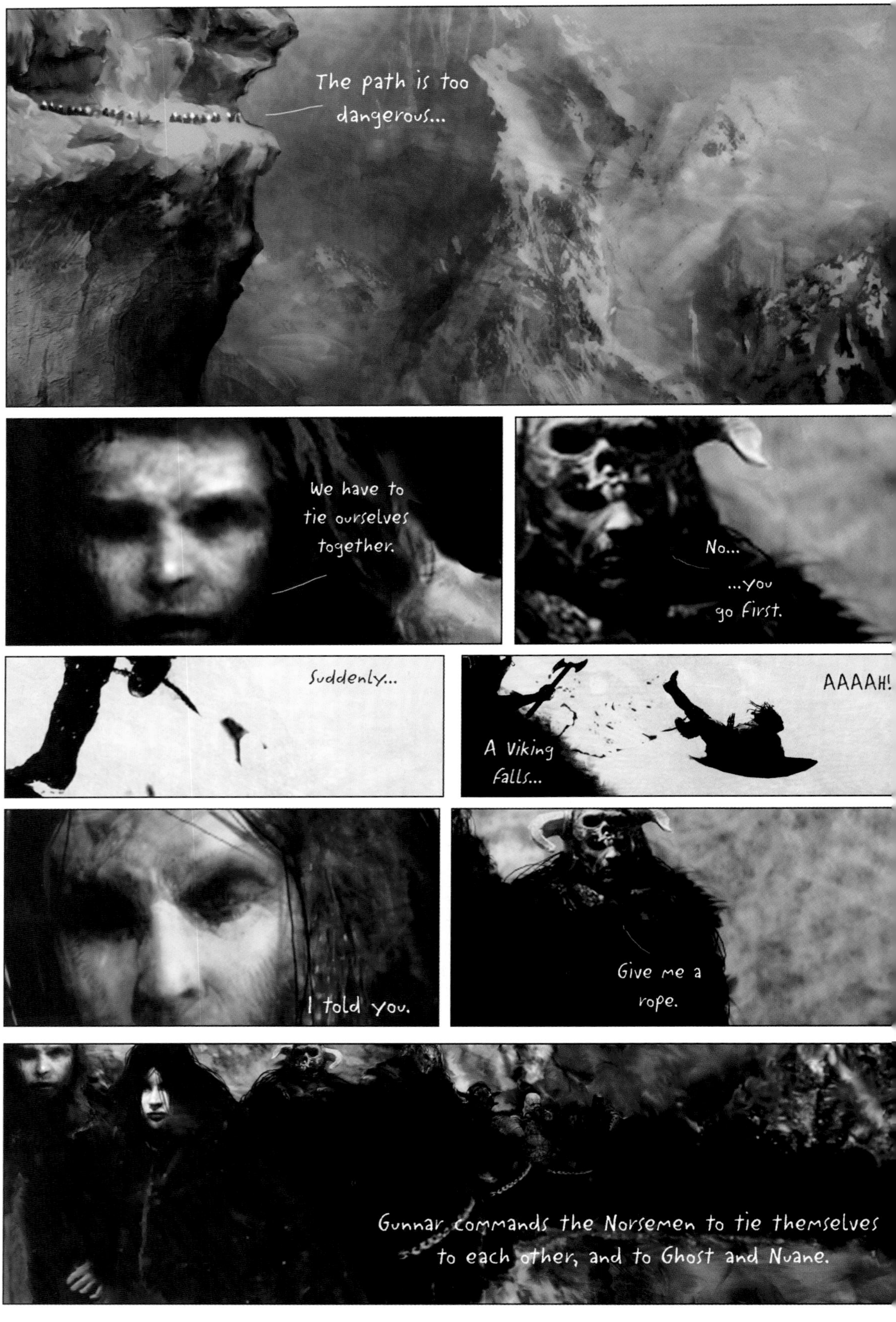
The path is too dangerous...
We have to tie ourselves together.
No...
...you go first.
Suddenly...
A Viking falls...
AAAAH!
I told you.
Give me a rope.
Gunnar commands the Norsemen to tie themselves to each other, and to Ghost and Nuane.

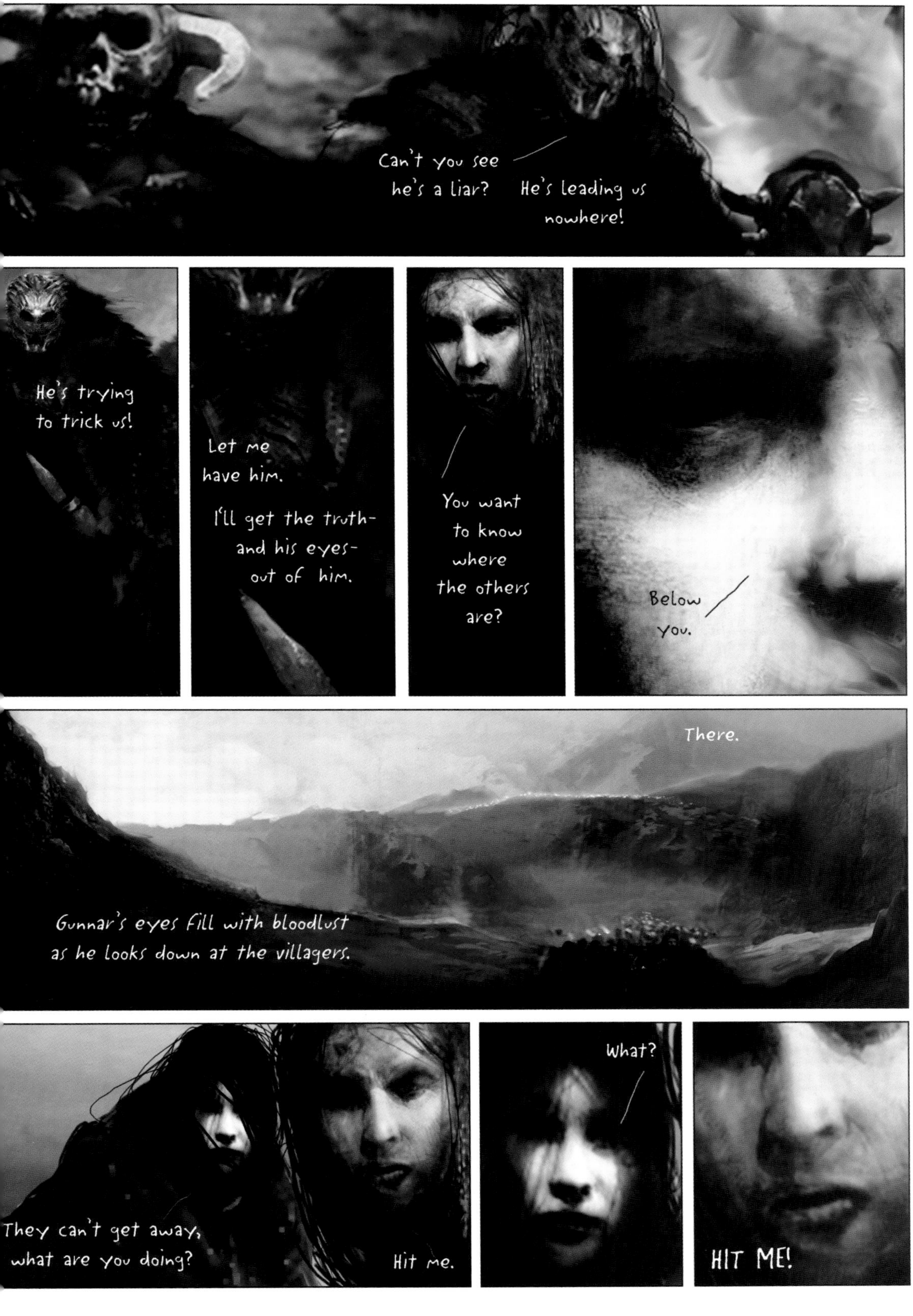
Can't you see he's a liar? He's leading us nowhere!
He's trying to trick us!
Let me have him.
I'll get the truth- and his eyes- out of him.
You want to know where the others are?
Below you.
There.
Gunnar's eyes fill with bloodlust as he looks down at the villagers.
They can't get away, what are you doing?
Hit me.
What?
HIT ME!

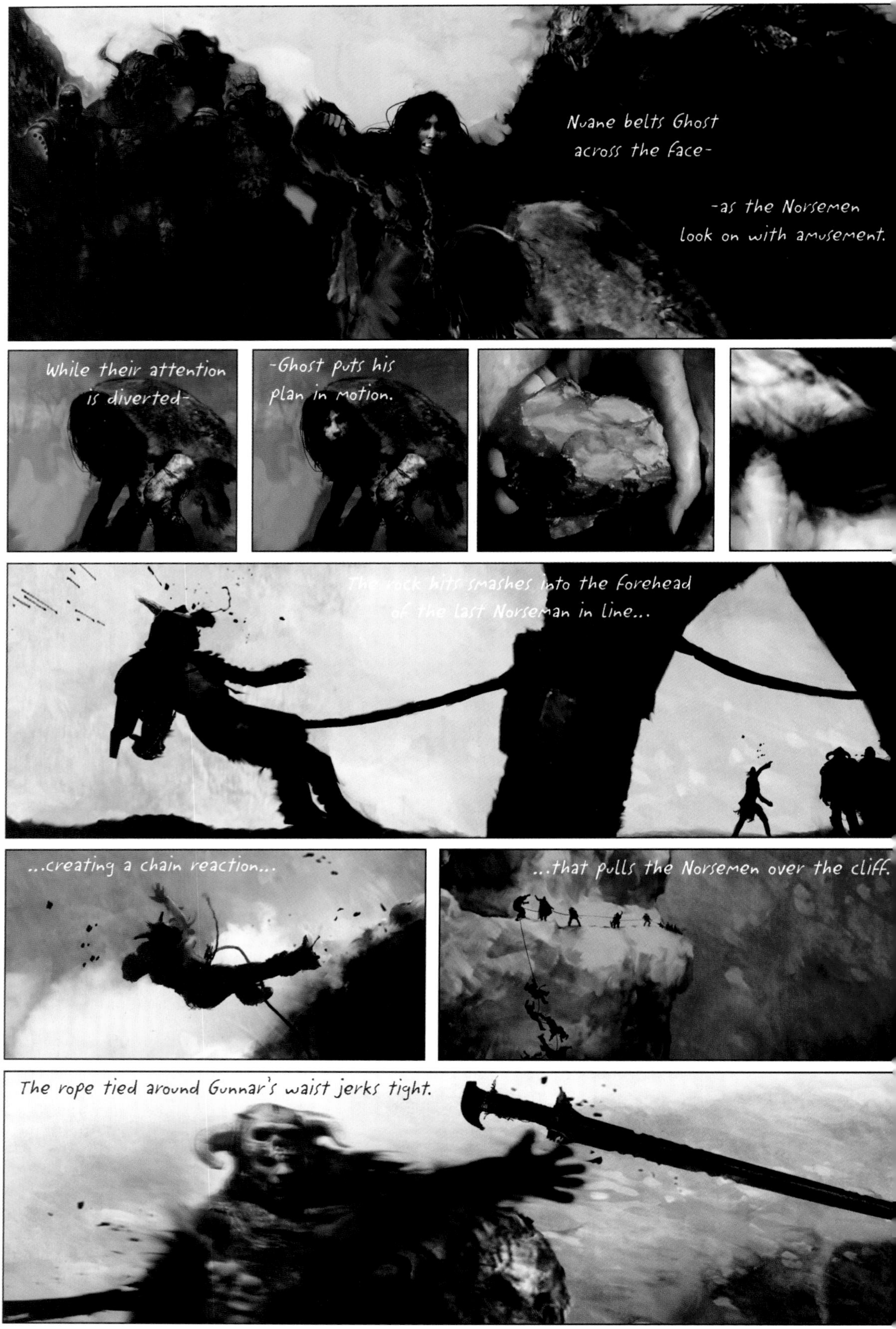
Nuane belts Ghost across the face-
-as the Norsemen look on with amusement.
While their attention is diverted-
-Ghost puts his plan in motion.
The rock hits smashes into the forehead of the last Norseman in line...
...creating a chain reaction...
...that pulls the Norsemen over the cliff.
The rope tied around Gunnar's waist jerks tight.

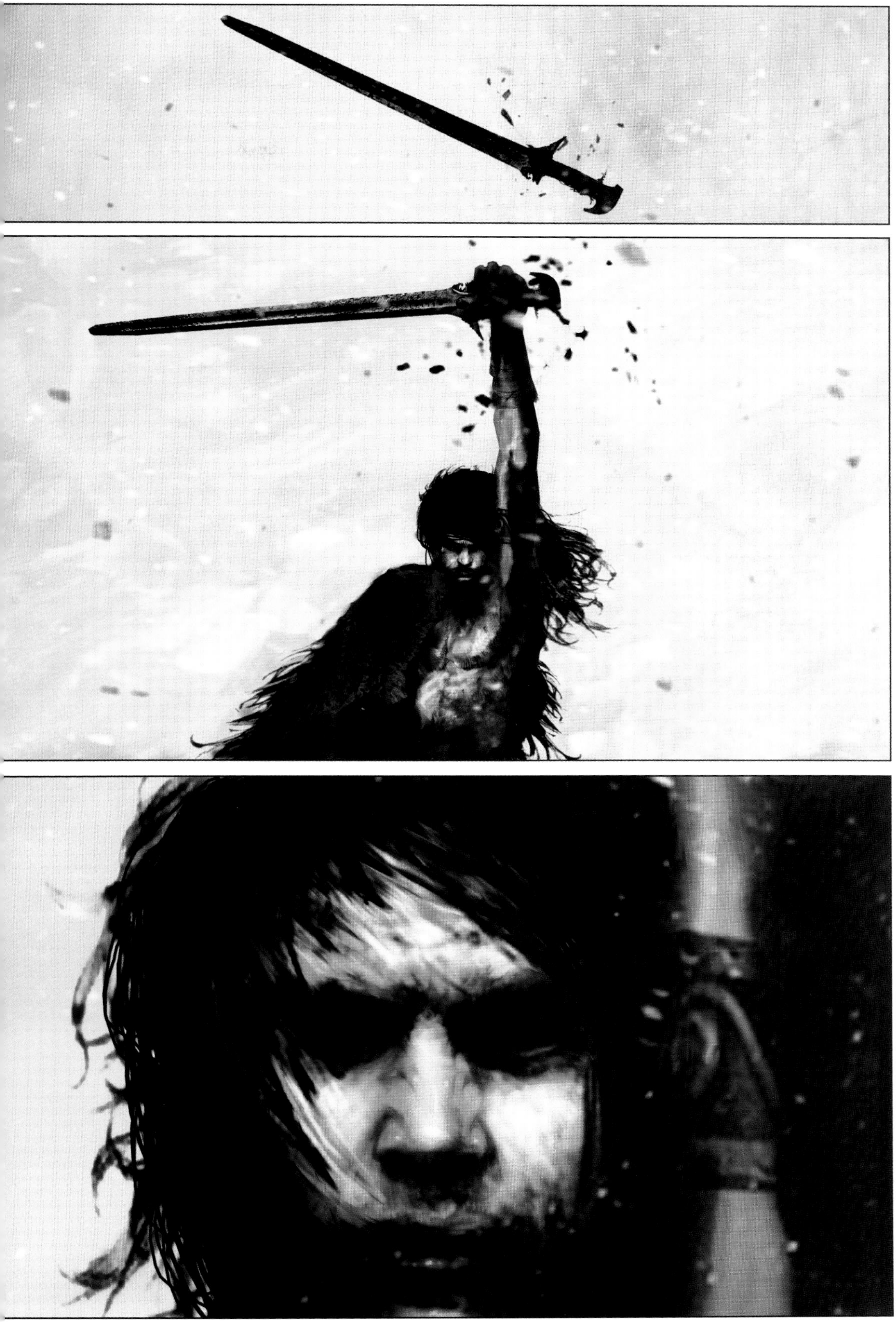

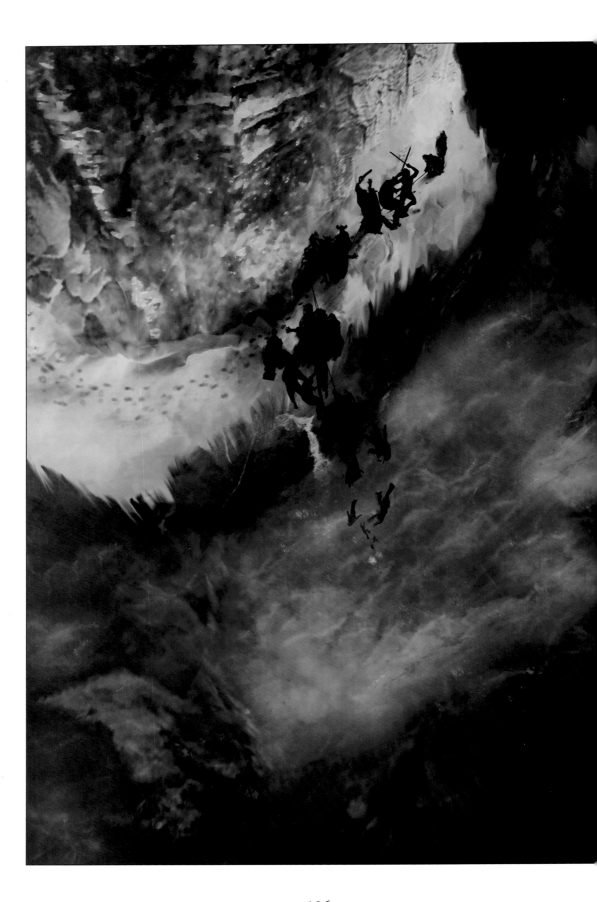

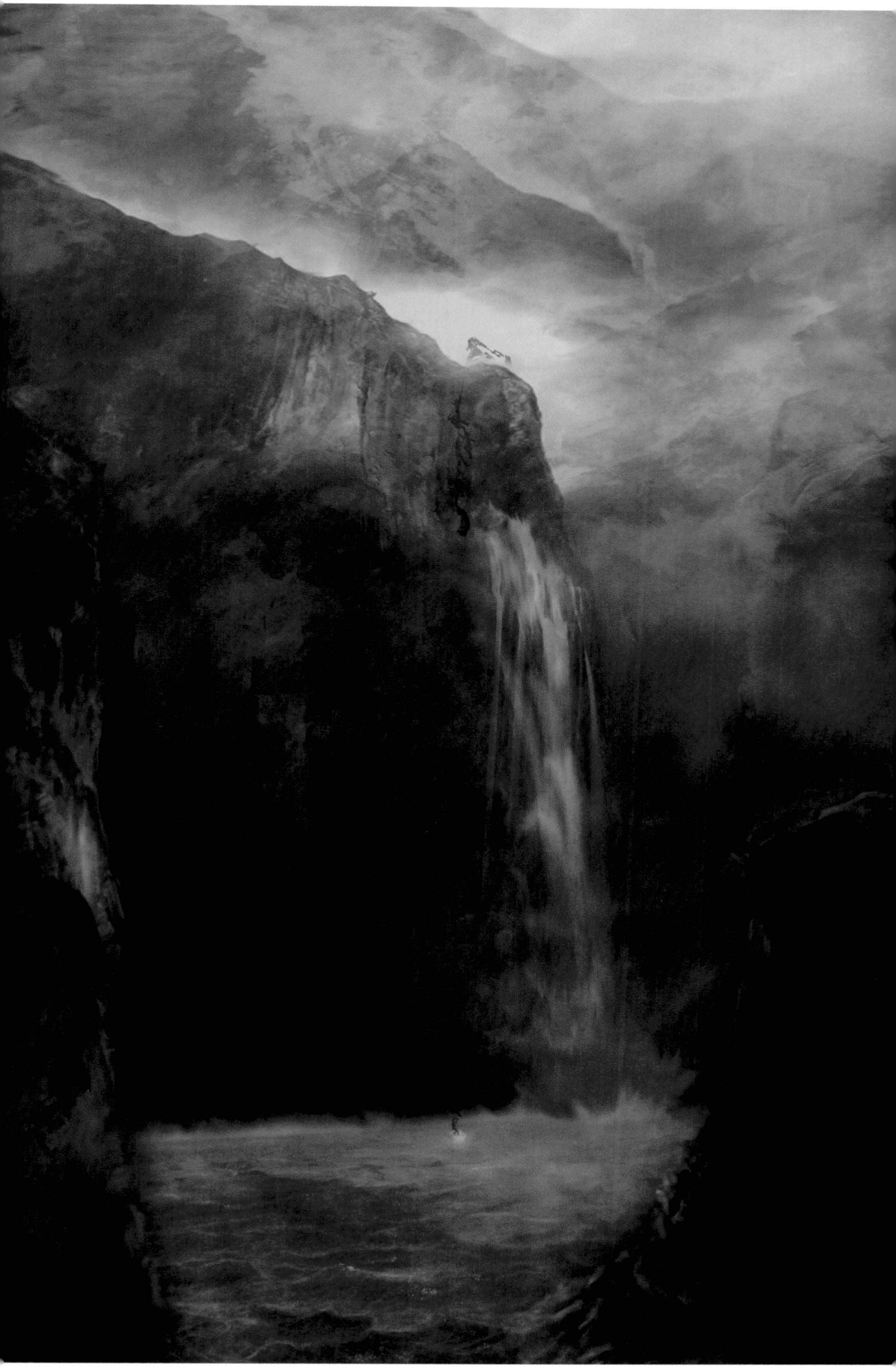

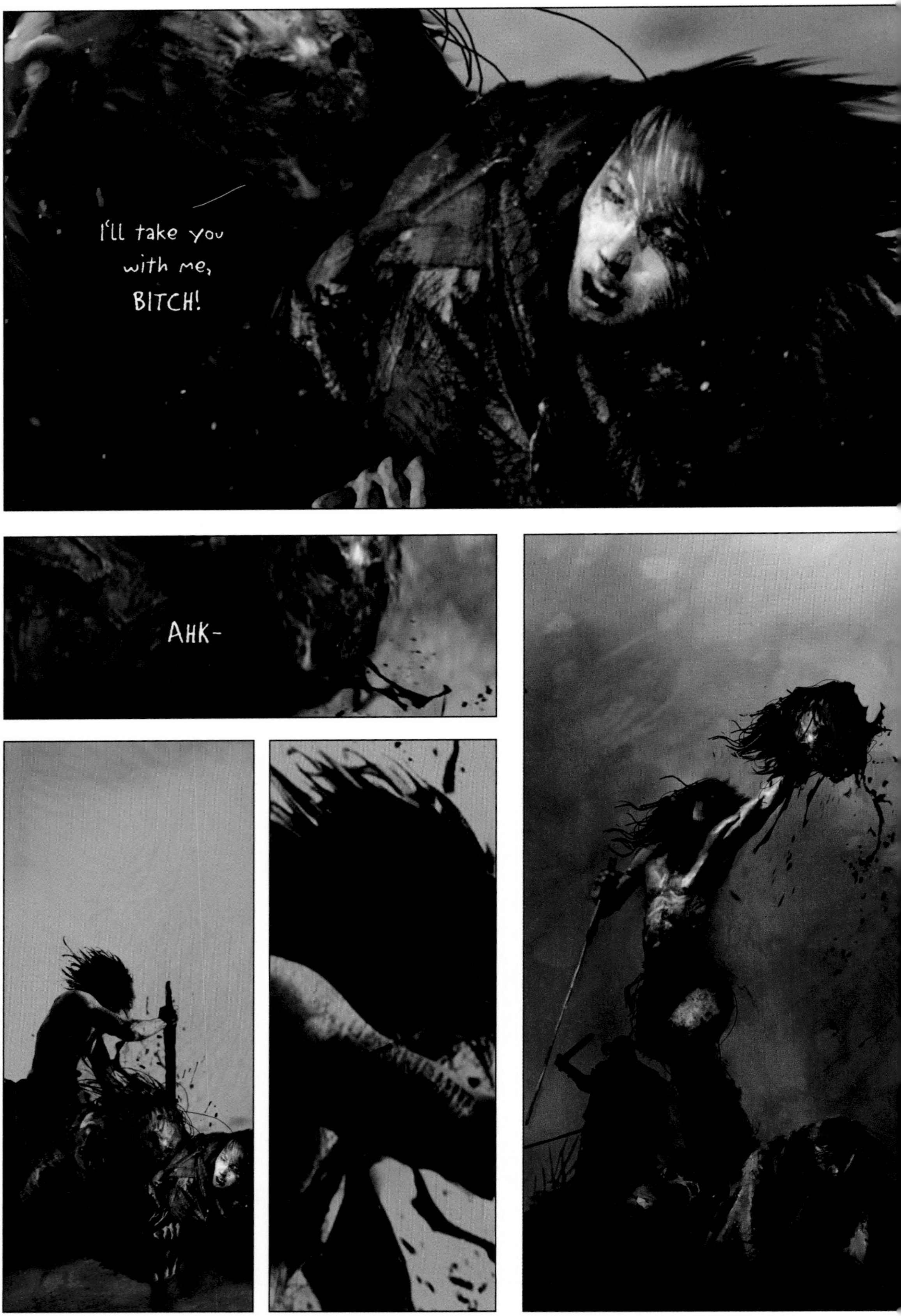
I'll take you with me, BITCH!
AHK-

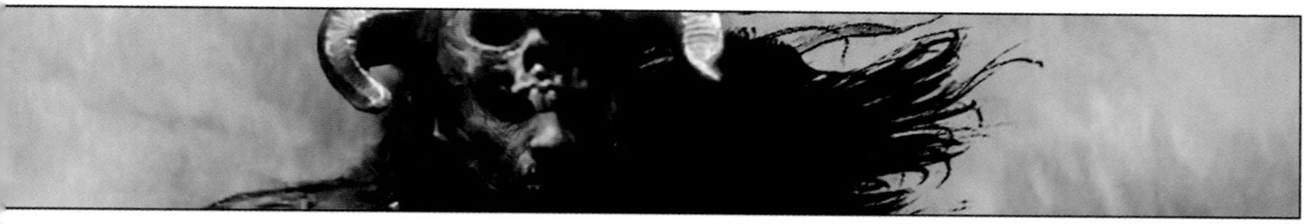

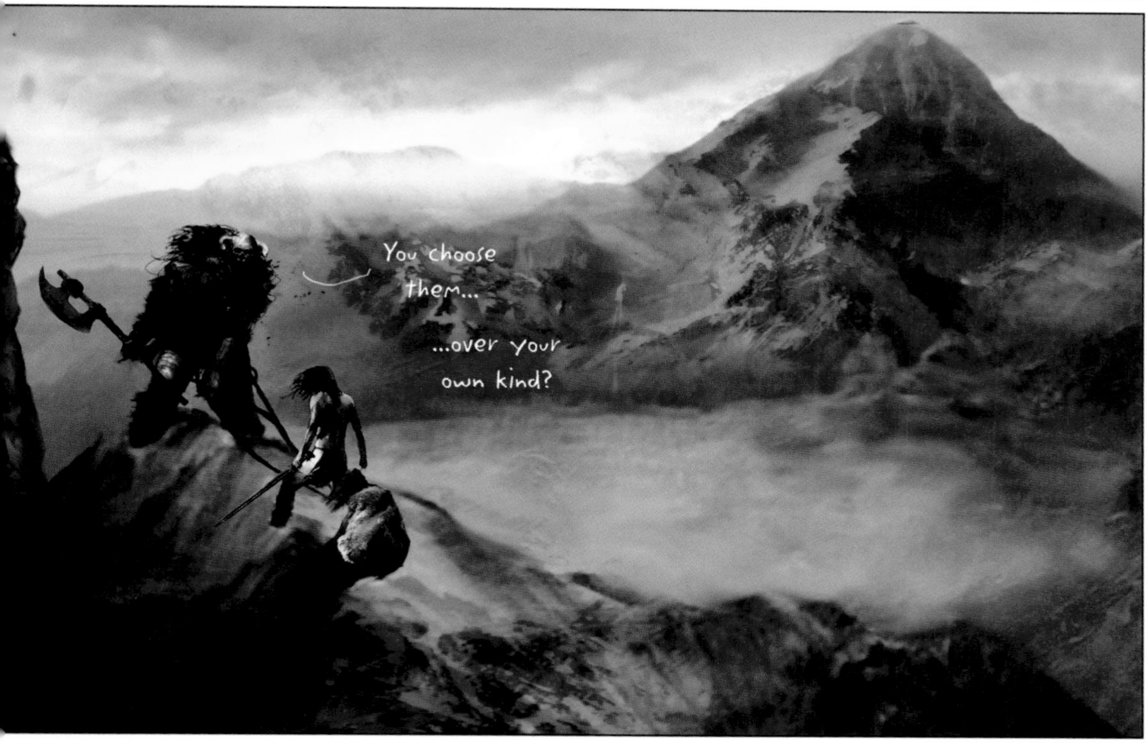
You choose them...
...over your own kind?

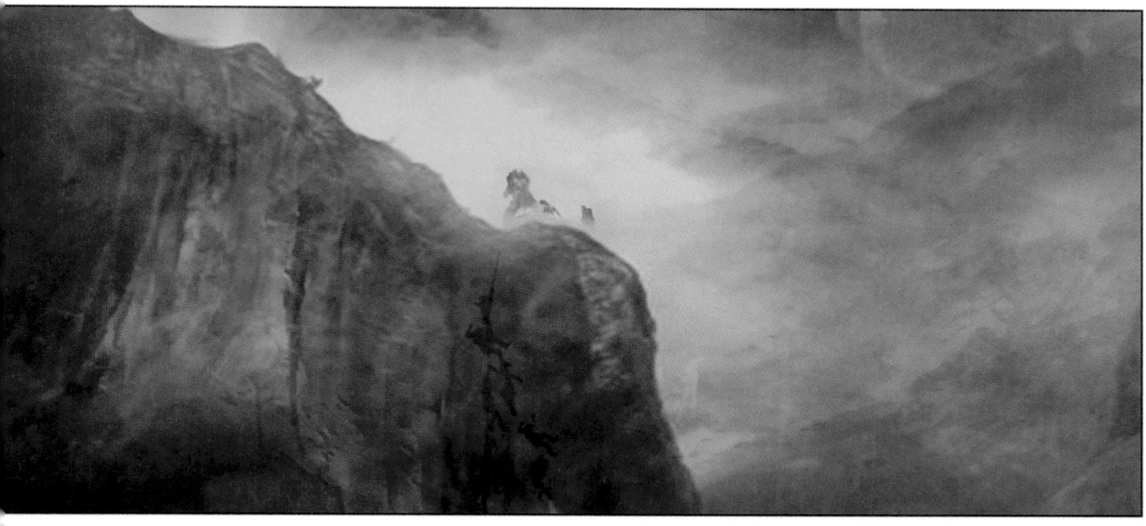

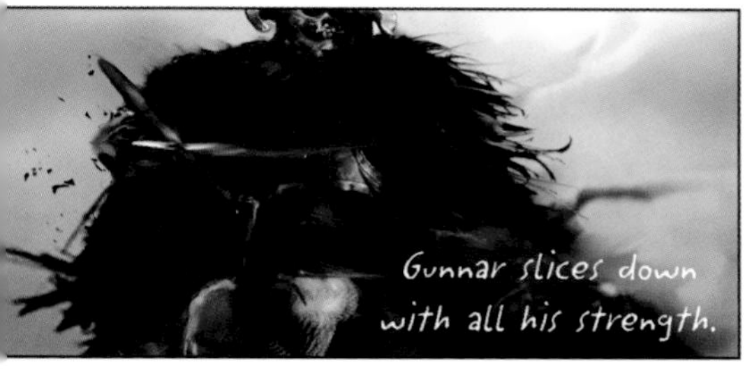
Gunnar slices down with all his strength.

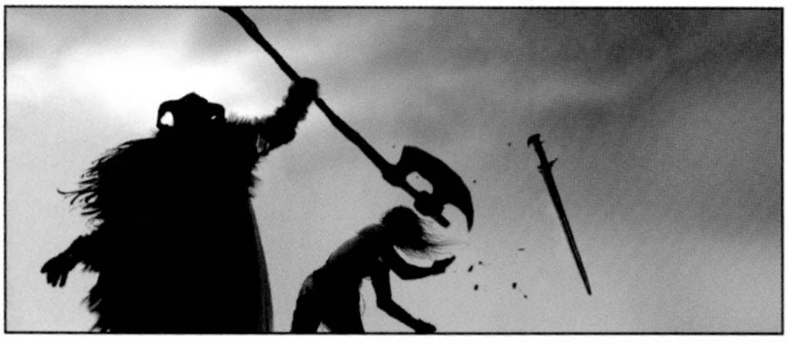

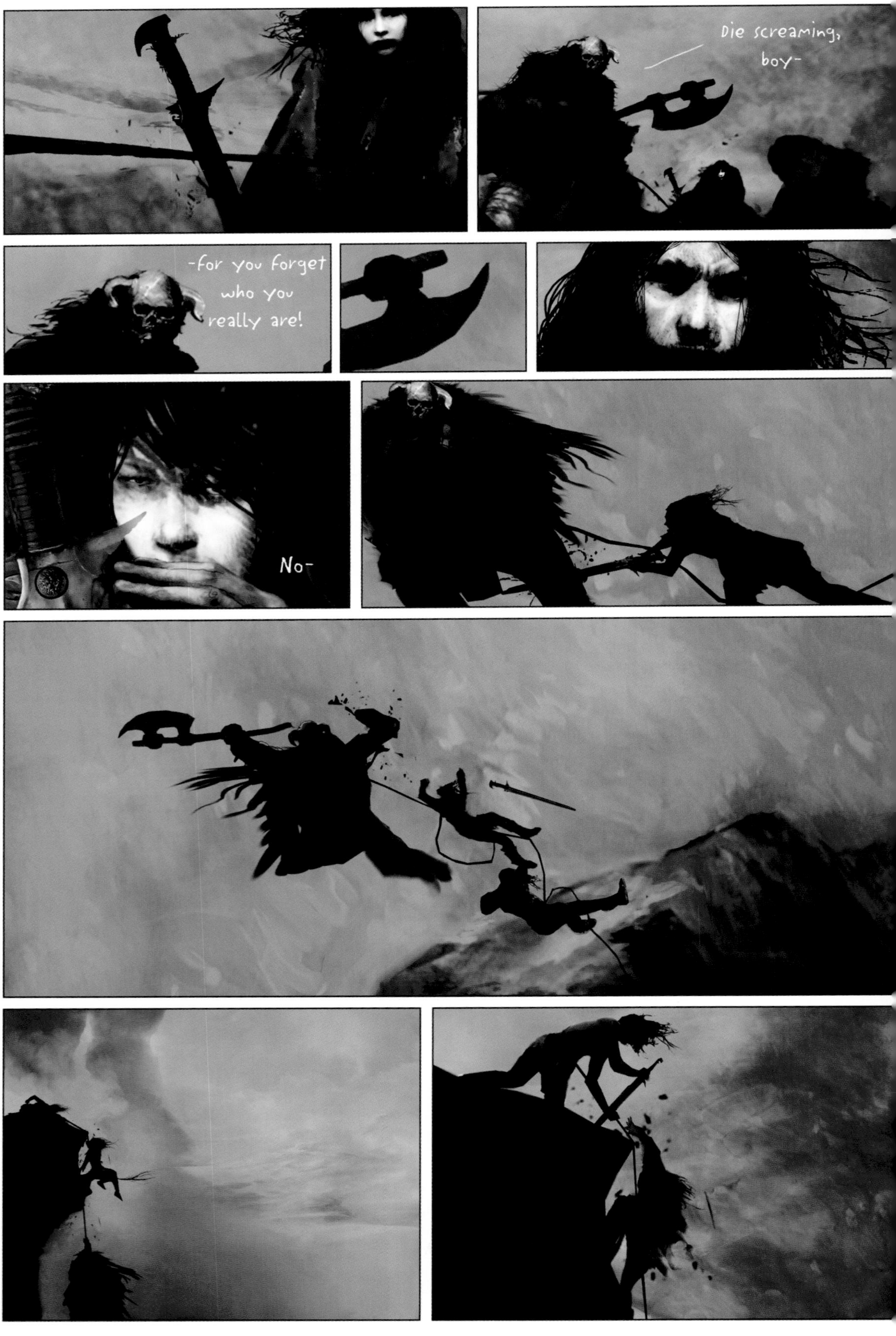
Die screaming, boy-
-for you forget who you really are!
No-

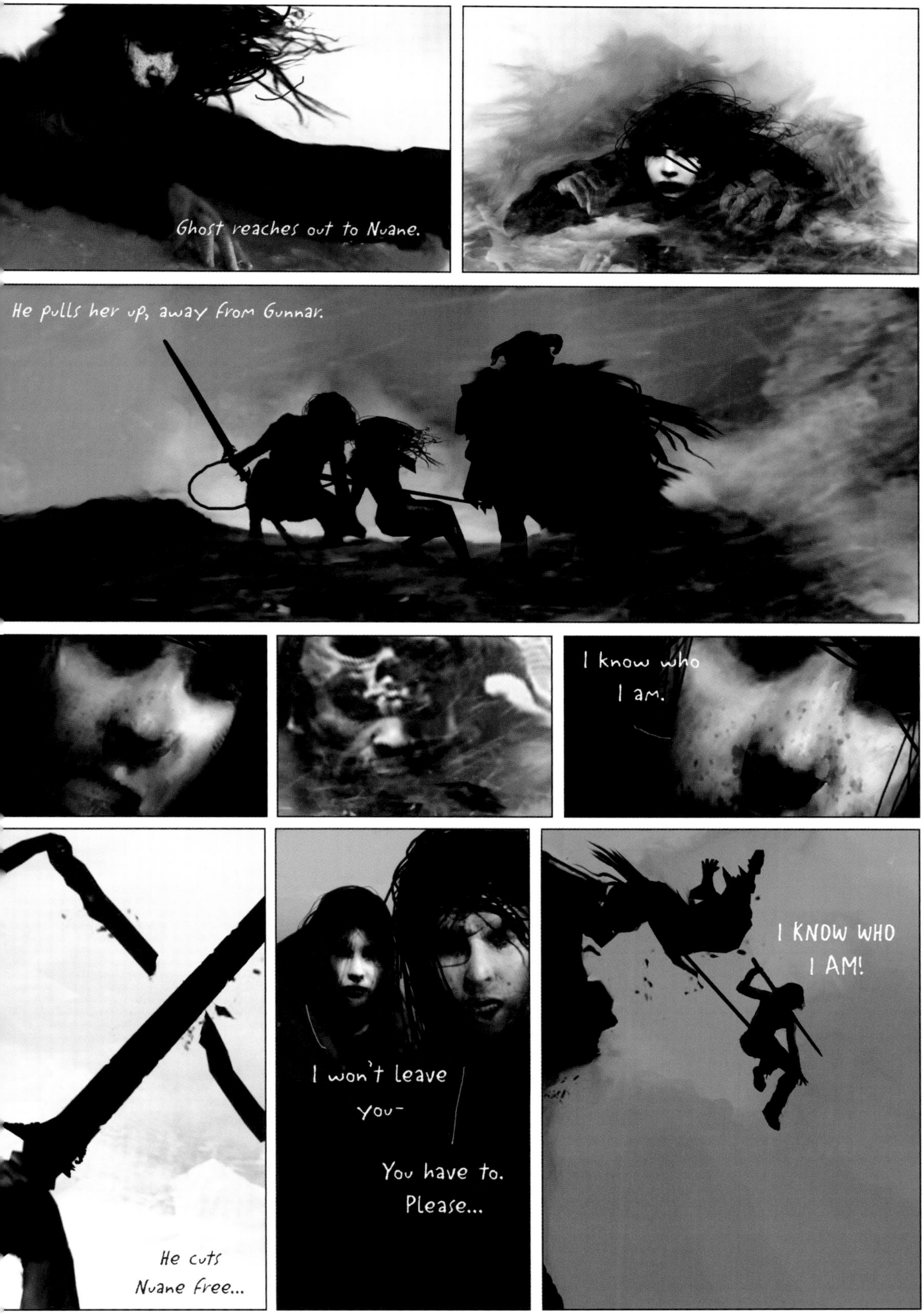
Ghost reaches out to Nuane.
He pulls her up, away from Gunnar.
I know who I am.
He cuts Nuane free...
I won't leave you-
You have to. Please...
I KNOW WHO I AM!

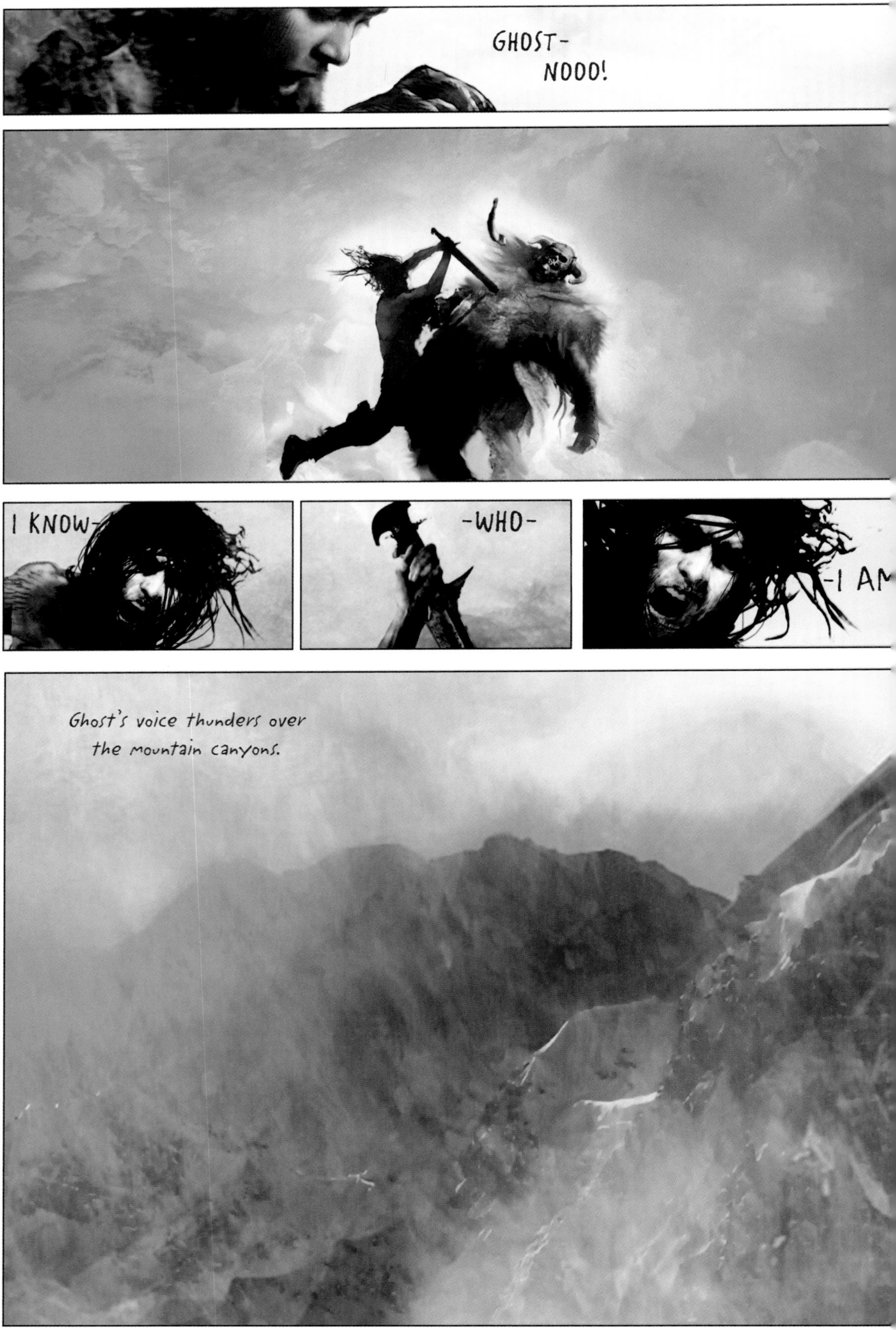
GHOST-
NOOO!
I KNOW-
-WHO-
-I AM
Ghost's voice thunders over the mountain canyons.

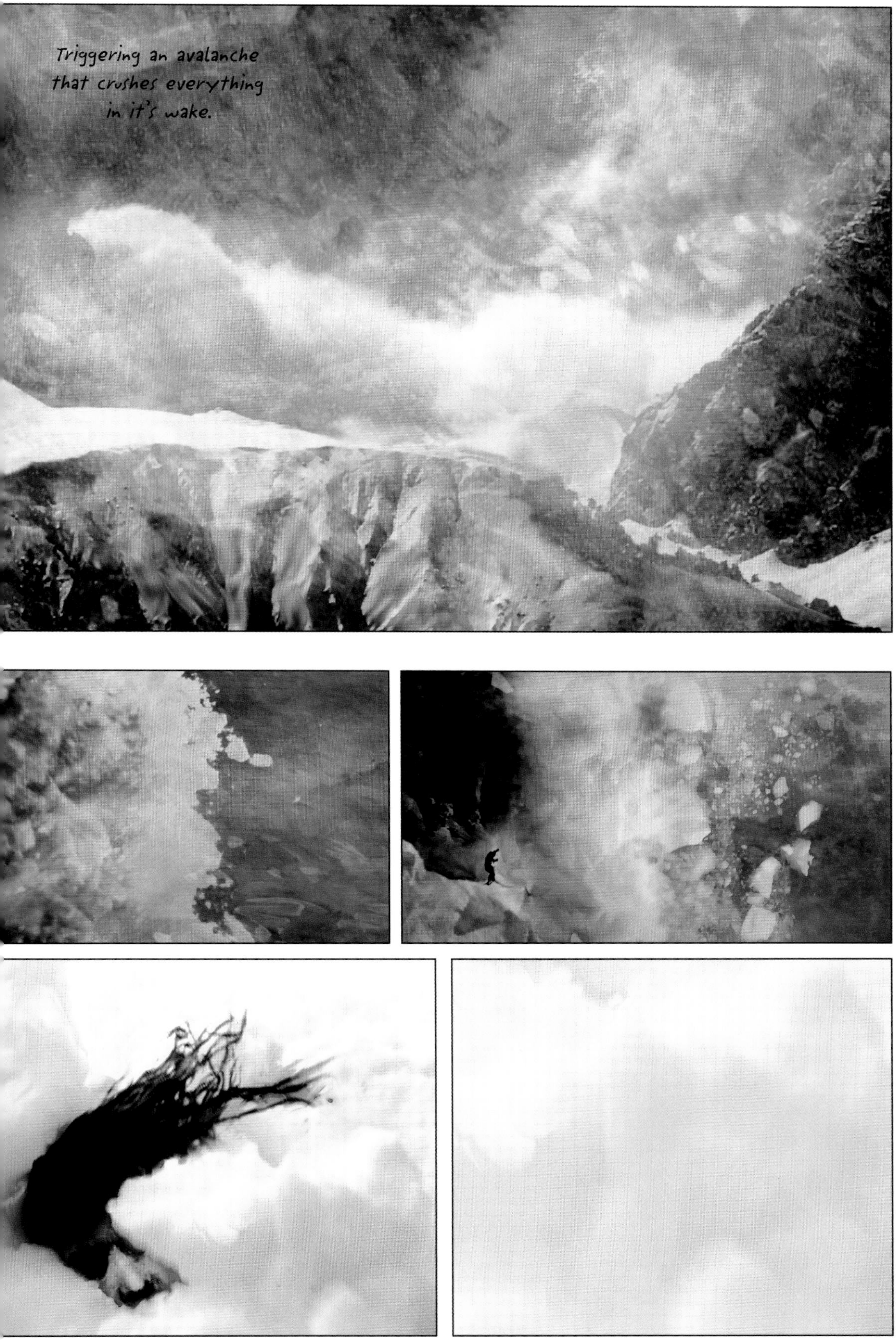
Triggering an avalanche that crushes everything in it's wake.

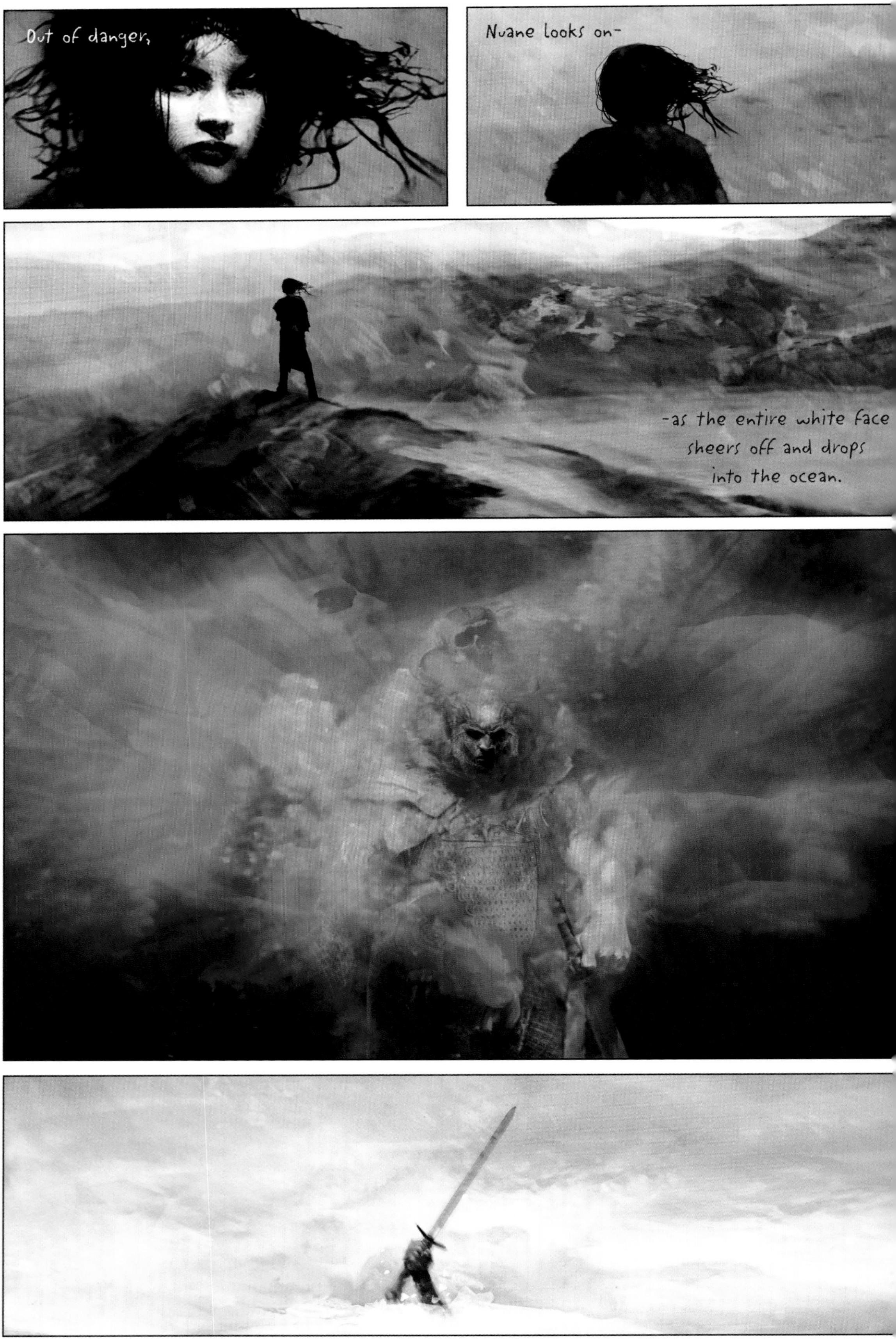
Out of danger,
Nuane looks on-
-as the entire white face sheers off and drops into the ocean.

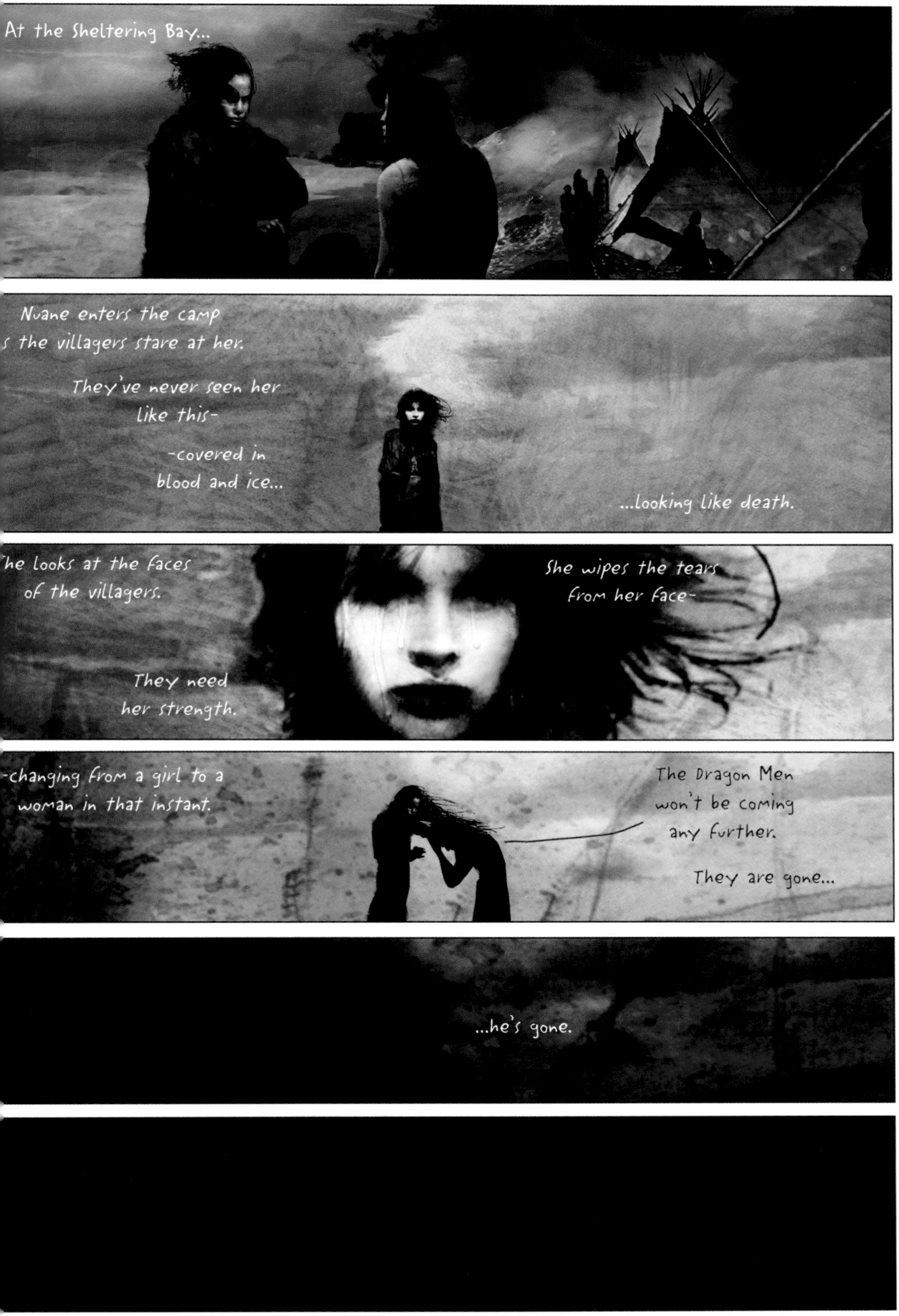
At the Sheltering Bay...
Nuane enters the camp
the villagers stare at her.
They've never seen her like this-
-covered in blood and ice...
...looking like death.
looks at the faces of the villagers.
They need her strength.
She wipes the tears from her face-
-changing from a girl to a woman in that instant.
The Dragon Men won't be coming any further.
They are gone...
...he's gone.

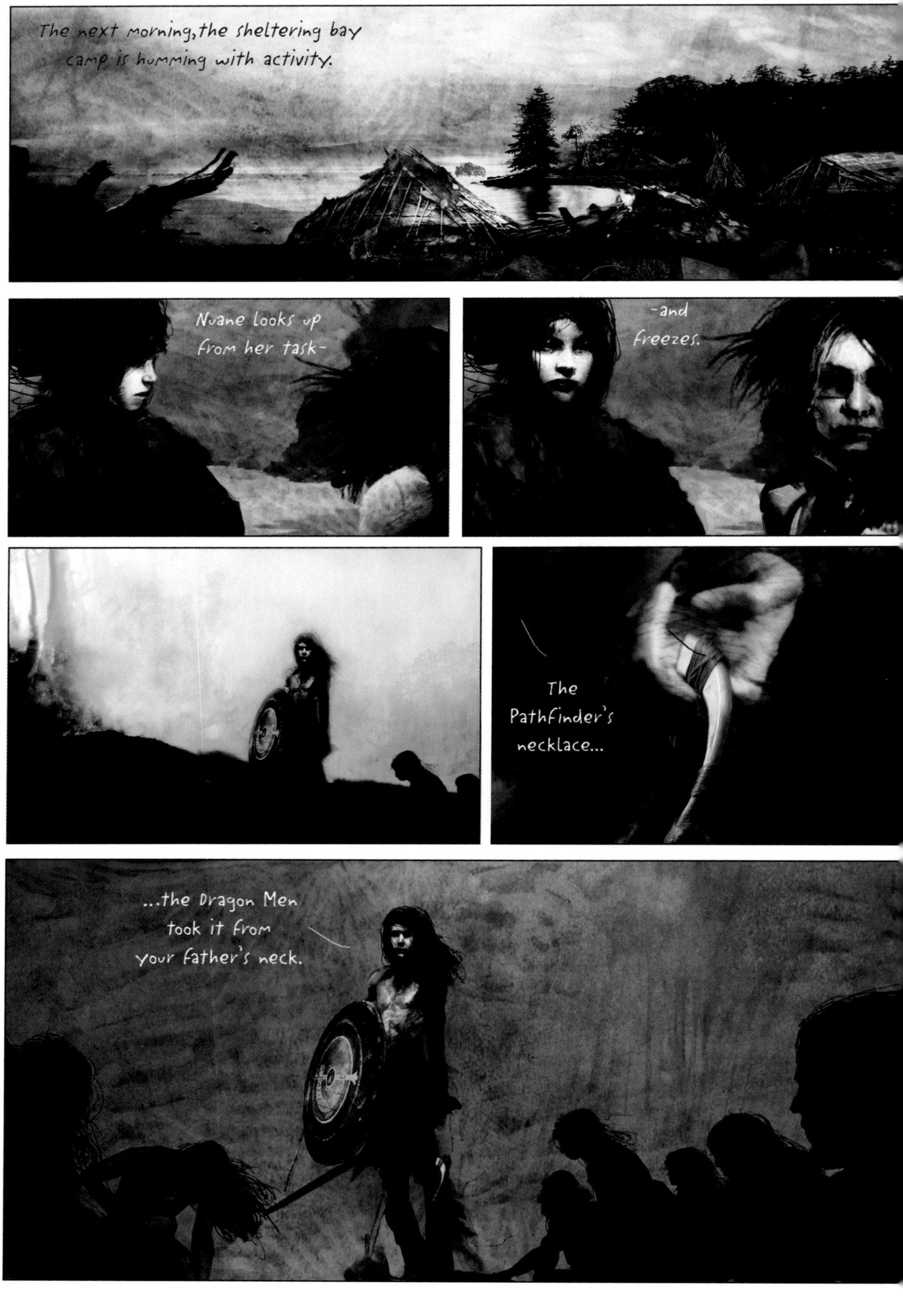
The next morning, the sheltering bay camp is humming with activity.
Nuane looks up from her task-
-and freezes.
The Pathfinder's necklace...
...the Dragon Men took it from your father's neck.

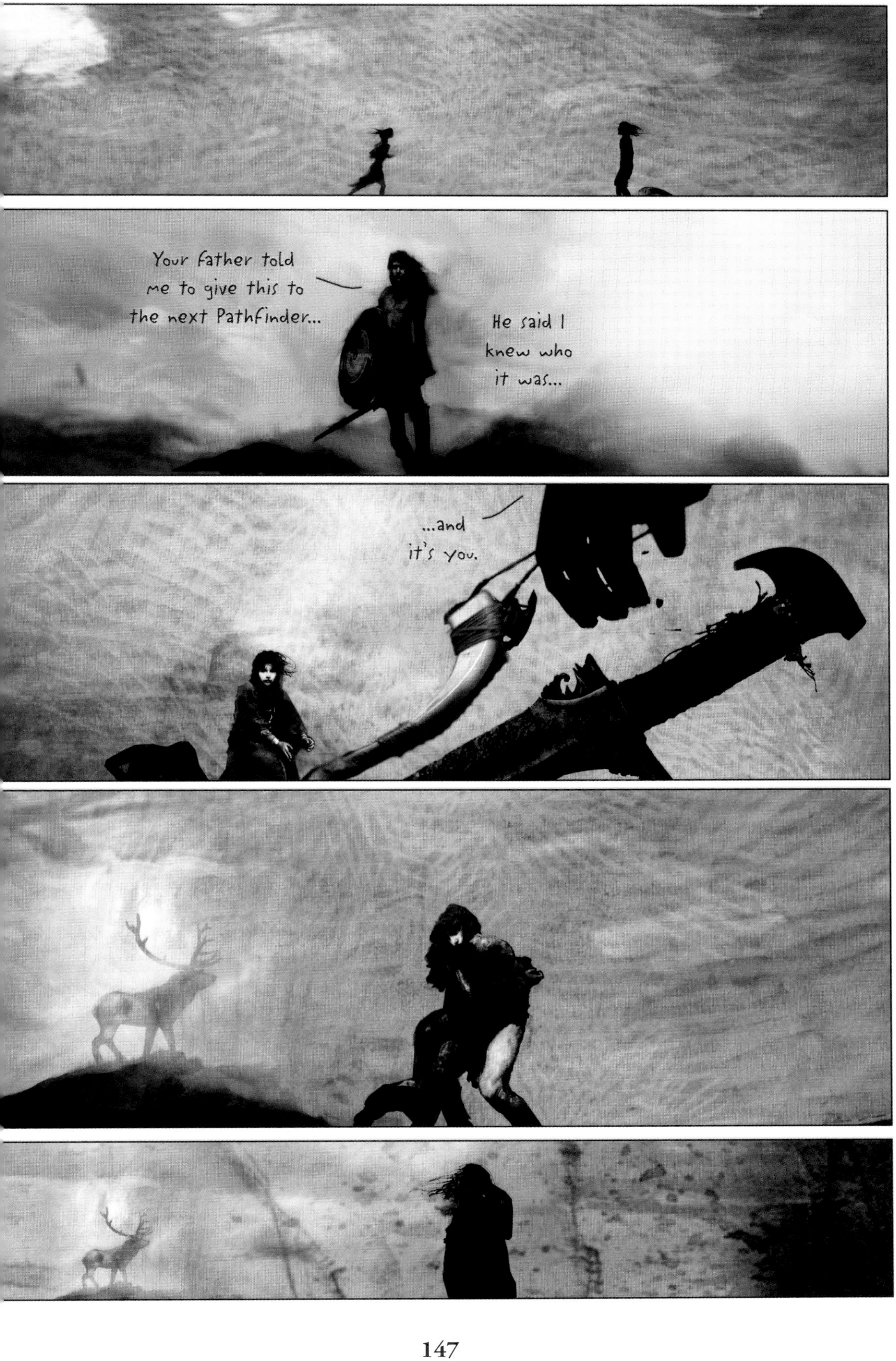
Your father told me to give this to the next Pathfinder...
He said I knew who it was...
...and it's you.

When I was old enough to understand—

—she told me the story, just as I tell you now.

And so my mother became a Pathfinder for the People...

...Like her father before her.

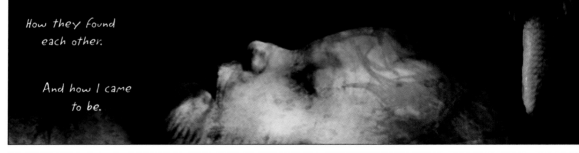

How they found each other.

And how I came to be.

My father went over the mountains, along the coast...

...always along the coast.

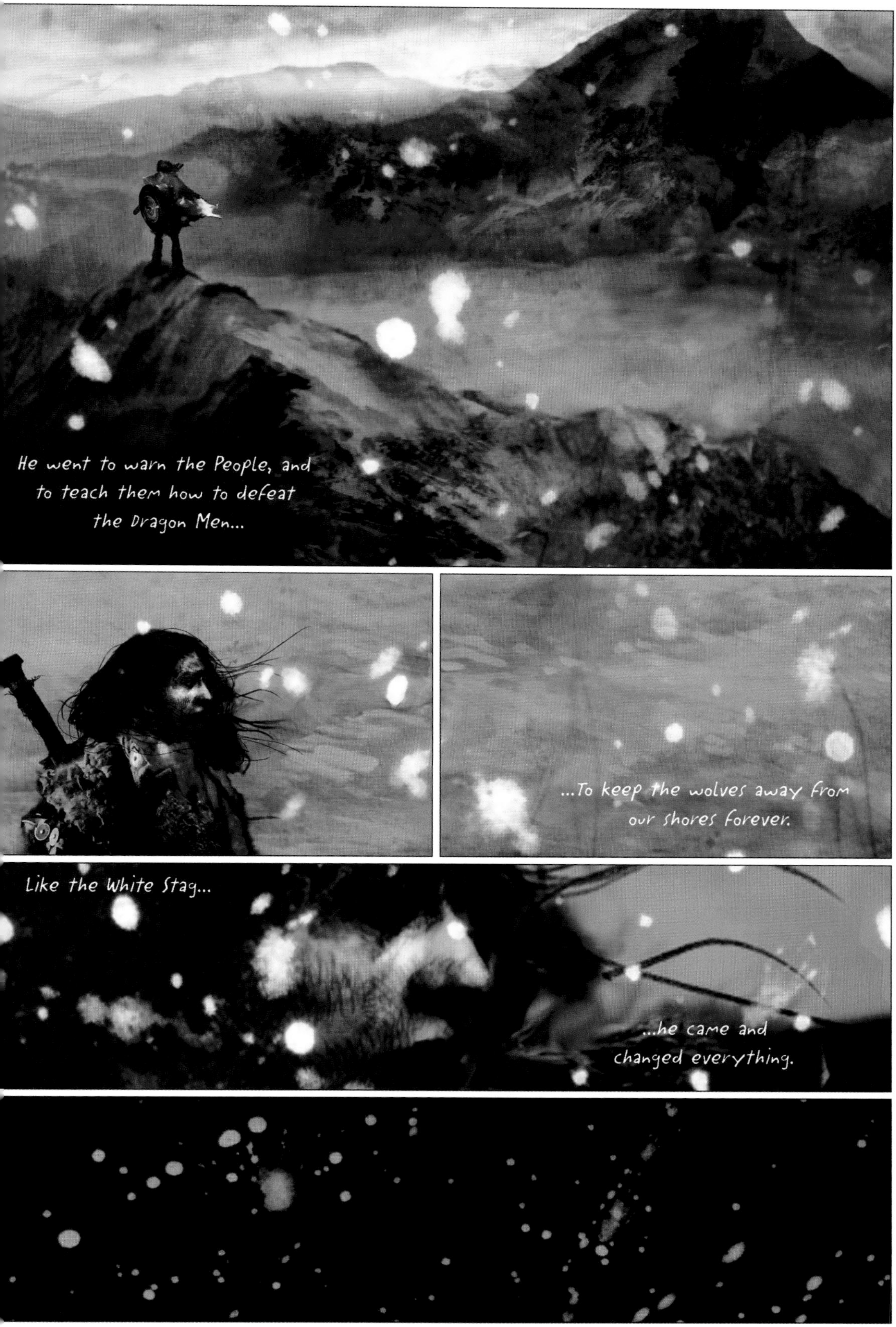
He went to warn the People, and to teach them how to defeat the Dragon Men...
...To keep the wolves away from our shores forever.
Like the White Stag...
...he came and changed everything.

"Courage is not the towering oak that sees storms come and go;
it is the fragile blossom that opens in the snow."

Alice Mackenzie Swain

For my grandfather Tott Reynolds. Peace be on your Soul.

Your son will remember everything you taught him.

Christopher Shy

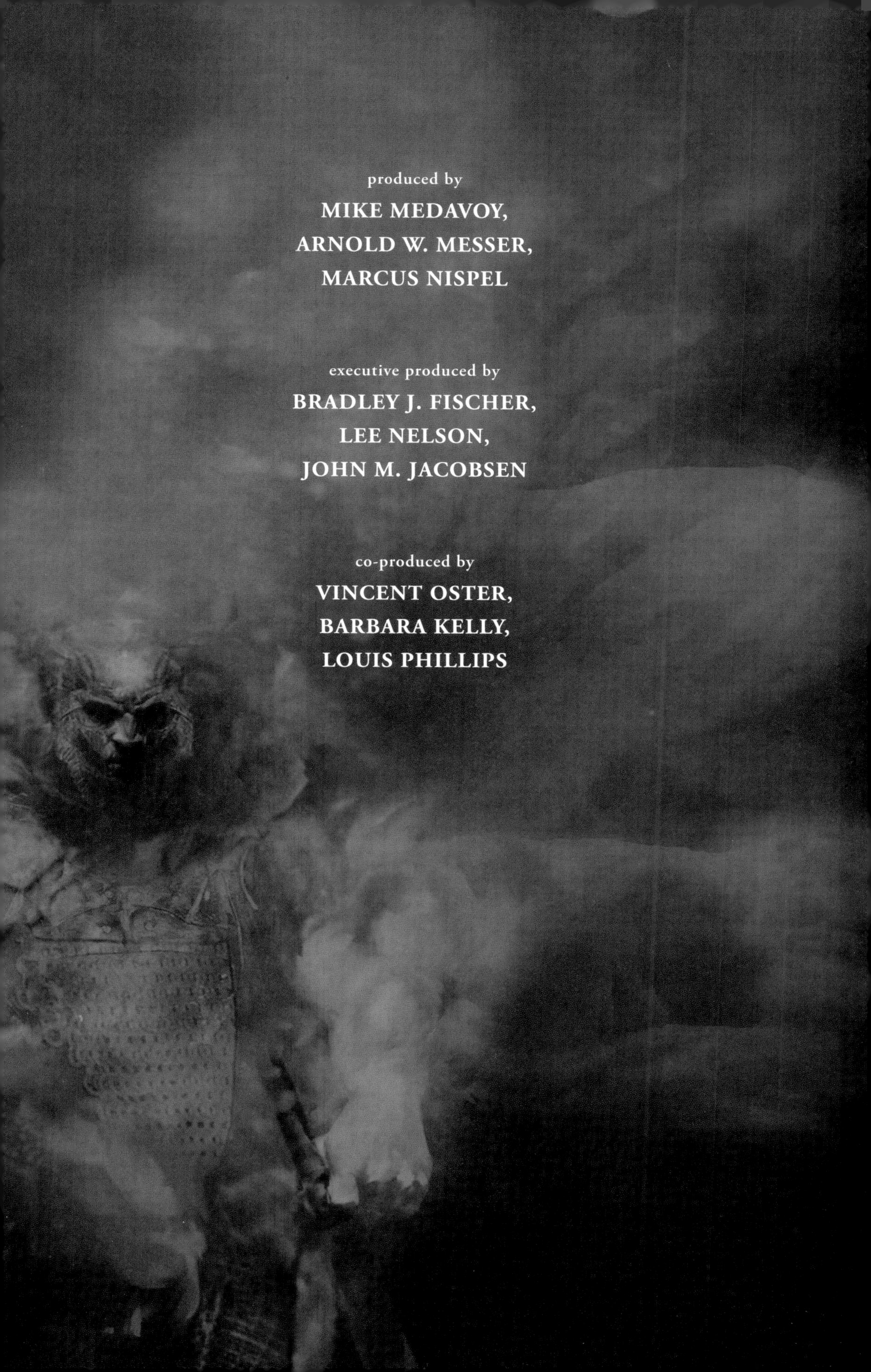

produced by

MIKE MEDAVOY,
ARNOLD W. MESSER,
MARCUS NISPEL

executive produced by

BRADLEY J. FISCHER,
LEE NELSON,
JOHN M. JACOBSEN

co-produced by

VINCENT OSTER,
BARBARA KELLY,
LOUIS PHILLIPS

publisher
Mike Richardson

designer
Joshua "Mjolnir" Elliott

Dark Horse Books
A division of Dark Horse Comics, Inc.
10956 SE Main Street
Milwaukie, OR 97222

darkhorse.com

To find a comic shop in your area, call the Comic Shop Locator Service: (888) 266-4226

First edition: July 2006
ISBN 10: 1-59307-671-1
ISBN 13: 978-1-59307-671-9

10 9 8 7 6 5 4 3 2 1

Printed in Canada